ENVISIONING
THE REIGN OF
GOD

PREACHING FOR TOMORROW

DEBRA J. MUMFORD

JUDSON PRESS
PUBLISHERS SINCE 1824
VALLEY FORGE, PA

Judson Press has made every effort to trace the ownership of all quotes. In the event of a question arising from the use of a quote, we regret any error made and will be pleased to make the necessary correction in future printings and editions of this book.

Unless otherwise noted, Bible quotations in this volume are from the New Revised Standard Version of the Bible, copyright © 1989 by the Division of Christian Education of the National Council of the Churches of Christ in the United States of America. Used by permission. All rights reserved. Scriptures marked KJV are from *The Holy Bible*, King James Version.

Interior design by Wendy Ronga, Hampton Design Group.
Cover design by Lisa Delgado, Delgado & Associates.

Library of Congress Cataloging-in-Publication data
Names: Mumford, Debra J., author. Title: Envisioning the reign of God: preaching for tomorrow / Debra J. Mumford. Description: first [edition]. | Valley Forge: Judson Press, 2019. Identifiers: LCCN 2019010981 (print) | ISBN 9780817018061 (pbk.: alk. paper) Subjects: LCSH: Eschatology. | Preaching. | Theology, Doctrinal. Classification: LCC BT823 .M86 2019 (print) | LCC BT823 (ebook) | DDC 236—dc23
LC record available at https://lccn.loc.gov/2019010981
LC ebook record available at https://lccn.loc.gov/2019980537

Printed in the U.S.A. | First printing, 2019.

Contents

Introduction: Preaching for Tomorrow   iv

Chapter 1   Dispensational and Premillennial Eschatology
             The Theology of John Nelson Darby   1

Chapter 2   Realized Eschatology—Radical Freedom
             The Theology of Rudolf Bultmann   17

Chapter 3   The Vision of the Beloved Community
             The Theology of Martin Luther King Jr.   34

Chapter 4   Presentative Eschatology—Creative Discipleship
             The Theology of Jürgen Moltmann   52

Chapter 5   Feminist Vision
             The Theology of Elisabeth Schüssler Fiorenza   69

Chapter 6   The Vision of the Social Gospel
             The Theology of Walter Rauschenbush   88

Chapter 7   Black Liberation Vision
             The Theology of James Cone   105

Chapter 8   Womanist Vision
             The Theology of Emilie Townes   125

Chapter 9   Mujerista Vision
             The Theology of Ada María Isasi-Díaz   144

Chapter 10   Disability Vision
             The Theology of Nancy Eiesland   161

Chapter 11   LGBTIQA/Queer Vision
             The Theology of Patrick Cheng   176

Chapter 12   A Vision of the Reign of God
             Perspectives for the Twenty-first Century   196

Afterword   A Chance of Reign   213

Bibliography   217

Index   228

Introduction
Preaching for Tomorrow

The rapture. The four horsemen of the apocalypse. The final judgment of the living and the dead. The Great Tribulation. The rise and fall of the anti-Christ. The pillowy clouds of heaven. The fiery gates of hell. These are just a few of the events and images that come to mind when many of us hear the term "eschatology," "last days," or "end times." Some of us have formed these images by reading or hearing sermons preached from apocalyptic texts such as Daniel, Ezekiel, and Revelation. Others have been influenced by popular movies such as the *Left Behind* series, *Rumors of Wars* or *Jerusalem Countdown*.

Even those of us who might not associate the term *eschatology* with the apocalypse also might not relate it to our day-to-day existence. However, Jesus told his followers that the kingdom of God is not just some far-off, future event. Rather, the kingdom was also near or at hand (Luke 10:11; Mark 1:15) and among them (Luke 17:21). The Greek term *basileia*, translated as "kingdom" in the New Testament, can mean kingship, dominion, rule, or reign. As a result, for Jesus, the rule, dominion, or reign of God is a part of our everyday existence.

While there are many books that provide visions of the end of the world as we know it, this book will provide visions of a better world. A more inclusive world. A world in which all people and all of God's creation not only survives but thrives. Theologian James Cone prioritizes the reign of God on earth over the reign of God in heaven. He defines eschatology as "joining the world and making it what it ought to be."[1] Cone contends that Christians should use the power at work in them through Jesus Christ to bring about the reign of God on earth. They should not look to the future as a time when they will reap rewards for godly living and see evildoers punished. Instead, since Christians have been set free through Christ, they should be ready to revolt against the powers and principalities of this world that oppress, marginalize, and enslave other people.

Theologian Jürgen Moltmann defines *eschatology* as the doctrine of Christian hope—hope in Jesus Christ and his future.[2] The once-crucified

Christ has a glorious future because he was resurrected from the dead. Because Christ has a glorious future, followers of Christ also have hope for the future through him. Hope for the future means this world is full of possibilities.

We can capture Jesus' vision of the reign of God in the Gospels. For example, the Gospel of Matthew offers a vision of the basileia of God in Jesus' Sermon on the Mount. We find a new way of being that is starting to take shape as Jesus unveils the connection between human relationships with God and human relationships with one another. In Matthew 5, Jesus says those who mourn, are meek, are merciful, are peacemakers, and are pure in heart will be blessed. We observe that each of these behaviors has a dual purpose: each facilitates good relationships among people and each pleases God. Jesus admonishes the crowd not to insult one another or commit adultery. He makes it clear that these behaviors not only displease God but are also detrimental to human relationships. Jesus tells people that when they are offering gifts at the altar, if they remember that their brother or sister has something against them, they should leave their gifts at the altar, go, and be reconciled with them. Then they can come back to give their gifts. Their offerings to God are unacceptable as long as they are not in right relationship with one another.

In Matthew 6, at the center of this Sermon on the Mount, Jesus teaches the crowd how to pray. Jesus teaches that if they would forgive their sisters and brothers when their sisters and brothers sin against them, God will forgive their sins. Therefore, our observation about the reign of God is that human spiritual well-being is integrally linked to our relationships with one another. If we cannot learn to treat each other in a godly way; if we cannot learn to love each other unconditionally the way God loves us; if we cannot learn to treat each other with dignity and respect (even people we do not like with every fiber of our being), then we cannot please God. In addition, by highlighting the intersectionality of human behavior and divine affirmation, Jesus' vision of the reign of God reminds us to take responsibility for the ways we behave in the world. Jesus' vision of the reign of God also reminds us that we must hold each other accountable for our actions. Our actions have consequences not just for ourselves but also for our families, friends, and people we don't even know.

The premise of this book is that by studying diverse eschatological views, pastors and preachers may be able to infuse their congregations with enthusiasm and a new sense of purpose by helping them to develop a vision of the way the world can be because of the person and work of Jesus Christ. Instead of thinking of eschatology as apocalyptic, catastrophic, divine in-breaking into human history, the congregations may be able to broaden their thinking. Eschatology is not just about how humanity will be judged on the Last Day but how we live our lives every day. Eschatology is not just about the fate of the earth as we know it but how we treat the earth and all its living treasures each and every day. Eschatology is not simply about our ultimate destruction but rather how we construct and conduct our human existence daily. Eschatology is an existential endeavor that every pastor and preacher who wrestles with the will of God for all of creation must take up with earnest intentionality.

While Jesus' teachings about the basileia of God offer guidance for relationships among individuals in communities, they also offer guidance for churches. The churches who claim to follow the resurrected Christ should be purveyors of resurrection hope. They should seek to realize a godly vision of the world. Instead, many churches today are going through the motions of worship, meetings, Bible study, and Sunday school. They sing familiar songs. They pray familiar prayers. They hear familiar sermons that encourage them to attend to their personal salvation by striving to be personally sin-free so they can reap personal rewards for their earthly faithfulness upon their deaths.

Some churches have praise and worship that is lively, exhilarating, and energizing. Yet after the dynamic sermons have been preached, after the praise team has sung its last song, after the benediction has been given, after the doors of the church have been closed and locked, the godly experiences of worship do not make their way outside of the doors. The world that exists outside of the church is no better off because of what took place inside.

By contrast, many churches have a resurrection hope that causes them to be deeply involved in issues of justice. They truly believe that those who claim to follow Christ should seek to eradicate the suffering and oppression caused by structural and systemic sin. But because they lack a focused vision, these well-meaning churches may find themselves engaged in social justice whack-a-mole. As soon as have they begun working on one social justice issue, others crop up that also need their attention. They drift from issue to issue without a vision to guide and focus their efforts. These churches often are so focused on systemic sin that they fail to remind their people of the personal responsibility and accountability required by those who are truly infected with resurrection hope.

In one chapter of Proverbs that venerates justice, wisdom, and personal discipline while denouncing foolishness, injustice, and misplaced pride, we read: "Where there is no vision, the people perish."[3] As we near the end of the second decade of the twenty-first century, we can easily make the argument that the world around us is perishing. Worldwide, millions are fleeing violence and fueling immigration crises in Europe, Africa, and North America. More than 85 million children are subjected to physical labor, exploitation, and trafficking each year. More than two million children are exploited in the sex trade each year.[4]

Consider the folowing U.S. statistics. Twenty-two school shootings occurred by July 2019.[5] In 2017, more than 39.7 million people were living in poverty.[6] The gap between the rich and the poor continues to grow. Ten percent of the population owns wealth equivalent to the income of 75 percent of the population.[7] Nearly forty-two thousand people died of opioid overdose in 2016.[8] African Americans make up 40 percent of the prison population while representing only 12 percent of the total population. Approximately 2.3 million people are incarcerated in jails and prisons. Another eight-hundred-and-forty thousand are on parole and 3.7 million are on probation.[9] Many of these almost 7 million people will never again be able to vote, bear arms, or serve on a jury. Finding employment and housing will be an uphill battle.

As the people perish, the world needs vision. Even more, the world needs godly people who are committed to realizing the vision. Studying diverse eschatological views helps the people of God see the breadth of God's creation and understand their connection to it.

I first developed a course entitled "Preaching for Tomorrow" while I was a PhD student at the Graduate Theological Union in Berkeley, California. During those years, I studied eschatologies developed by several different theologians. I was fascinated by them because they presented disparate views of the kingdom or reign of God developed from varied methods of biblical interpretation and cultural experiences. It was Jürgen Moltmann who first inspired me to think differently about eschatology. He argued that "Christianity is eschatology, is hope, forward looking and forward moving, and therefore also revolutionizing and transforming the present."[10] He further defined eschatology as *Christian hope* engendered by Jesus' resurrection or resurrection hope. Because Christ, through the power of God, defeated death, the Christian's daily existence is infected with a "mobilizing, revolutionizing, and critical" hope that imbues the people of God with the love of God.[11] People who hope in Christ are a transformed people. They are a restless people. They are a people who cannot abide the world as it is. People who hope in Christ find themselves in conflict with the world as they seek to realize God's future for the world. People who hope in Christ are led by the love of God and seek fulfillment of the promises of God not solely in the "sweet by and by" but also in the here and now. People of God who hope in Christ strive to fulfill a vision of what God's world can be.

Ten of the eleven eschatological perspectives included in this book offer a vision of the reign of God that transforms human relationships to better reflect the love of God for all of God's people by striving for justice and eliminating oppression. Two of the theologians relate the basileia of God to the environment as well.

While I was studying these diverse views, I noticed that many factors helped to shape the eschatological views of each theologian. Like all of us, theologians begin their work with presuppositions inherited from their life experiences, denominational affiliations, ecclesial motivations, and theological education and training. In the years since I first developed the course, I have required students to research the biographical information of each theologian in addition to thoroughly reading his or her work. Consequently, they began to understand that every eschatology is a product of many different factors. By understanding the life experiences and social and economic circumstances that influenced the development of each of the eschatologies, preachers and pastors are thereby able to understand that no theology is neutral or without social and cultural context and human motivations. Therefore, each of the first eleven chapters begins with a brief biography. The biography of each theologian includes childhood development and influences, education and theological training, and relevant life experiences.

The content of this book has also been shaped largely by my five years of summer teaching a course entitled "Preaching for Social Transformation" in the ACTS Doctor of Ministry program in Chicago under the leadership of Rev. Dr. Gennifer Brooks. I also had the honor of co-teaching the course with homileticians Dawn Ottoni Wilhelm and Karyn Wiseman, who helped me develop my approaches to teaching and applying the various eschatological perspectives to the lived experiences of our students. While teaching these visions of the reign of God over the years, diverse groups of students have insisted that I not only teach the specifics of each eschatology and how to preach them, but also how to use them as points of departure for biblical exegesis. Therefore, the section "Implications for Preaching" at the end of each chapter provides preachers and pastors with ideas of how to incorporate the visions into their preaching and ministries. The "Questions for Exegesis" lists questions that preachers can use to interrogate their chosen texts from each theological perspective as they prepare their sermons. Therefore, when they read the word "text" in this section, it applies to the text they have chosen to exegete.

My final chapter highlights important aspects of each theology that pastors may be able to use to shape their visions of the reign of God. By calling attention to specific tenets, I am not suggesting that others be ignored. Rather, these tenets are among those that make the various eschatologies unique. Each pastor or preacher may add to or take away aspects that have more or less appeal to their communities of faith. One sermon I developed and preached for and during the ACTS DMin course is included in the Afterword. I used the eschatological perspective of Elisabeth Schüssler Fiorenza for this sermon.

Throughout this book the terms *eschatology, vision,* and *reign of God* will be used interchangeably to refer to the will of God for all of God's creation on earth.

Chapter 1: Dispensational and Premillennial Eschatology

Premillennialists and dispensationalists believe in the literal Second Coming of Christ before the millennium to take the saints of the church from the earth (Revelation 20:1-10). The kingdom of God is realized during a one-thousand-year period of peace, justice, righteousness, and long life. After this period of peace, the world as we know it will be destroyed. We will examine the eschatology of John Nelson Darby, the father of dispensationalism.

Chapter 2: Realized Eschatology—Radical Freedom

For adherents of realized eschatology, the kingdom of God is realized in each individual in the form of radical freedom from the past through the grace of God available in the person and work of Jesus Christ. Though the Christ event is historic in that it happened in the past, it is at the same time an eternal event that happens in the souls of believers in which "Christ is born, suffers, dies, and is raised to eternal life." Christian existence becomes eschatological existence in which the Christian's attitudes toward the world change. We will examine the eschatology of German theologian and New Testament scholar Rudolf Bultmann.

Chapter 3: The Vision of the Beloved Community
The vision of the beloved community challenges the United States to live up to the true meaning of its creed. If indeed all people are created equal, then racial injustice, poverty, and all forms of oppression are anathema to the American dream. In the beloved community, any oppression or injustice is a distortion of the image of God. We will examine the eschatology of Martin Luther King Jr.

Chapter 4: Presentative Eschatology—Creative Discipleship
The theology of hope is founded in hope born of the resurrection of Jesus Christ. Because God raised Jesus from the dead, the world is faced with new possibilities that can and should be met through the "creative discipleship" of those who claim to follow the risen Christ. Creative discipleship is not content with supporting the existing world order but rather goes about transforming it. We will examine the eschatology of Jürgen Moltmann.

Chapter 5: Feminist Vision
Feminist eschatology envisions a world in which women and men are equal partners in realizing the reign of God. By tracing the integrative discipleship of women in the early church, feminists make the case that the equal voice of women has been important in Christianity since its founding and remains essential to its future. We will examine the eschatology of Elisabeth Schüssler Fiorenza.

Chapter 6: The Vision of the Social Gospel
Proponents of the social gospel believe that the kingdom of God can be realized only when Christians broaden their conceptions of Christian responsibility. Christians should be concerned not only about personal sins and their personal relationship with God but also about systemic sins that

oppress and marginalize the people of God. We will examine the eschatology of Walter Rauschenbusch.

Chapter 7: Black Liberation Vision
Black liberation theology emerged during the black power movement and
the Detroit riots of the 1960s. During this period of civil unrest, African
American seminary students demanded a theology that evolved from the
lived experiences of African Americans rather than from the experiences
of Europeans or Americans of European descent. Black liberation theology contends that God is particularly on the side of the poor and oppressed. We will examine the eschatology of James Cone.

Chapter 8: Womanist Vision
Womanist theology has its impetus in the lived experiences of African
American women who have historically been, and are still currently being,
oppressed by racism, sexism, and classism, which seeks to deny their full
humanity. Hope for a liberated future for these women is found in the
reign of God in Jesus Christ, in whom they find the support and resolve
they need to resist injustice and oppression. We will examine the eschatology of Emilie Townes.

Chapter 9: Mujerista Vision
Mujerista theology has its impetus in the voices of Latin American
women expressed through narratives that relate how prejudices such
as ethnocentrism, racism, classism, sexism, and heterosexism affect
their lives. By faith, Mujerista theologians believe in the possibility of
the realization of a new heaven and a new earth in which prejudice of
all types will be no more. We will examine the eschatology of Ada
María Isasi-Díaz.

Chapter 10: Disability Vision
A theology of disability evolved from the disability rights movement,
which resulted in the Americans with Disabilities Act (ADA) of 1990.
People with disabilities have been biblically characterized as cursed in Mosaic law and in need of healing in the New Testament. In contemporary
society, they are rendered invisible from public view. Disability theologians
envision a world in which people of different abilities are valued for their

humanity rather than their able-bodiedness. We will examine the eschatology of Nancy Eiesland.

Chapter 11: LGBTIQA/Queer Vision

Lesbian/gay and queer theology has roots in the emergence of liberation
theologies in the 1960s. Each is concerned with the oppression of persons
who are lesbian, gay, bisexual, transgendered, intersex, questioning, and
asexual in the church and larger society. LGBTIQA people envision a
world in which multiple sexualities and gender identities are socially accepted and affirmed. We will examine the eschatology of Patrick Cheng.

Chapter 12: A Vision of the Reign of God

This chapter highlights important and unique tenets of each eschatology
that can serve as a foundation for a new vision of the reign of God. The
section "Using Visions of the Reign of God for Exegesis" takes preachers
through the process of using the visions of the reign of God for preaching
by working through the exegesis of Mark 1:40-45. The sermon is included
as an Afterword.

Notes

1. James H. Cone, *Black Theology and Black Power* (Maryknoll, NY: Orbis Books,
1997), Chapter 5. Kindle Edition.

2. Jurgen Moltmann, *Theology of Hope: On the Ground and the Implications of a
Christian Eschatology* (San Francisco: HarperSanFrancisco, 1991), 15–18.

3. Proverbs 29:18, KJV.

4. "Fast Fact: Child Protection and Development," UNICEF USA (2018), accessed September 11, 2018, https://www.unicefusa.org/mission/protect.

5. Michelle Lou and Christina Walker. "There Have Been 22 School Shootings in the
US So Far This Year." CNN (2019). https://www.cnn.com/2019/05/08/us/school-shoot-
ings-us-2019-trnd/index.html.

6. Kayla Fontenot, Jessica Semega, and Melissa Kollar, "Income and Poverty in The
United States: 2017 Current Population Reports, United States Department of Commerce," (Washington, DC: U.S. Census Bureau, 2018), 11.

7. Pedro Nicolaci da Costa, "The Richest US Families Own a Startling Proportion of
America's Wealth," Business Insider (2017), accessed September 11, 2018, https://www.busi-
nessinsider.com/richest-us-families-own-a-startling-proportion-of-americas-wealth-2017-6.

8. Centers for Disease Control and Prevention, Opiod Overdose: Understanding the
Epidemic (Atlanta: U.S. Department of Health and Human Services, 2018).

9. Peter Wagner and Wendy Sawyer, "Mass Incarceration: The Whole Pie 2018," Prison
Policy Initiative (2018), accessed September 11, 2018, https://www.prisonpolicy.org/re-
ports/pie2018.html.

10. Moltmann, 16.

11. Ibid., 15.

1
Dispensational and Premillennial Eschatology
The Theology of John Nelson Darby

A Brief Biography

John Nelson Darby was the eighth child born to Anne Vaughan and John Darby on November 18, 1800, in London, England.[1] Anne was the daughter of a wealthy Unitarian retailer who owned several sugar plantations in Jamaica. John Darby was a merchant who belonged to the Church of England. Their son John Nelson's middle name was taken from Lord Horatio Nelson, an officer and hero in the British Royal Navy.[2] John Nelson attended a public boarding school in the Westminster neighborhood of London, where he was an average student. In 1815, John Darby sent John Nelson to Trinity College in Dublin, Ireland. Trinity, associated with the Church of Ireland, trained young men in classical studies and mathematics. There his academic gifts began to emerge. In 1819, he graduated with a bachelor of arts and was awarded the Classical Gold Medal, which was the highest honor awarded in the classics. He attended law school in Dublin and was admitted to the bar in 1822.

Though Darby converted or became a believer in Christ in 1820 or 1821,[3] he believed that he did not receive deliverance until another six or seven years had passed. Darby made a distinction between conversion, which he contended was forgiveness of sins upon confession in accordance with Scripture, and deliverance, which was inward assurance that he had been forgiven of his sins.[4] During this period he spent a lot of time fasting and praying but experienced little inner peace. For a while, after his conversion, he was attracted to the Roman Catholic Church. However, it was Hebrews 9–10 that convinced him that the Roman church was out of line with Scripture. He particularly did not agree with the Mass and its suggestion of perpetual sacrifice. Christ had been offered only once as a sacrifice for many.

In his quest for peace, he changed his occupation from barrister (lawyer) to ordained minister. He believed that since Jesus gave his life for him, he should give his life back to God in gratitude for what Jesus had done. Upon hearing of John Nelson's career change, his father disinherited him. (Father and son did eventually reconcile.) Darby had a particular desire to work among the poor Roman Catholic population of Ireland. However, he decided to seek ordination in the United Church of England and Ireland, in which he was ordained in 1825.[5] Since there is no record of Darby having attended the divinity lectures usually required by United Church clergy for ordination, it is believed he may have received a waiver because of his legal training. He also had the support of church officials. He spent the next two years living the life of a poor minister among his poor parishioners in the town of Calary, Ireland. He lived frugally and used an inheritance from an uncle to build schools and enhance the lives of people in his parish.

While he was in Calary, the archbishop sent a letter to all clergy in his diocese stating that all Roman Catholic converts to Protestantism in the diocese were required to take an Oath of Supremacy and Allegiance to the British Crown. For Darby, this request was unconscionable. It was his belief that people who professed to follow Christ should have allegiance only to Christ and not to any human political structure. One of the issues he had with Roman Catholicism was the perceived practice of veneration of the pope. Therefore, to have converts from Catholicism to the Church of England and Ireland, also known as the Anglican Church, replace veneration of the pope with veneration of the king was unacceptable and unbiblical.[6]

He wrote an article in protest of the request of the archbishop that had little impact on the clergy. While he was still considering what to do next, he was severely injured when his horse got frightened one night while he was visiting his parishioners and threw him against a doorpost. While recovering, he stayed with his sister and brother-in-law, who also lived in Ireland, for three months. While there, he thought at length about his many objections to the established church of which he was part: forcing converts to declare allegiance to the state, not allowing unordained people to preach, and generally replacing ministry of God with the will of humanity. He struggled to reconcile his emerging views.

After healing from his injuries, he returned for a short time to Calary before formally tendering his resignation. Even after leaving the congregation, he preached in Anglican churches when invited. Somewhere around 1827 or 1828, Darby began meeting with four other men in

Dublin and with other like-minded clergy for worship in a home. Their worship was simple and reminiscent of the worship of the early church described in Acts. Very soon others began to join them. The group became known as the Plymouth Brethren.[7] These men used Matthew 18:20 as a foundation for their gathering: "Where two or three are gathered in my name, there I am in the midst of them." Darby and the other founders were clear that the Plymouth Brethren was not a denomination. They were a gathering of like-minded believers who were committed to Christ, to simple and plain teaching of Scripture, and to being separate from the world.

Darby was a prolific writer and linguist. In addition to many volumes of sermons and biblical interpretations, he wrote hymns and completed three biblical translations from the Greek and Hebrew into German, French, and English.[8] It was Darby's teachings about prophecy, and his doctrine of the Rapture in particular, that set Darby and the Plymouth Brethren apart from other Christian assemblies. Darby traveled throughout Europe, Canada, New Zealand, and the United States to preach and share his beliefs. He first introduced his teachings in the United States in 1863. Darby died of health complications from a fall on April 29, 1882.

A Theological Overview

John Nelson Darby is renowned for being the father of the eschatological perspective known as premillennial dispensationalism. This is the belief that God will rapture the saints of God from the earth before the millennium and a Jewish remnant will have an inheritance on the earth. Therefore, while his view of the kingdom of God (and kingdom of heaven) has an otherworldly focus, it also has an earthly orientation that makes it unique among other apocalyptic doctrine. The times in which Darby lived may help to explain the attraction of his apocalyptic doctrine in his day and its continued attraction in ours.

For people living in Great Britain, the times leading up to the formation of the Plymouth Brethren were rife with revolution and tremendous change. Through the Revolutionary War, the thirteen colonies finally won their freedom from British rule in 1783. The West African slave trade was abolished in 1833. French emperor Napoleon Bonaparte's defeat at Waterloo by Britain and Prussia marked the end of the high taxes, high food prices, and perpetual unemployment experienced during the years of war.[9] The Industrial Revolution compelled many people to migrate to cities in search of employment. On the one hand, some encountered poverty, poor working conditions, overcrowding, and lack of hygiene that led to health problems.[10] On the other hand, others experienced prosperity made possible through technology that was transforming agriculture, textile and metal manufacturing, transportation, evolving social structures, and economic policies.[11]

Another revolution, the Enlightenment, impacted the church through people known as Dissenters. Dissenters fully embraced new rationalism and scientific worldviews. They no longer believed in the doctrine of total depravity in which humans were weak and sinful creatures who needed to be saved from themselves. They also did not believe in the concept of heaven and the afterlife. They believed that Jesus Christ was the head of the church and Scripture was the only rule of faith and practice. However, from their perspective, the impact of faith on the lives of believers should be left to their own judgment and discretion through reason. Dissenters objected to the creeds and offices of the Church of England.

During this period non-Anglican populations throughout Ireland and England began to contend for their civil rights. Despite the official standing of the Anglican Church as the state church, the majority of the population was Roman Catholic. However, only Protestants were allowed to be members of the parliament.[12] The representation of Protestant Dissenters was also restricted. Catholics, Dissenters, and Jews were denied specific civil and political rights.[13] An organization called the Society of United Irishmen emerged to fight for the inclusion of Irish of all religious persuasions in the parliament. Dissenters also fought for the inclusion of Catholics and Jews in the parliamentary process in addition to fighting for their own rights.

Other areas of discontent within the Anglican Church included the belief that some of the practices and traditions in the Book of Common Prayer were contrary to the Word of God.[14] Dissenters also rejected the mandate that converts to Christianity were to declare allegiance to the state, the denial of unordained people the right to preach, and the replacement of the ministry of God with the will of humanity. Like the Dissenters, Catholics, and Jews, Darby had issues with the established church. His cofounding of the Plymouth Brethren was evidence of his belief that the Anglican Church was conforming itself more to the image of the world than to the image of God.[15]

However, Darby's objections were not related to civil authority. Rather his objections were biblical and theological. While Dissenters rejected the validity of narratives of the biblical text such as the Fall in Genesis and the concept of heaven in the New Testament, Darby believed that all Scripture came directly from God. He rejected the scientific view of the Bible advanced by the Enlightenment in favor of more literal views. Of prophecy in particular, Darby contended that "holy men of God spake as they were moved by the Holy Ghost."[16]

Therefore, Darby believed that words found in Scripture have authority simply because they are found in the Scriptures. The Scriptures are holy writings provided by God for the people of God as a sure and certain guide. Though some of the Scriptures were written to clergy, he believed that most were written with regular people in mind.[17] In addition, Darby did not believe that the impact of faith on the lives of believers was a personal choice. All people who claim to be followers of Jesus Christ are mandated to be obedient to God in every way. The responsibility of Christians in their daily lives is to behave as if they are already Christians rather than as if they are aspiring to be Christians.[18] Therefore, behaving according to one's own will is a sin. Likewise, any human behavior that contradicts the will of God is also sin.

Salvation for Darby was a state of being that occurs when a person becomes conscious of her or his own sin and guilt and through Jesus Christ has his or her past sins erased and assumes a new, righteous condition before God.[19] Being in a new condition means that believers are now "in Christ" rather than "in the flesh." As a result, they live life anew in obedience to God. Darby, as part of the Plymouth Brethren, believed that followers of Christ should have nothing to do with the world. Christians are supposed to get through the world "unspotted" by it, or blameless. Christ's life on earth serves as a model of how Christians should live their lives.[20] Just as Jesus lived a life that was holy and without blame, so humans are to be holy and without blame before God.[21] Darby further clarifies his position by writing that the life in which God saw the Christian as a sinner is past, done, complete. Once people accept Jesus as Lord and Savior, they embark on a new life. The condemnation and death that were the consequences of their sinful lives before their conversion no longer exist for them.

As a result of all Christ has done, Christians are to no longer live according to the standards of the world. They instead should live according to the Word of God under the guidance of the Holy Spirit.[22] When Jesus ascended to the right hand of God, the Holy Spirit descended to dwell in the people of God. The Holy Ghost provides full knowledge of the Christian's place and blessedness in Christ.[23] Christians should strive daily to conform to the image of Christ while making Christ the motive for everything they do. Conforming to Christ can be accomplished through the power of the Holy Ghost that dwells in all Christians. In those times when the saints of God fall short of the will of God in their daily living, they have the blessed assurance of the intercession of Christ on their behalf. Christ, the great high priest, maintains the communion of saints and restores the communion of saints when needed.[24]

For the Christian, living in the world is an ongoing test of faith. Just as the Israelites had to go through the wilderness before they got to the promised land of Canaan, Christians must get through life in the world in order to reap the reward of eternal life with Christ.[25] The good news about the tests of faith is that God does not leave Christians on their own when these tests occur:

> God's way is to put us through the wilderness, as He did the Israelites, but He never forgot them, never left them without manna. He puts us through this process in bringing us to glory, that we may know ourselves, but He interweaves His grace with all our trials and difficulties. Not only has God wrought eternal redemption for us, but "He withdraweth not his eyes from the righteous."[26]

Through the tests of faith, Christians get to know themselves. Most of all, they can better understand the faithfulness of God.

As it relates to love, Darby believed there are two kinds, both of which are divine: downward and upward. Downward love works in human hearts toward other people. Upward love is love toward God and directly affects that state of the human soul.[27] He believed that it is not enough for a Christian to love others as they love themselves. They must love in a way that is above all the evil and sin in the world. They must love as Christ loves them. Downward love feels the pain of those who are suffering, just as Christ did.

It is Darby's views of the kingdom of God and kingdom of heaven that set him apart from other conservative churchmen and theologians of his day. He believed the kingdom of God to be "the exercise or exhibition of the ruling power of God under any circumstances in the wisdom of God."[28] The kingdom of God was present when Jesus was on earth. The kingdom of heaven, by contrast, is the kingdom of God in its heavenly character or form. The kingdom of heaven came into being because the Jews rejected Jesus as the Messiah and was set up for the saints of God until Jesus' Second Coming. At that point, the saints will experience the blessedness of the rule of the Son of Man. If the Jews had not rejected Jesus, the earth would have continued to be the kingdom of God. The earthly powers that had once rejected Jesus will be under his rule in the end times.

Therefore, the primary hope of the Christian is that Jesus will come back. Christians are in a constant state of waiting for Christ.[29] When Jesus returns, the saints of God will inherit a future with Christ in the kingdom of heaven. However, those who rejected Christ or did not accept him as their Lord and Savior will receive God's wrath at the Final Judgment. While there is hope for individual followers of Christ, Darby believed that the church was in ruin. By "in ruin" he meant that the church did not bring glory to God as it should have.[30] The church in his day seemed to value the tradition of humans over the Word of God. The church encouraged veneration of church officials over veneration of God. He identified eras in history, or dispensations, in which God repeatedly gave humanity opportunities to live according to God's will. In each dispensation, the people of God failed. It is from the term "dispensations" that part of the term "premillennial dispensationalism" (Darby's brand of apocalypticism) is derived.

Darby wrote and lectured that human history is marked by five eras or dispensations, while expecting that there would likely be an additional dispensation that marked the end of human history. Also, not included in the five dispensations is the paradisiacal state (state of Adam and Eve in Paradise), which he claimed could not properly be called a dispensation. Each dispensation declares some leading principle, interference of God, or condition in which God has placed humanity. Though the principles are sanctioned by God, the responsibility for fulfilling God's expectations is put in the hands of the people of God in order to display and discover who they are. Unfortunately, in every dispensation, humanity has completely and immediately failed to meet God's expectations.

Some dispensations have experienced revival. However, throughout history, no dispensation has ever been restored.[31]

Darby conferred upon the first dispensation the name **Noah**. In this period Noah is drunk, his son mocks him, and a curse descends on him. Also part of this dispensation is Abraham. Abraham asked Sarah to lie about their relationship by claiming to be a sister rather than his wife. With this dispensation emerged the issue of idolatry. Overall the behavior of the patriarchs was shameful.

The second dispensation is **Moses (the Law)**. During this dispensation, the children of Israel were supposed to be obedient to the Law. However, even while Moses was on the mountain with God (after the Israelites had pledged to be obedient to the words of God under a blood covenant), the children of Israel succumbed to worldly influences. All around them were cultures that worshiped many gods. So the people had Aaron make a golden calf for them to worship and to which to sacrifice. With this one act, the foundation of the commandments and ordinances of God were destroyed.

The third dispensation, **Aaron (priesthood)**, was marked by the disobedience of two of Aaron's sons, Nadab and Abihu. As part of the priesthood, they offered an unholy sacrifice to God and were subsequently consumed by fire. Two other sons of Aaron, Eleazar and Ithamar, displeased God because they did not follow his explicit instructions for them to eat a grain offering by the altar. The offering was supposed to make atonement for the congregation. God spared their lives, but the consequence of this disobedience was recession of the privilege of regularly wearing beautiful and ornate garments. Because of their disobedience, priests were allowed to wear their ornate garments only during priestly consecration. Though the priesthood lasted for some time, there was no remedy for their disobedience.

The fourth dispensation was **Kingly**. For Darby, David and Solomon represented the kingship with victory and peace. The problems with the kingship emerged with Rehoboam and Jeroboam. When Rehoboam ascended to the throne after the death of his father, Solomon, he disobeyed the wise counsel of older men to lighten the heavy yoke of service that Solomon had placed on the people. Rather, he made it heavier. The people rebelled and Rehoboam fled Jerusalem. Jeroboam subsequently ascended to the throne. However, he made idol gods, set up altars for the idol gods to be worshipped, and appointed priests who were not Levites. It was finally the actions of Manasseh, son of Hezekiah, that eliminated all hope that this dispensation could bring glory to God. Manasseh rebuilt high places for worship of idol gods that his father had destroyed. He forced his son to pass through fire, practiced soothsaying, and consulted with mediums and wizards.

Darby's fifth dispensation was that of **Spirit (Gentiles)**. This dispensation arose upon the death of Stephen. Stephen witnessed the resistance of the Jews to the Holy Ghost. At the outset of the dispensation, there was resistance by some of the disciples, such as Peter, to spreading the gospel to the Gentiles. It was only when God provided a special revelation (Acts 10:28) that Peter and others obeyed. Even after the revelation, the twelve disciples of Jesus never fulfilled the Great Commission. In fact, Darby noted that the Great Commission still had not been fulfilled in his day. He believed that any attempt to set the Spirit or Gentile dispensation on a path for success was a sign of ignorance of the principle of God that actions that do not continue in the goodness of God are cut off.[32] In addition, within the organized church Darby noted issues and concerns—such as failure to teach the doctrine of justification by faith, an exchange of a doctrine of works for salvation, ascription to derived rather than divinely assigned authority, and the integration of the church into the world—that further led to the failure of the current dispensation.

When asked whether the Spirit or Gentile dispensation in which he was living would pass away into a new one, Darby responded in the affirmative with an appeal to prophetic texts. He felt that the change in dispensation was very near. He refuted postmillennialist assertions that the earth will one day come to the full knowledge of the glory of God.[33] His primary argument was that there was no prophecy in Scripture that attested to a gradual diffusion of the gospel to convert the world to Christianity. In addition he noted that prophecies usually indicated there would be godly judgment for sin and wickedness. He believed that the incoming dispensation, which he thought would be during his lifetime, would be the final dispensation—the end of the world as we know it. He quoted Revelation 14:7: "Then I saw another angel flying in mid-heaven, with an eternal gospel to proclaim to those who live on the earth—to every nation and tribe and language and people. He said in a loud voice, 'Fear God and give him glory, for the hour of his judgment has come.'"

For Darby these verses highlighted what was happening in the world of his day and was a "solemn warning" and testimony that the current dispensation, Spirit (Gentile), would inherit judgment rather than the world, as postmillennialists supposed. Rather than being a system through which the world is blessed, this dispensation will be cut off. Since this, and every other dispensation, has failed under the power of Satan, this dispensation will give way to the millennium or the final dispensation. In other words, Darby believed that God had given up on humanity.

The final dispensation, which Darby did not name, would reflect the glory of God both on earth and in heaven. God's kingdom in heaven would be centered on followers of Christ. God's kingdom on earth would be centered on Jerusalem and a Jewish remnant. To justify his contention that Jewish people would inherit the earthly kingdom, he contended that the entire collection of Psalms points to the godly promise of a Jewish remnant. He also cited many other texts, including Isaiah 65:17-19:

> For, behold, I create new heavens and a new earth: and the former shall not be remembered, nor come into mind. But be ye glad and rejoice for ever in that which I create: for, behold, I create Jerusalem a rejoicing, and her people a joy. And I will rejoice in Jerusalem, and joy in my people: and the voice of weeping shall be no more heard in her, nor the voice of crying. (KJV)

Darby noted that each dispensation failed to accomplish the will of God very soon after it had begun. Though humans repeatedly failed to honor God in each dispensation, God proved faithful and patient throughout the entire history. However, Darby believed that at some point—it could be any day—God would end human history. Since humanity had continually failed, God would bring an end to human history, starting with the rapture of the saints.

The Rapture is another unique feature of Darby's apocalyptic interpretation of biblical texts. He cited Colossians 3:4 as evidence of the Rapture. In this text, the saints of God are already with Jesus when he appears in the Last Days and will be raptured before Christ appears to judge the world. Though the saints of the church form part of those who will be caught up to meet Christ in the air, the Rapture does not consist exclusively of formally recognized church saints. Saints include all of those who believe in Jesus Christ. As members of the body of Christ, the saints reign with him, suffer with him, and are glorified together with him. They are conformed to Christ's image. Though all the saints will stand before the judgment seat of Christ to give an account of themselves, they will each enjoy the special privilege of being received by Christ himself. Nobody knows when the Rapture will occur. Texts cited as evidence of the Rapture included Zephaniah 13:8-9, Ezekiel 20:33-38, Colossians 3:4, 1 Thessalonians 4:15-18, and Revelation 7:14; 12:10-12.

Since the Rapture could occur at any time, Christians should always be ready for Christ to come. Darby's general principle around waiting is that constant waiting for Jesus as a present possibility, as well as spiritual preparation for Jesus' arrival, characterizes those people who will be blessed when Jesus comes and who will reign over all things. Those who deny Jesus' coming may be led into wickedness. The premillennial portion of "premillennial dispensationalism" indicates that the Rapture will occur before the thousand-year period found in Revelation 20:1-15. During this period Satan will be bound.

Another element of Darby's doctrine is his belief that Jews are part of God's final plan for humanity. Judgment came upon the Jews as a nation when they rejected Jesus as the Messiah. However, members of a Jewish remnant were the faithful among an unfaithful people. In prophetic texts, the remnant is those who feared Jehovah's name and who triumphed over their wicked oppressors in their day. He argued that God is faithful to fulfill God's promises made to the Jews. God did not set aside those promises when they rejected Jesus. Rather God extended grace to them.[34] Darby cited texts such as Joel 2, Zachariah 9, Romans 16:25-26, Ephesians 3:4-5, and Colossians 1:24 as biblical evidence that the Jews would be grafted into their own olive tree and become the nation—the "all Israel."[35] The throne of God will be established in Jerusalem. This throne will be a source of happiness for the entire earth.

For Darby, the Great Tribulation is not just the period mentioned in Revelation 7:14. It is the period that Jesus spoke of in Matthew 24:3-8 when the disciples asked him about a sign of his coming and of the end of the age. Jesus responded to them that they will know the end was near when false messiahs arise and lead people astray, there are wars and rumors of wars, nations rise up against nations, and there are famines and earthquakes in various places. He contended that the people who will have to go through the Great Tribulation are not Christians but rather Jews.[36]

Darby believed that in the Last Days, an antichrist will rise up in political prominence. Darby cited Revelation 13, along with many other texts, such as 2 Thessalonians 2:9, Acts 2:22, and 1 Kings 18, as evidence of the existence and nature of the antichrist. The antichrist will be able to perform signs and wonders as Christ did during his ministry on earth. However, he will pursue an evil and anti-Christian agenda. He will have Christ-like power while using Satan-like language.[37] He will be defeated at the Judgment.

Implications for Preaching

Hope is at the core of the premillennial dispensationalist view of the end of human history. There is hope that those who are faithful to the will and Word of God will be raptured and rewarded with eternal life. There is hope that death of the physical body is not the end of human existence. Rather, life with Christ in the afterlife is the next phase of existence for those who love and worship Christ. Belief in the life to come can serve as comfort for those facing their own death or the death of loved ones. Preachers can remind their people of Darby's traditional perspective to give their people hope. Hope for receiving a reward in the next life for faithfulness to the will of God in earthly life can serve as inspiration for living a life that is pleasing to God in the present.

Darby's view of love is a call for people of God to love in a way that is above all the sin and evil in the world. Though he does not provide details about what this type of love might look like in his writings, his life may bear more evidence. When he was a pastor of his mostly Catholic congregation in Calary, he used his inheritance to help meet the many needs of the people, leading a minimalist existence so that the resources he had could be used to help those who did not have much. The Catholics in his parish were denied many basic civil rights simply because of their denomination. Though he could not change the law, he did what he could to positively affect their lives. Perhaps his actions can provide an example for preachers to use of loving beyond the sin and evil in the world—with sin in this case being the marginalization and disenfranchisement of people for their religious beliefs.

Darby believed that the church was in ruin because of its failure to embrace and embody the Word of God as exemplified by Christ and as guided by the Holy Spirit. He believed that after giving humankind so many chances to change through dispensations, God had given up on humanity. This sense of hopelessness seems to contradict the hopefulness for redemption brought about through the resurrection of Christ. Humankind has been redeemed by God through Christ. Rather than giving up hope and believing that God will end the world because humans will never measure up to God's will, preachers should remind their people of the Good News of the gospel: our sins are forgiven. We are a redeemed people. Our charge is by the power of God to live lives that reflect our new status.

In addition, Darby's belief in dispensations seems to contradict Jesus' own message of forgiveness. In each dispensation, the sins of humanity caused God to give up on them. The God who created humanity with its imperfections gave up on imperfect humanity. When asked by Peter in Matthew 18:21 how many times he should forgive, Jesus said not seven times but seventy times seven. Preachers should remind their people that there should be no limit to the number of times we forgive others because God has no limit for the number of times God forgives us.

Darby believed that being faithful to the will of God in this life meant attending to issues of personal piety and separating oneself from the world in hopes of remaining unspotted by it. He claimed that this model of existence was the one lived by Christ himself. However, while Jesus was concerned with personal piety and even modeled it by separating himself from his disciples to commune with God (Mark 1:35), he was also concerned about the troubles of the world. Jesus associated with publicans and sinners (Luke 19:1-10). He walked, talked, and ate with those who were deemed to be the outcasts of society (Matthew 9:10). While on earth Jesus attended to the needs of others by healing those who were sick (Mark 2:9-12; Luke 17:12-16; John 9:6-7), feeding those who were hungry (Matthew 15:32-39 and Mark 8:1-13), and encouraging his disciples to do the same (Matthew 14:15-21; 25:37-40). When Jesus saw political and religious leaders who were abusing and oppressing the poor, he confronted them and challenged their interpretation of the will of God (Mark 7:1-21). Preachers can share with their congregations the Jesus who lived his life in the world while providing for us a godly example of how to do it.

Darby was a futurist. He interpreted many biblical texts as applicable for future circumstances. He often ignored the messages that the prophets and other biblical writers were attempting to convey to the people in their day. Through their interpretation and preaching, preachers can emphasize the importance of historical context for biblical interpretation. Every biblical text was written for a particular people in a particular time and place. We learn about God and God's will through biblical stories of God's interactions with others. If we ignore what God is doing in a text with a particular people in order to speculate about what God may do in the future, we may miss the lessons God has for us for today.

Questions for Exegesis

1. How do the people in the text live out their faith in God? Are they separating themselves from the world in an attempt to remain unspotted by it? Are they living their lives in the world while also trying to be faithful to God?

2. Is the love of God being experienced in the text in the ways the people live and relate to one another? What are some examples of rightly living and relating to others?

3. Is the hope of God present in the lives of the people in the text? If so, in what forms? Is their hope that God will help them in their earthly lives? Is their hope that God will reward them in the life to come?

4. How did people in the text experience the salvation of God? Through a personal conversion experience? Through deliverance from some form of peril or persecution?

5. What is the relationship of the people in the text to Scripture? Do they live according to a strict interpretation of it? Do they use it loosely to provide parameters in which to live and move and have their being?

6. Hermeneutical Bridge Question: How is God calling us to live in our world today? Are we called to separate ourselves from the world so that we can remain unspotted by it? Are we called to live godly lives in the world while providing examples for others? What are the consequences of each?

Notes

1. Max S. Weremchuk, *John Nelson Darby* (Neptune, NJ: Loizeaux Brothers, 1992), 21.

2. Marion Field, *John Nelson Darby: Prophetic Pioneer* (Surrey: Highland Books, 2008).

3. Weremchuk, 32.

4. Ibid., 34.

5. Field.

6. Ibid.

7. Weremchuk, 70–71.

8. Ibid., 170.

9. Ruth Mather, "The Impact of the Napoleonic Wars in Britain," *Discovering Literature: Romantics and Victorians*, May 15 (2014), https://www.bl.uk/romantics-and-victorians/articles/the-impact-of-the-napoleonic-wars-in-britain.

10. Field.

11. Joseph A. Montagna, "The Industrial Revolution," (1981), http://teachersinstitute.yale.edu/curriculum/units/1981/2/81.02.06.x.html.

12. Patrick Buckland, "The Act of Union, 1800," *The Warrington Project* (1998), http://www.iisresource.org/Documents/0A5_02_Act_Of_Union.pdf., 5.

13. Steven Kreis, "A Note on Protestant Dissent and the Dissenters," *The History Guide* (2004), http://www.historyguide.org/intellect/dissenter.html.

14. Andrew Jukes, "The Way Which Some Call Heresy or Reason for Separation from the Established Church," *Brethren Archive* (1844), http://brethrenarchive.org/media/357772/the_way_which_some_call_heresy_or_reason.pdf. 48.

15. John Nelson Darby, "The Closing Days of Christendom," *Sound Teaching on Electronic Media*, http://www.stempublishing.com/authors/darby/New7_96/Closing_Days.html.

16. John Nelson Darby, "Scripture: The Place It Has in This Day," *Stem Publishing*, http://www.stempublishing.com/authors/darby/DOCTRINE/23005E.html.

17. Ibid.

18. John Nelson Darby, "What Is the Responsibility of the Saints?," *Stem Publishing*, http://stempublishing.com/authors/darby/PRACTICE/17012E.html.

19. John Nelson Darby, "Salvation and Separation," *Stem Publishing*, http://stempublishing.com/authors/darby/NOTESJOT/40010E.html.

20. John Nelson Darby, "Not of the World," *Sound Teaching on Electronic Media*, http://stempublishing.com/authors/darby/EXPOSIT/27008E.html.

21. John Nelson Darby, "Obedience," *Stem Publishing*, http://stempublishing.com/authors/darby/PRACTICE/16001E.html.

22. Ibid.

23. John Nelson Darby, "Christ in Heaven, and the Holy Spirit Sent Down," *Stem Publishing*, http://stempublishing.com/authors/darby/DOCTRINE/31018E.html.

24. Darby, "What Is the Responsibility of the Saints?"

25. John Nelson Darby, "The Christian's Life in Christ: Colossians 1," *Stem Publishing*, http://stempublishing.com/authors/darby/DOCTRINE/31015E.html.

26. Ibid.

27. John Nelson Darby, "1 Corinthians 13," *Stem Publishing*, http://stempublishing.com/authors/darby/EXPOSIT/26020-6E.html#a13.

28. John Nelson Darby, "The Dispensation of the Kingdom of Heaven," *Stem Publishing*, http://stempublishing.com/authors/darby/PROPHET/02004E.html.

29. Darby, "Christ in Heaven, and the Holy Spirit Sent Down."

30. John Nelson Darby, "The Public Ruin of the Church," *Stem Publishing*, http://www.stempublishing.com/authors/darby/MISCELLA/32026E.html.

31. John Nelson Darby, "The Apostasy of Successive Dispensations," *Biblecentre.org*, http://biblecentre.org/content.php?mode=7&item=613.

32. Ibid.

33. John Nelson Darby, "Evidence from Scripture of the Passing Away of the Present Dispensation," *Stem Publishing*, http://www.stempublishing.com/authors/darby/PROPHET/02007E.html.

34. John Nelson Darby, "The Rapture of the Saints and the Character of the Jewish Remnant," *Stem Publishing*, http://www.stempublishing.com/authors/darby/PROPHET/11007E.html.

35. Ibid.

36. John Nelson Darby, "What Saints Will Be in the Tribulation?," *Stem Publishing*, http://stempublishing.com/authors/darby/PROPHET/11006E.html.

37. John Nelson Darby, "Signs of Antichrist," *Stem Publishing*, http://www.stempublishing.com/authors/darby/PROPHET/05038E.html.

2
Realized Eschatology— Radical Freedom
The Theology of Rudolf Bultmann

A Brief Biography

Rudolf Bultmann was born the first of four children in 1884 in Wiefelstede, Germany, a village made up primarily of Protestants near the northwestern agrarian countryside of Oldenburg.[1] His family lived in a parsonage with a garden surrounded by trees "amidst fields and woodlands."[2] His father, Arthur Kennedy Bultmann, was a liberal Evangelical Lutheran pastor. His mother, Helene Stern, while also a Lutheran, was a pietistic conservative. Bultmann's parents had both been raised in families that valued education and embraced a certain "pietistic-revivalist religiosity."[3] Stern's father was educated at Erlangen, Tübingen, and Heidelberg.[4] Arthur Kennedy was educated at Erlangen, Tübingen, and Göttingen.[5] While Helene Stern remained firm in her theological stance throughout her life, in subsequent years, Arthur Kennedy diverged from the path upon which he entered his marriage to one in which he embraced a liberal eschatology. The liberalism of Bultmannn's day was an approach to reinterpreting the Christian faith through the new scientific worldviews that had emerged during the Renaissance and Enlightenment.[6] Liberalism understood aspects of the Bible such as the miracles Jesus performed and the virgin birth to be part of a worldview that was unrealistic or out of touch with the new scientific reality. How could people who confessed to be Christian, but who also embraced science and scientific worldviews, keep their faith in the Jesus Christ of the Bible? Arthur Kennedy wrestled with his beliefs. His liberal perspectives influenced his eschatology. While his wife believed that the kingdom of God would be realized in the future through divine intervention, Arthur Kennedy came to believe that Christians were called to play a role in the building of the historical kingdom of God through their actions in the world or "religio-ethical activity."[7]

In 1890, Arthur Kennedy began pastoring in Oldenburg. As the son of a pastor and therefore part of the middle class, Rudolf Bultmann was eligible to be educated in the German Gymnasium, an educational institution dedicated to the study of ancient languages (Latin, Greek, and Hebrew) and ancient literature. Religious instruction was not part of the Gymnasium curriculum. The Gymnasium was also committed to the study of German culture, including literature and grammar, history, geography, mathematics, and nature. He began his education there in 1895 at the age of ten. Since most students completed their studies in nine years, Bultmann proved himself exceptional when he completed his studies in just over seven.

During his seventh year at the Gymnasium, Bultmann developed what would become a lifelong friendship with Leonhard Frank, who happened to be Jewish. It was through his relationship with Frank that Bultmann began to ponder the future of Judaism and Jews in a German culture that was profoundly anti-Semitic.[8] After completing studies at the Gymnasium, Bultmann attended Tübingen, the University of Berlin, and the University of Marburg, where he subsequently began his teaching career in 1912 as a lecturer in New Testament.[9] While at Marburg, Bultmann was inspired to concentrate his studies in the New Testament after attending lectures of Adolf Jülicher and Johannes Weiss. Of the courses in practical theology that he took at Marburg, homiletics was his favorite. It was while he was a student at Marburg that he began to ponder the relationship between theology and praxis in general, and theology and preaching in particular. In 1916 Bultmann was called as associate professor of New Testament in Breslau followed by a call to Giessen in 1920. It was in 1921 that Bultmann answered his last call as full professor of New Testament to the faculty at the University of Marburg. He served at Marburg from 1921 to 1951.

In 1933, a pivotal year in the political rise of Adolf Hitler and the Nazi Party, Bultmann joined with other pastors of the Confessing Church to denounce the demand of the Nazis to terminate faculty who were not of Aryan ancestry from state institutions. The Confessing Church was a group of pastors and theologians who objected to the Civil Service Reconstruction Law that legalized the purging of Jews from civil service. Civil service in Germany during this time included ordained pastors and ecclesiastical officers. Members of the Confessing Church were primarily concerned with church autonomy and the interference of the law theologically with the sacrament of baptism. They said very little about the discrimination against Jews who had not converted to Christianity.[10] The Marburg theological faculty developed a report in which they declared the Reconstruction Law incompatible with the essence of the Christian church.

At the end of World War II, Great Britain, the United States, France, and the Soviet Union divided Germany into four occupied zones and began a denazification process.[11] The denazification process included the prosecution of high-profile officers and low-level offenders in Hitler's National Socialist Party. It also included subjecting individuals to hearings before panels to determine Nazi affiliations and stripping those found with Nazi pasts of their businesses and estates. After World War II, Germans lived at the mercy of the Allied forces and the Soviet Union.[12] Bultmann and other philosophers and theologians of his day believed that not being able to control their own fates led Germans in particular and human beings in general to nihilism or hopelessness. It is Bultmann's political context and his attempt to help Christians avoid nihilism that compelled him to develop his realized eschatology.

Bultmann received many honors for his scholarship during his lifetime, including a *Festschrift*, an edited book that honors the life and work of a scholar and is composed of chapter contributions by friends, former students, and colleagues. The Festschrift was presented to him on his seventieth birthday. He also received honorary memberships to the Academia Goetheana in Sao Paolo in 1949, Society of Biblical Literature in 1962, and the Academic Study of Theology in 1969. He received the Superior Cross of the Order of Merit with star and shoulder sash in 1974, the day before his ninetieth birthday. Bultmann died in 1976 at the age of ninety-one in Marburg, Germany.

A Theological Overview

Rudolf Bultmann's vision of the reign of God is a realized eschatology in which Christians experience "radical freedom"—freedom from their own pasts through the grace of God available in the person and work of Jesus Christ. A realized, authentic, Christian existence is one in which people are able let go of anxieties and concerns about their daily existence. Rather, they trust in God to guide their lives and provide for them as they faithfully pursue God's will. Realized eschatology rejects the coming of a dramatic, cataclysmic, eschatological event in which God breaks into human history and ends the world as we know it. For Bultmann, Jesus Christ himself is the eschatological event that is ever-present in the lives of humanity through preaching.[13]

Preaching was important to Rudolf Bultmann. He had grown up hearing his father preach every week. When he was a student at university and graduate school, homiletics was his favorite subject within practical theology. He believed that it is in the preaching moment that decisions about faith are made. His concern throughout his career was how to make Christianity relevant to the people in his twentieth-century context. The reality that many people in his German context were steeped in the scientific worldview of the Enlightenment made the challenge of relevancy complex. Many no longer believed in the mythological worldview of the Bible, which includes the existence of heaven as a place where God and the angels dwell and hell as a place of torment; the intervention of God and Satan into the affairs of humanity; the catastrophic end of the world by divine interference; Jesus' ascension to sit at the right hand of God; and the return of Jesus to complete the work of salvation on some future judgment day.[14] Bultmann referred to these beliefs as mythological because they were are not based in scientifically verifiable facts. There is no way to verify scientifically the existence of heaven, hell, or Satan. There is no way to distinguish divine intervention from a stroke of good luck. These beliefs could not be proven through historical documentation or anthropological data collection. As a result, Bultmann believed that the major challenge of preachers in modernity was how to inspire Christian faith while simultaneously embracing the advent of the scientific worldview.

By the time Bultmann began his teaching career in Germany, all academic disciplines, including biblical studies and theology, were grounded in scientific principles and reason. For Bultmann, the question that needed to be asked and answered in the age of modernity was: Is it necessary to believe the mythical worldview of the Bible in order to be Christian, or is there a truth in the New Testament that is independent of the worldview of its time?

The way Bultmann made the case for the gospel in the age of modernity was through a process he termed *demythologizing*. Understanding his concept of demythologizing is key to understanding his approach to eschatology. For Bultmann, demythologizing the biblical text means critiquing the mythological world of the New Testament in order to reveal its true intention. Myth was used in the Bible to express the belief that human existence is grounded in and limited by a Higher Power. Critique is necessary because myth represents God and Satan as being located in heaven above the earth and in hell beneath it. From a scientific perspective, this belief is not grounded in reality. Bultmann believes that myth limits the powers of God to the realm of human ability through its use of human language to describe a transcendent God. For example, in mythology God is represented as omnipotent and omniscient rather than by any qualities different from those of humans. In addition, by becoming so involved in the affairs of humans, God becomes immanent rather then transcendent.[15] Myth also defies natural laws and psychological occurrences while linking them together. For example, Jesus turned water into wine in the Gospel of John, thus defying natural laws. By performing this miracle, Jesus enabled his newly chosen disciples to believe in him.

Demythologizing means translating and recontextualizing the mythological language of the Bible into language and contexts that people can understand. For example, mythological language that Jesus was with God from the beginning actually means that God was present in Jesus' words and deeds. Jesus being born of a virgin actually means that Jesus is the Son of God. The phrase "the word became flesh" represents a paradox by being at once an historical and an eschatological event. The coming of Christ put an end to the world and its history. Therefore, for Bultmann, the Christ event cannot be made present through remembrance. The Christ event becomes present through proclamation.

By demythologizing the text, people of faith are able to understand that God is calling God's people out of their own anxieties and attempts to secure their own lives and into a more authentic existence. A more authentic existence for people of faith is one in which they adopt a "nevertheless" or "over against the world" attitude in which their understanding of God's will guides every decision they make.[16] In order to fully understand Bultmann's eschatology, we must understand some of the terminology that he uses to better appeal to those with a scientific worldview and then understand his approach to interpreting the Bible.

Bultmann often redefined common theological terms in ways that people with scientific worldviews could understand and relate to. For example, with great detail he clarifies what he means by the term "flesh." Often the term is translated to mean the human body and actions associated with it, such as adultery and fornication. Bultmann contended that flesh does not refer to just the body. Rather, the flesh is the world-at-large—the sphere of everything that is transient (the visible, available, disposable, and measureable) in human existence. Flesh also includes activities such as all human creating, accomplishing, and achieving that is done to advance in the world. When we are successful in the world, we become secure in our own achievements and may even become boastful. This world exerts power over humanity when we live according to its ways rather than the ways of God. When we allow the world to exert power over us we lose our God-intended life—our authentic existence. Seeking security in the world brings us into conflict with others who are doing the same, which leads to envy, anger, jealousy, strife, and compacts and conventions (i.e., governmental agreements that privilege some while disenfranchising others). Conflicts lead to anxiety as we try desperately to hold on to our successes and achievements while secretly feeling that our lives and everything we hold dear are slipping away from us.

Bultmann contrasts life in the world with genuine human life or "life in the Spirit," which is lived out of what is invisible and nondisposable. Life in the Spirit is made possible through God's grace, which we experience as love. Bultmann defines *grace* as forgiveness of sin and liberation from our pasts, which threaten to hold us in bondage. The grace of God allows us to let go of things of the flesh that prevent us from embracing the future that God has in store for us.

Sin for Bultmann is the attitude with which we try to secure our own futures without God. Sin includes being highhanded and rebellious. Sin is grabbing hold of that which we should let go and clinging to that which is in the process of perishing or has already perished. Sin is closing off God's future by refusing to let go of the past. Our sins are forgiven when we open ourselves to grace and renounce all attempts to be acceptable by the standards of the world. Our sins are forgiven when we act in faith and obedience by putting our trust solely in God. Being free from sin means prioritizing the will of God over the cares and concerns of the world.

Being a new creation in Christ Jesus means allowing the fruits of the Spirit (love, joy, peace, patience, kindness, goodness, faithfulness, gentleness, and self-control) to shape the ways we interact with others. When we are no longer anxious about our own futures, we can be open to others and their needs. However, the others to whom we should be open, for Bultmann, are only our true neighbors to whom we are historically bound. He does not believe that true neighbors include all people.

How can the cross, crucifixion, and resurrection of Christ be demythologized? Bultmann first acknowledges that though Jesus has been characterized as a preexistent divine being, he was actually an historical person. Though his mythological destiny was resurrection and ascension, his actual destiny was death on the cross through crucifixion. Therefore, Bultmann believes that the significance of the story of Christ does not lie in mythical language used in the New Testament to describe Jesus' life and death. Rather the significance of Jesus' story lies in what God wants to say to humanity through it. According to 1 Corinthians 2:6, the cross is the judgment of the world through which the rulers of this age are brought to nothing. Therefore, everything that happens at the cross is judgment against all of us who have fallen under the powers of the world. When God allowed Jesus to be crucified on the cross, God was establishing the cross for us. Believing in the cross of Christ means accepting the cross as our own and allowing ourselves to be crucified with him. The cross is not an act of salvation that happened to the mythical person of Christ. Rather, the cross is an event that is always present in the lives of those who understand its significance for their faith.

It is God's liberating judgment of the world through the cross that robs death of its power. Therefore, the resurrection is not a literal raising from the dead of the Crucified One. Rather, the resurrection literally means that genuine new life in Christ has been and is being created.[17] Sharing in Christ's resurrection means living a life in which one struggles to be free from sin and put off works of unrighteousness (Romans 6:11-14).

The significance of the cross of Christ is in the sacraments of baptism and the Lord's Supper. We are baptized into Christ's death (Romans 6:3) and crucified with him (Romans 6:6). Taking part in the Lord's Supper means participating in the crucified body and the shed blood of Jesus (1 Corinthians 10:16). The cross of Christ is present in the lives of believers as they endeavor to crucify their passions and desires (Galatians 5:24). Crucifying passions and desires also means overcoming fears of suffering when being persecuted for the sake of Christ (2 Corinthians 4:10-11).

Bultmann also contended that demythologizing is existential interpretation because it seeks to clarify the intention of myth to talk about human existence.[18] He believed that knowing God and Christ does not mean contemplating their natures or Christ's mode of incarnation. Instead, knowing God and Christ means knowing what they do to us as individuals. Existentialist interpretation attempts to free the texts from statements that objectify their meaning rather than apply their meaning to real human life. In an essay he wrote after retiring from a thirty-year career as a professor, Bultmann invites his readers to have an existential encounter with the text.[19] An existential encounter is one in which the preacher brings all of who he or she is to the text for the purpose of discovering as much as possible about the world of the text. By advocating for existential encounters, Bultmann is in essence saying that authenticity in preaching begins not in sermon delivery but in the exegetical process itself.[20]

Bultmann understood that no preacher is a *tabula rasa* or a blank slate. Every one of us comes to the text with particular life experiences while also standing in particular social locations—both of which shape our perspectives and worldviews. As a result, when preachers question the text out of their own historical situations, the text comes alive. When they are formed from their personal experiences, questions they raise are significant and meaningful—so much so that the thought of finding the answers to their questions generate excitement about the exegetical process itself. The preachers' questions can then guide their research by employing a handy stash of interpretive tools such as knowledge of original languages and resources that reveal the social and political forces at work in the world of the text. In an existential encounter, exegeting biblical texts becomes a lively and stimulating experience.

Bultmann advocates an existential encounter because biblical texts are like treasure troves full of valuable gems and an abundance of riches that reveal themselves only to explorers who are alive with questions and embark on their quests with great expectations. As a proponent of historical criticism, Bultmann contends that though ancient texts are awash with knowledge of the past, "they speak anew to every present situation."[21] While the exact dates and details of events may be fixed, their meaning is not. The meaning of events that happened in the past can only be known in the future. And even that future meaning varies depending on who is doing the interpreting.

Bultmann's invitation to an existential encounter is not without caution. While he believed that preachers should bring their perspectives to the exegetical process, he also believed that they should put their prejudices in check. Prejudice is very different from perspective. Prejudice prejudges and limits interpretive possibilities. When operating with prejudice, the preacher refuses to consider that some outcomes are possible. By contrast, perspective focuses the interpretive lens while remaining open to possibilities. When operating from this perspective, the preacher remains open to all the possibilities that the text may yield. Therefore, preachers should learn to recognize their particular biases and prejudices so as to not taint the results of their exegetical work.

It follows that when Bultmann wrote and lectured about eschatology, he did so through his own existential encounter with Old and New Testament texts. He also incorporated his encounters with human (European) history. Bultmann examined many manifestations of human existence and self-perceptions. He acknowledged that in each era and context, human existence was at the mercy of historical circumstances. The turbulent political circumstances of Bultmann's day compelled many philosophers to ponder the meaning of history. One even went so far as to posit, "Today, history is our biggest problem."[22] Bultmann himself participated in such pondering in his seminal work, *History and Eschatology*.

During the mid-twentieth century, some philosophers felt humanity was at the mercy of history in two senses. First, people were living and struggling not only with situations they created for themselves but also with situations created by those who came before them. They were not completely in control of their fates.

> [They] have comprehended that they are dependent on circumstances, and that the achievement of a plan of life involves a struggle with opposing powers, which are often stronger that man's own virtue. They know that history takes shape not only through the actions of men but also by fate or destiny. This perception in our day acquired special urgency in consequence of the events of world-history. Men have become conscious not only of their dependence but also of their helplessness. They have come to feel that they are not only interwoven with the course of history but are also at its mercy.[23]

Second, many people were experiencing nihilism or a sense of hopelessness. Bultmann raised the question, "Can there be salvation from nihilism?"

In response, he embarked on an existential journey that began by contrasting the mindsets of ancient Greeks (before Christ) with the ancient Israelites, segued to the Gospels and Pauline epistles, took a detour into Enlightenment philosophy, and then ventured back into the New Testament for the finale. In each of the movements of his lectures, he highlighted the ways human conceptions of existence change throughout the centuries in order to maintain some sort of hope for a better future. Guiding his journey is the presupposition that historical knowledge is existential knowledge (history is simply a reflection of the state of human existence).

When examining the evolution of biblical views of eschatology, Bultmann noted that they shifted over time. The early Christian community understood themselves to be an eschatological community with its impetus in the incarnation, crucifixion, resurrection, and glorification of Christ.[24] This eschatological view dictated their view of the world as well as ways they lived in it. Since Christians had their ultimate citizenship in heaven, they saw the earth as a foreign land toward which they bore no responsibility. One of their primary tasks was to keep themselves untainted by the world's sin so they would be blameless on the Day of Judgment, which was imminent. Therefore, they occupied themselves with matters such as abstinence and other pursuits of righteousness rather than efforts to transform society such as social programs.

In the ensuing centuries, since Christ had not yet returned, the mindset of Christian communities shifted to meet the demands of their new existential realities. Rather than continuing to exist as if there would be no future, Luke and writers of the pastoral epistles acknowledged the possibility that the Christian community might be around at least for the foreseeable future. As Christianity continued to evolve, so did the biblical view of human existence. The effect of baptism shifted from the Pauline sense of an act that freed humans from the past and the power of sin to a means of forgiveness of sin with the requirement to avoid new sin in the future. After baptism, Christians had a limited amount of time to prove their virtue by fulfilling godly demands before imminent judgment.[25] The meaning of obedience also shifted. Obedience was no longer believed to be simply the fruit of salvation but also the action taken to remain saved. Salvation became a new opportunity for continual justification through good works.

During this period, eschatology was not abandoned. Rather, its status changed from imminent to indefinite. Christians got used to waiting.

While waiting for the end, they developed sacramentalism in which the destiny of the world became less of a priority than the salvation of the individual soul. A blessed afterlife was deemed available through sacraments (communion, baptism, marriage, ordained ministry). In addition, the powers of the beyond that would bring an end to the world were working in the present world through the sacraments administered by the church.[26] Sacramental worship began to be ruled by church officials, thereby shifting the church from a community of the saved to an institution of salvation.[27] Over the years the degree to which the church was able to forgive sins changed. At one point, the church forgave only smaller sins while teaching adherents that gross sins, especially apostasy, lost the grace of baptism. Over the years this teaching changed. The church began to offer forgiveness of gross sins through the sacrament of penance.

In addition to analyzing the evolution of the eschatology of worshipping communities, Bultmann also examined secular philosophical views. He highlighted the work of Emmanuel Kant, who differentiated between biblical views of eschatology in the religion of revelation and the view of eschatology in the religion of reason. In the religion of reason, the goal of the kingdom of God is the emergence of an ethical community on earth rather than a world outside of history.[28]

Bultmann also considered the writings of Karl Marx, who believed that the course of history was guided by the economic-social conditions and the struggle between opposing groups, crises, and catastrophes. Marx's eschatological vision was a realm of economic freedom—a kingdom of God without God. In Marx's vision, the kingdom would be realized when the opposition between the bourgeoisie (ruling class) and the proletariat (working class) resulted in a revolution in which the proletariat emerged victorious. In the Marxist secular vision of the kingdom, differences between the oppressors and the oppressed would disappear.[29]

Ultimately, Bultmann concluded that salvation from nihilism can be found in Christianity. In Christianity, humans can experience "radical freedom"—freedom from their own pasts through the grace of God available in the person and work of Jesus Christ. Jesus Christ is the eschatological event by which the old world of believers has come to an end. Once believers accept Christ as their Savior, they are new creatures in Christ Jesus.

Bultmann was clear that the eschatological event is not a "dramatic cosmic catastrophe."[30] He argued that, although the Christ event is historic in that it happened in the past, it is at the same time an eternal event that happens in the souls of believers in which "Christ is born, suffers, dies and is raised to eternal life." Christian existence therefore becomes eschatological existence. In this new existence, it is not history and the world that changes but rather the newly converted Christian's attitude towards the world that changes.[31] In this new existence, Christians decide on a new self-understanding for their own responsible acting. Responsible acting is grounded in Christian love. In this sense, Christian life is one lived from the future where humans find freedom from themselves. This new life of freedom is the result of a conscious decision to accept a new life grounded in the grace of God. "Christian faith is the power to grasp this gift" of freedom. For Bultmann, eschatological moments are realized in Christian faith and preaching.[32]

It is in the act of preaching that eschatological existence or the reign of God is truly realized. Preaching is an address that demands decisions of faith. In decisions of faith, individuals develop new understandings of themselves—understandings in which they are free from the old self. In this new understanding, the believers make decisions that are born of love—love of neighbor.[33] Being able to truly love one's neighbor is possible only when humans become free from themselves. For Bultmann, philosophy corrects the Christian mandate to love all people and "exposes what is truly natural" by teaching people to love those who are closest to them.

Implications for Preaching

For Bultmann's German audience, his understanding of Christianity as freedom from one's past would have been very good news. Many people who had lived through the reign of the Third Reich were feeling guilty for not speaking out or doing more to impact the fate of millions. Germans may have felt ashamed that such an atrocity happened in their nation. "Radical freedom" was just what they needed on many levels.

Preachers today can share the availability of radical freedom with their congregations. Radical freedom from one's past is good news for people in all times and places. No one has to allow anything they have done in the past to mar their futures.

For those who preach in congregations in which there are people who may be skeptical about the reality of traditional theological conceptions such as the resurrection and the virgin birth, Bultmann's demythologizing approach could be very helpful. Preachers can inform their people that these theological concepts have a deeper meaning. The cross and the resurrection of Christ point to a new life. One of the gifts that Bultmann's realized eschatology makes to the larger conversation is his conceptualizing of eschatology as a state of existence, a way of being and living made possible through the cross and the resurrection. Unlike some eschatologies in which Christians are rewarded for their faithfulness and fidelity to the will and ways of God only in the afterlife, such as dispensationalism, in realized eschatology accepting Christ yields an immediate reward of an altered state of earthly existence.

Through Bultmann's realized eschatology, preachers can remind their congregations that Christians need to act responsibly in their daily lives while being guided by love. Each person must make conscious decisions to be guided by godly principles every day of their lives. Consequences of our human actions often have implications and repercussions that reach far beyond our personal domains.

The question "Can there be salvation from nihilism?" is a timeless one that transcends culture and space. Unfortunately, Bultmann's realized eschatological solution provides an individualistic and perpetrator-centered response to a question that also has communal, systemic, and victim-centered implications. Preachers can remind their congregations that while God certainly forgives us of our sins, our actions are not without consequences.

Bultmann's simplistic characterization of "radical freedom" as liberation from one's past at best appears to overlook the impact of our sins on others. Victims of sin are also people of God who need to experience the "radical freedom" of God by escaping the threat of nihilism that ensues when they find themselves embroiled in situations and circumstances that are not of their own making. Bultmann's supposed solution to nihilism not only fails to resolve the issue but also further ensconces victims into nihilistic states by offering them no redress for their issues and concerns. Salvation itself becomes a perpetrator-centered existence. Preachers can remind their congregations that salvation is for all of God's people and includes liberation from the sins of others.

In Bultmann's realized eschatology, he contends that Christian faith is the power bestowed on every human to grasp the gift of freedom from their own existence. However, his conception does not address whether Christian faith includes the power for each individual to help secure freedom for those who are unable to help themselves. Bultmann's Christology is narrowly focused on the eschatological implications of Jesus' crucifixion as it enables Christians to experience freedom from the guilt and responsibility for personal sin versus freedom to help others who are victims of personal and corporate sin. Preachers can remind their people of the responsibility to treat others as they wish to be treated. When we see others being oppressed, we have a responsibility to address and eliminate the cause of their oppression.

Bultmann's omission is even more startling when recognized in light of his political and social context. He wrote the lectures contained in *History and Eschatology* after the rise and fall of the Third Reich. He had personally witnessed and fought against the demonization and dismissal of Christian Jewish scholars from academic institutions based solely on their race. Yet the need for all Christians to emulate his actions by embodying their Christian sensibilities was not included in his eschatology. Again, Bultmann's solution for nihilism breaks down when his conception of Christian faith includes no mandate for radically free Christians to help anyone other than themselves.

Another concern about realized eschatology is the loss of the value of the life of Jesus in Bultmann's radical vision. By treating the Bible solely as a historical document from which to extract historical models of human existence, Bultmann ignored potential influences that Jesus' earthly life can have on those seeking a model for Christian living. Bultmann writes in *New Testament and Mythology* that Jesus' significance for humanity cannot be contained by regular historical observation because of the historical unreliability of Scripture. Yet he admitted that mythology has value beyond the realm of historical reality. Preachers can highlight the centrality of Jesus' life as a model for those committed to following him. It is from his life that we learn how we should think and how we should relate to God and to one another.

Even if we believe Bultmann's contention to be true, should historical unreliability negate the significance of the life of Jesus presented in the tradition of Scripture? There is existential value in observing and modeling

Jesus' behavior throughout his earthly ministry as recorded in the Gospels. When Bultmann wrote that Christians should act out of love, he does not define what acting responsibly and out of love looks like. The life of Jesus provides such a model.

Bultmann's realized eschatology is thoroughly Eurocentric, androcentric, and anthropocentric. He developed his perspective in a European physical context, in conversation with other European males (Greek and German), while using European history and context as his point of departure and by privileging humanity over all of God's creation. Consequently, there are issues and concerns not raised and addressed in his scholarship that impact the rest of the world's human populations and other parts of God's creation. Many godly experiences and perspectives are not honored or even acknowledged. Preachers should often invite their hearers to see and understand the experiences and worldviews of those who are different from them.

The limited worldview of Bultmann's theology is a reflection of the state of academic theology as a discipline in the mid-twentieth century worldwide. In the seventy years since Bultmann wrote these lectures, theology as a formal academic discipline has trained and embraced scholars from many parts of the world and represents genders, races, ethnicities, and perspectives that were marginalized and underrated in Bultmann's day (as some still are in our day). Many of these academics are producing scholarship that addresses issues that were not part of the lived experiences of academic theologians seventy years ago. The writings of diverse theologians can be invaluable resources for those seeking to broaden the worldviews of their congregations.

Whether Bultmann and other German theologians of his era believed their scholarship had universal implications can be debated. Today, we are called to acknowledge and embrace the value and particularities of Bultmann's eschatology while also acknowledging its limitations. Bultmann's vision of the reign of God is good news for some of God's creation. It is not good news for all.

Questions for Exegesis

1. Are there people mentioned in the text whose suffering is caused by the sins of others who have created the situations and circumstances in which they live? If so, who? Who is the source of their suffering?

2. Are there people in the text who live in a state of hopelessness? If so, is God acting on their behalf to relieve their suffering? How?

3. Are there people in the text striving for success in their world that leads them into envy, anger, jealousy, strife, and compacts and conventions? If so, who are they and what are they doing?

4. Are the fruits of the Spirit (love, joy, peace, patience, kindness, goodness, faithfulness, gentleness and self-control) shaping the ways the people in the text are interacting with one another? If so, how?

5. How do people in the text understand their relationship to the world? Are they citizens of heaven who see the world as a sin-filled stopover on their way to heaven, or are they citizens of the world who are charged to live godly lives that shape and positively impact everything around them?

6. Hermeneutical Bridge Question: What is the spiritual significance of mythological (as termed by Bultmann) concepts such as heaven, hell, and the virgin birth for us today? Does the significance differ based on whether they are understood as myth or reality? Describe the significance.

Notes

1. William D. Dennison, *The Young Bultmann: Context for His Understanding of God, 1884–1925*, American University Studies VII, Theology and Religion (New York: P. Lang, 2008).

2. Konrad Hammann and Philip E. Devenish, *Rudolf Bultmann: A Biography*, First English edition. ed. (Salem, OR: Polebridge Press, 2013), 6. Hammann is Professor of Systematic and Historical Theology and its Didactic in the Evangelical-Theological Faculty of the University of Munster, Germany. Throughout this biography Hammann deftly intertwines Bultmann's personal history gleaned from personal letters and letters of close friends and associates with a thorough knowledge of Bultmann's biblical and theological writings, while contextualizing both in German history to develop a comprehensive portrait of Bultmann's life and legacy.

3. Ibid., 2.

4. Ibid., 3.

5. Ibid., 2.

6. Philip Edgcumbe Hughes, *Creative Minds in Contemporary Theology: A Guidebook to the Principal Teachings of Karl Barth, G. C. Berkouwer, Emil Brunner, Rudolf Bultmann, Oscar Cullmann, James Denney, C. H. Dodd, Herman Dooyeweerd, P. T. Forsyth, Charles Gore, Reinhold Niebuhr, Pierre Teilhard De Chardin, and Paul Tillich* (Grand Rapids: Eerdmans, 1966), 136.

7. Hammann, 3.

8. Ibid., 12.

9. Hughes, 132.

10. See Matthew D. Hockenos, "The Church Struggle and the Confessing Church: An Introduction to Bonhoeffer's Context," *Journal of the Council of Centers on Jewish-Christian Relations* 2, no. 1 (2007), 9. See Hammann, 291.

11. Louisa McClintock, "Facing the Awful Truth: Germany Confronts the Past, Again," *Problems of Post Communism* 52, no. 6 (2005): 32–45. Though Great Britain, the United States, France, and the Soviet Union were supposed to be facilitating a denazification process to identify and punish people who had participated actively in the Nazi regime, they engaged in their own political agendas. For example, the United States used qualified people to further its goal of establishing democracy and capitalism in their occupied territory.

12. Mitchell G. Bard, "World War II: Denazification," *Jewish Visual Library* (2008), http://germanculture.com.ua/germany-history/the-nuremberg-trials/.

13. Rudolf Bultmann, *History and Eschatology: The Presence of Eternity* (New York: Harper Torchbooks, 1957), 152.

14. Rudolf Bultmann, "New Testament and Mythology (1941)," *New Testament and Mythology and Other Basic Writings*, ed. Schubert M. Ogden (Philadelphia: Fortress Press, 1984), 2–5.

15. Rudolf Bultmann, "On the Problem of Demythologizing (1952)," *New Testament and Mythology and Other Basic Writings*, ed. Schubert M. Ogden (Philadelphia: Fortress Press, 1984), 98–99.

16. Rudolf Bultmann, "On the Problem of Demythologizing (1961)," *New Testament and Mythology and Other Basic Writings*, ed. Schubert M. Ogden (Philadelphia: Fortress Press, 1961), 158–59.

17. "New Testament and Mythology (1941)," 25.

18. "On the Problem of Demythologizing (1952)," 113.

19. Rudolf Bultmann, "Is Exegesis without Presuppositions Possible? (1957)," *New Testament and Mythology and Other Basic Writings*, ed. Schubert M. Ogden (Philadelphia: Fortress Press, 1984), 152.

20. See Mumford, Debra J. "An Existential Encounter with the Text." *Working Preacher* (2015). https://www.workingpreacher.org/craft.aspx?post=3478.

21. *History and Eschatology*, 142.

22. Ibid., 1–7.

23. Ibid., 2

24. Ibid., 36–37.

25. Ibid., 50.

26. Ibid., 51–52.

27. Ibid., 53.

28. Ibid., 67.

29. Ibid., 69.

30. Ibid., 151.

31. Ibid., 153.

32. Ibid., 154.

33. Ibid., 152.

3
The Vision of the Beloved Community
The Theology of Martin Luther King Jr.

A Brief Biography

Martin Luther King Jr. was born Michael King Jr. in Atlanta, Georgia, on January 15, 1929.[1] His father, Michael King Sr., was senior pastor of the Ebenezer Baptist Church. His mother, Alberta Christine Williams King, was an organist, and gifted choir director who was in demand for her musical gifts throughout the state of Georgia and within the National Baptist Convention.[2] Alberta's father, A. D. Williams, served as pastor of Ebenezer for forty years and had grown Ebenezer from thirteen members to more than seven hundred and fifty by the time he died in 1931. Michael King Sr. assumed pastoral duties a few months after his father-in-law died.

Michael King Jr. was brought up in a household with a father who believed that injustice should be resisted. When he was an adult, King Jr. recalled an incident in which his father walked out of a shoe store rather than be forced to go to the back of the store to be served. He recalled another incident where his father was stopped by a white police officer. King Sr. corrected the officer when the officer called him "boy." He pointed to King Jr. and told the officer, "This is a boy, I am a man. I will not speak to you until you call me a man."[3] The police officer wrote the speeding ticket quickly, got in his car, and drove away. Resistance was in King Jr.'s DNA.

It was after returning from a World Baptist Alliance meeting in Berlin, Germany, that King Sr. changed his name—and his son's name—to Martin Luther King. Some say he did so because he was inspired by the work of Martin Luther as a reformer. However, in his autobiography, King Sr. wrote that his father preferred to call him Martin Luther when he was a boy. Martin Luther was the combined name of two of his uncles.[4]

Martin Luther King Jr. attended elementary school in Atlanta. After completing the sixth grade, he attended the Atlanta University Laboratory High School, which was a private, experimental program for African

Americans who were seeking an alternative to crowded public schools. After the school closed, he skipped the ninth grade and started the tenth grade at Booker T. Washington High School.[5] In his second year of high school, he won his first oratorical contest in Dublin, Georgia, with a speech entitled "The Negro and the Constitution." On the way home from the contest he and some other students were cursed by a bus driver when they refused to give up their seats to whites on a bus. Their speech teacher advised them to move so that the situation would not escalate. Reflecting on this incident twenty years later, King Jr. stated that when he was standing on the bus on his way back to Atlanta, "I was the angriest I have ever been in my life."[6] He had just finished delivering a speech in which he had said, "We cannot be truly Christian people so long as we flaunt the central teachings of Jesus: brotherly love and the Golden Rule. . . . So as we gird ourselves to defend democracy from foreign attack, let us see to it that increasingly at home we give fair play and free opportunity for all people."[7] Even at such a young age, he fully understood the irony of his situation.

After completing the eleventh grade, King entered Morehouse College. His early entry was made possible by a program instituted by the president of Morehouse, Benjamin Mays. Enrollment had declined because of the wartime draft. Mays allowed qualified high school juniors to complete the entering class of 1944. By entering Morehouse during the Mays era, King became part of an institution committed to helping students understand the relationship of religion to real life. Mays taught his students that "a religion which ignores social problems will in time be doomed."[8]

King Jr.'s goal when enrolling at Morehouse was to become an attorney. Though he felt inclined toward ministry, he resisted because he rejected the emotionalism and literal biblical interpretation that was so pervasive in traditional Baptist preaching and worship. He believed religion should appeal to the intellect while being applicable to the lives of the people in the pews. King Jr. wrote years after graduating from Morehouse that during his first two years there, "the shackles of fundamentalism were removed from my body." While enrolled at Morehouse, King Jr. preached his trial sermon and was licensed to preach at Ebenezer. He graduated from Morehouse in the spring of 1948 and entered seminary later in the fall at Crozer Theological Seminary in Chester, Pennsylvania.

At Crozer, theologian George Washington Davis had a profound influence on King Jr.'s thinking. Davis emphasized the social implications of the gospel and was himself greatly influenced by the social gospel of Walter Rauschenbusch. While at Crozer, King Jr. was elected student body president and became class valedictorian. Upon graduation he was accepted into the doctoral program in systematic theology at Boston University School of Theology. While at Boston University he met and married Coretta Scott on June 18, 1953, who was pursuing a graduate degree at the New England Conservatory of Music.[9] He earned his PhD in five years and graduated in 1955.

Upon graduating, King Jr. had a number of career options. He had offers to pastor churches in integrated cities in Massachusetts and New York. He also had three offers to serve in the academy as a dean, a professor, or an administrator. He and Coretta could have chosen one of those positions and lived very comfortable lives. However, they chose to go back to the segregated South when the offer of the pastorate of Dexter Avenue Baptist Church in Montgomery, Alabama, was made. King Jr. and Coretta felt a call to try to make a difference in the part of the country they felt needed it the most.

It was the Montgomery bus boycott that launched King Jr. into national prominence. He worked with Ralph Abernathy and many other dedicated men and women to develop and sustain the boycott for 381 days. After the success of the boycott, sixty ministers and faith leaders met in 1957 to establish the Southern Christian Leadership Conference (SCLC) to take the movement national. They decided that their motto needed to be something that not only reflected the purpose of the group but also the state of the nation in which the group would function. They chose as their motto "To save the soul of America." King was selected to be the president of the SCLC. He led a coalition of civil rights groups in 1963 in a nonviolent campaign to gain civil rights in Birmingham, Alabama, and delivered his "I Have a Dream" speech on August 28, 1963, at the March on Washington. The March on Washington in large part led to the signing of the Civil Rights Act in 1964. In 1964 Martin Luther King Jr. became the youngest recipient of the Nobel Peace Prize. In 1965 he led the Selma to Montgomery, Alabama, march that led to the passing and signing of the Voting Rights Act. Between 1965 and 1968, King Jr. focused his efforts on achieving economic justice and international peace, which culminated in the Poor People's Campaign. He also spoke out against the war in Vietnam.[10]

King Jr. described himself as a drum major for justice.[11] Though he spent much of his public life fighting racism, his fight for justice transcended the bounds of race. He fought against poverty, spoke out against the Vietnam War, and fought for the rights of workers whose voices were unheard and whose human worth and value were unacknowledged by the white majority. Though his public ministry spanned a period of only twelve and a half years, his sermons, speeches, books, and YouTube videos have motivated millions to fight for justice and equality for all people.

Martin Luther King Jr. was assassinated at the Lorraine Motel in Memphis, Tennessee, on April 4, 1968.

A Theological Overview

Martin Luther King Jr. believed that people who are followers of Christ, and those who believe in God generally, should vehemently resist injustice wherever it is found. God is a God of justice, as can be witnessed in biblical texts. Therefore, at the heart of everything King did and said and worked for so diligently was his vision of the kingdom of God, which he called the "beloved community." He developed his formal theological foundation for the beloved community during educational experiences at Morehouse, Crozer, and Boston universities. The beloved community for King was not a utopian vision in which people continuously gathered to join hands and sing "We Shall Overcome." The beloved community was a state of being in which every person would be recognized as being created in the image of God by the one and same creator God.[12] The "image of God" is a biblical term that refers to the inherent dignity and innate worth of all humans. Since all humans are created in the image of God, there is "no graded scale of essential worth."[13] No one race has more divine right than any other. The "indelible stamp" of the Creator is etched in the personality of every human.[14] In the beloved community, all people have access to resources they need—job opportunities, education, training, health care, safe and adequate housing, and so on—so they can not only survive, but thrive.

Since King believed that all people are created in the image of God, he also believed that the social constructs of race and racism are anathema to the will of God. King understood that the pain inflicted on individuals, families, and communities by racism is, unfortunately, central to African American life. It is evident in every moment of African American existence because it is pain that derives from a trait that they cannot control—the color of their skin.[15] King believed white society put a curse on black skin that causes African Americans to shed "invisible tears that no hand can wipe away."[16]

In the beloved community, every child should grow up understanding her or his worth in the eyes of God. Therefore, the reality that "every Negro child suffers a traumatic emotional burden when she or he encounters 'color shock'" or "the reality of his black skin"—and the social stigma that accompanies it—is not God's will for God's people.[17] King first became aware of the existence of race at the age of six when he was no longer allowed to play with his best friend, who was white. After playing together for three years, his friend's father told his son that he could no longer play with King. This happened as the boy was entering Atlanta's segregated school system. King was shocked. His parents took that moment to inform him about racism and how their lives were affected by it. He recalled that, though he wanted to hate all white people, his parents taught him that it was his Christian duty to love them. The question arose in his mind, "How can I love a race of people who hate me and cause me to break up with my best friend?"[18]

Segregation, which is a by-product of racism, prohibited African Americans from experiencing an essential aspect of the beloved community—freedom. Segregation denied individuals the ability to deliberate, decide, and respond. They could not deliberate and decide when they had no alternatives. Segregation impeded the ability of people to choose for themselves where they would live, how much they could earn, or the types of careers they would pursue, thereby reducing them to animals. Animals, by their nature, have a limited capacity to make decisions. Therefore, since segregation treated African Americans as if they were incapable of deliberating, deciding, and taking full responsibility for their own lives, it reduced their existence to the level of animals. They merely existed.[19]

In addition to treating African Americans like animals, segregation treated them like social lepers—people ostracized or outcast because of physical conditions or characteristics over which they have no control. Being treated as social lepers inflicts immeasurable psychological harms and creates fears, resentments, anxieties, and sensitivities that "make each day of life a turmoil."[20] Social lepers never know what to expect from social encounters, which causes them to walk on tiptoe through life rather than walk assuredly based on the lived reality of shared humanity. For King, only complete integration could unchain the spirit and mind and provide the highest quality of human freedom. People cannot be truly free until they have the opportunity to fulfill their "total capacity" without socially imposed hindrances and barriers.[21]

In addition to treating African Americans like animals and social lepers, segregation treated African Americans as if they were a means to an end or mere tools to get jobs done. When the Southern gentry used the term "hands" to refer to African Americans, they were betraying their perception of the Negro's purpose—labor. Lost in the practice of segregation was the sacred worth of all people. Using the words of Martin Buber, King asserted that segregation substitutes an *I-it* relationship for the *I-thou* relationship. Only when society was truly integrated could African Americans be returned to the thou-ness intended by God.[22]

The ethos of the beloved community further distinguishes itself from secular society for King through its mandate to be guided by love in all things. Since all people are loved by God, all people must be respected. It is not a person's intellect, race, or social position that determines human worth. Rather, each person is valued simply because they are valued by God.

Being guided by love in all things includes the achievement of goals such as justice. The means that one uses to achieve a goal should directly correlate with the goal itself. Since the end goal of resisting injustice is the beloved community, love should be the means through which the goal is accomplished: agape love. King defined "agape love" as the kind of love that seeks nothing in return. People who have agape love do not love others because they are likeable. They love because the love of God is working inside of them. They love others because God loves them. Agape love enables the people of God to love the person who does evil while abhorring the evil they do.[23] Agape love seeks good for one's neighbor and not just for oneself. Those who have agape love don't discriminate with their love by deciding who is worthy and who is not. Their love is not contingent on the particular qualities people possess. They make no distinction between friends and enemies.

Another point about agape love is that it emanates from the need of the other person. King often used the example of the Samaritan on the Jericho

Road. The Samaritan demonstrated agape love because he saw a person with a need and responded to that need. "Need" in the case of racial segregation was with the soul of the oppressors: white people in the United States. King believed that the soul of white people was greatly distorted by segregation. As a result, whites need African Americans for the sake of their own souls. It is the agape love of African Americans that could remove the "tensions, insecurities, and fears" of whites.[24]

Agape love also means going through any length to restore community. The person who works against community works against the whole of creation. The resurrection, for King, symbolizes God's victory over all forces that seek to obstruct community.[25] Agape love recognizes that all life is interrelated. When humans harm each other, they harm themselves. An example of this for King was when whites refused to receive federal aid for education in order to deny African Americans their right to education. When they harmed African American children, they also harmed their own.

While at Crozer, King happened upon the life and teachings of Mahatma Gandhi. Gandhi's form of nonviolent resistance, which he deemed *satyagraha*, truth-force or love-force, served as an effective approach in the struggle for freedom.[26] King's rationale for his nonviolent strategy was very practical. Any minority group in the United States who decided to pursue an armed conflict would have to deal with a majority that was well-armed and wealthy. They would also have to deal with a fanatical right wing that would willingly exterminate the entire African American population if they felt the survival of white Western materialism was at stake.[27]

In addition to preserving life, nonviolence was also the means by which the beloved community could become a reality. In the struggle for racial justice, nonviolent resisters show just as much strength when opposing evil as those who use violence. While they are not physically aggressive, they are spiritually aggressive and dynamic. They do not seek to defeat or humiliate those opposing them. Rather, they seek to change their minds, to win their friendship and understanding. Through nonviolent resistance, adherents attempt to awaken a sense of shame in the opponent. Nonviolent resistance is aimed at the evil itself rather than those who perpetrate it. It recognizes that perpetrators are victims of the very evil they perpetrate. Nonviolent resistance avoids not only physical violence but also the internal violence of the spirit. Through oppression, the dignity of the oppressed is often lost, and they can become consumed by hatred and bitterness. Nonviolent resisters, by contrast, operate with an ethic of love for all.[28]

A key element of nonviolent resistance is suffering. King believed that (voluntary) unearned suffering, or "self-suffering," is redemptive because it has the potential to educate and transform. He quoted Gandhi when teaching and preaching about suffering: "Things of fundamental importance to people are not secured by reason alone, but have to be purchased with their suffering."[29] For King, suffering is powerful because it has the potential to shame the opponents into a change of heart.[30] When nonviolent adherents refuse to physically attack their oppressors, they expose the barbarity of the oppressor for the world to see.[31] The act of self-suffering, or suffering as a voluntary act, is the sacrificial offering of a person who sees the misery of people so clearly that she or he is willing to suffer on their behalf to bring an end to it.[32] King distinguishes between suffering resulting from violence and suffering from nonviolence as social forces for change. Both violence and nonviolence are weapons that can bring about social change. War is an example of the implementation of violence to bring about a desired result. However, those who choose nonviolence as their weapon willingly allow violence to be inflicted on them because they believe the situation can be transformed by it.[33]

Peace is an integral aspect of the beloved community. However, King clarified the type of peace that would be present by differentiating between negative and positive peace. To those who criticized him for disturbing the peace in communities when he joined people in their struggle against injustice, he said they misunderstood the true meaning of peace. A case in point was the eight pastors who penned the letter that inspired him to write his letter from the Birmingham jail. He responded that there had never been peace in Birmingham, Alabama.[34] He contended that there had never been peace in the South. There was a negative peace or an absence of tension because African Americans had not yet risen up to struggle for their rights. Negative peace existed in the presence of "stagnant passivity and deadening complacency."[35] When people were too scared or too apathetic to fight for their basic human rights, there existed a negative peace. The beloved community for King is a place of positive peace in which the hard-fought battles for justice and equality have been won.

It is also a place where people contend in good faith to work with one another to maintain those hard-fought gains.[36]

Also at the heart of King's concept of the beloved community is his expanded conception of salvation. Like his father, King believed that salvation was not just for the spirit; it was for the mind and body as well. For Martin King Sr., God was a holistic God. Both A. D. Williams, his father-in-law, and King Sr. preached a social gospel. Both believed in personal salvation. They also believed that the teachings of Jesus should be applied to the lived experiences of the African Americans in their congregations. King's ministry completely embraced and embodied this ideal.

We can also look at motto of the Southern Christian Leadership Conference, of which he was president for many years, to further discern his conception of salvation. By using faith language of salvation and soul ("To save the soul of America"), the SCLC leaders of King's day used their lenses of faith and demonstrated that they understood that America did not just have a justice problem. America did not just have a civil rights problem. America had a deep spiritual problem. The SCIC leaders believed that all people were fearfully and wonderfully made in God's image. Unless America began to treat all its people equally, its very soul would be lost.

For King and the founders of SCLC, America needed to be saved from itself. Their goal was not only securing civil rights for black people; they sought to have America live up to the true meaning of its creed that all people are created equal. America never had lived up to that standard. The SCIC leaders were determined to help this nation become what it was intended to be: a place of equality and equal opportunity for all people.

We can surmise from the motto of the SCLC and King's embrace of it that he did not believe a person who had accepted Christ but experienced oppression, inequality, or racism is fully saved from all sin. Rather, they are victims of societal sin. Therefore, for King, salvation was not just about the sins perpetrated by individuals; it was also about structural sin that kept people in bondage and kept them from experiencing the fullness of God's love in their daily lives. King would also say that the perpetrators of oppression, even when they too have confessed Christ as Savior, are not fully saved from sin. Their souls are at stake when they continuously oppress people who are created in the image of God.

King's concept of salvation was also not limited by geography. He said in some of his speeches that Christ died for the communist as well as the capitalist, for the Vietnamese as well as the American. Christ died for all. People who claimed to follow Christ had to seek the welfare of all people, not just a select few.

In the beloved community, remaining silent in the face of injustice is unacceptable. He said in many of his speeches, "We will have to repent in this generation not merely for the vitriolic words and actions of the bad people, but for the appalling silence of the good people."[37] King often reminded his listeners that human progress is not inevitable. Rather, progress comes from "the tireless efforts and persistent work" of people who are willing to be coworkers with God.[38] Coworkers with God speak up in the face of injustice.

Some of King's harshest words were aimed not only at people who actively try to obstruct the causes of justice but also at those who sit back, watch injustice happen, and say or do nothing while the rights of others are being trampled. His words were often aimed at Christian people: saved, sanctified, and filled-with-the-Holy-Ghost people. He criticized both white Christians and African American Christians for their silences. He criticized Christians for being so heavenly focused they were no earthly good. He criticized those of all races who were so afraid to lose their status and positions in society and their respectability that they refused to become involved in a movement to help other people.

Throughout his years in prophetic ministry, he continued to hope that America as a nation would one day live up to the true meaning of its creed that all people are created equal. He kept hoping, working, and believing that when people witnessed the voluntary redemptive suffering of those willing to put their lives on the line for justice and not retaliating with violence against their enemies, the government and the people of this nation would change—that they would see the error of their ways and eventually accept African American as brothers and sisters. As the years progressed, King began to lose faith in the will of the government in particular to do what was necessary to live up to the true meaning of its creed. In some of his speeches, he admitted his own disillusionment with the government.

The war in Vietnam was the case in point. Through his speeches and sermons about the Vietnam War, more of King's conceptions of the beloved community came into view. In the last year of his life, King took every opportunity he had to speak out against the atrocities of the Vietnam War. He had many theological reasons for his objections. First, he felt the war in Vietnam was one of the most unjust wars ever fought in the history of the world. He felt it was unjust because just wars are fought to free people from oppression rather than take away their freedom. Just wars are fought to secure brighter and more hopeful futures for the people rather than bring about their demise. He saw the war in Vietnam as the opposite of a just war. Rather than fighting the war to liberate the Vietnamese from oppression, America was fighting the war to advance its own economic agenda, siding with the South Vietnamese dictator and his regime that brutalized and marginalized its people while helping the United States achieve its own economic ends.[39]

Second, the war violated the biblical mandate of helping the poor. Billions of dollars were being appropriated by Congress for mass murder in Vietnam that could have been used to address issues of poverty and unemployment at home. Before the escalation of the war, King had hope that the nation would begin to concentrate on meeting the needs of the poor through the anti-poverty program.[40] The program would have offered new beginnings for white and black poor alike. But when the government began to build up troops in Vietnam, King realized that the nation was more committed to war than to the eradication of poverty.[41]

He was against the war in Vietnam because economically poor soldiers, who made up the majority of enlisted military personnel, were dying in record numbers. The poor soldiers who were fortunate enough to return home often did so physically or mentally impaired. After fighting in a war for their country, those who were already poor when they enlisted were often left worse off (financially, physically, and mentally) than they were before the war began.

He was against the war in Vietnam because even in combat, the government refused to treat all people as those created in the image of God. For example, the same Congress that authorized money to fight the war in Vietnam refused to allocate funds to include African American veterans in a fair-housing bill. White veterans were provided low-interest loans to purchase homes after they returned from war. African Americans were denied those loans.

Also, the U.S. government and people of this nation failed to see the humanity of people our government had declared our enemy. The United States destroyed two of the most cherished institutions of the Vietnamese: the family and the village. King repeatedly reminded his audiences and congregations that the U.S. government poisoned Vietnamese crops and forced Vietnamese children to become beggars and Vietnamese women to become prostitutes. What the United States was doing was the opposite of liberation. It was full-scale colonization.

For King, a nation that was as morally bankrupt as the United States needed to undergo a revolution of values in order to finally become a beloved community. A true revolution of values would cause the United States to shift from a thing-oriented society to a people-oriented society, from a society solely focused on material prosperity to a nation focused on meeting the needs of its people.[42] A nation seeking to become the beloved community will give up the privileges that evolve from tremendous profits in favor of engaging in activities in the best interest of the poor and marginalized.

A true revolution of values calls into question past and present policies that develop or maintain poverty. King often likened this aspect of the revolution to the Jericho Road in the parable of the Good Samaritan. King believed that the people of God are called to be Samaritans on life's highway by helping their sisters and brothers who are in distress. However, he also believed that the Jericho Road needs to be transformed so that people will not be constantly in danger of being robbed. True compassion is more than giving a beggar a coin. True compassion is restructuring the system that produces beggars in the first place. In like manner, he believed that a revolution of values seeks to dismantle structures that give rise to poverty and oppression.[43]

A true revolution of values finds ways of settling conflicts other than always going to war. Wars create orphans and widows and people with lifelong mental and physical impairments. Wars siphon off resources that could be used to lift up those who are outcast. Instead of always resorting to arms when conflicts arise, a nation seeking to become the beloved community will try to understand the root causes of the conflicts and develop positive and sustainable solutions.

When speaking of the need for a revolution of values, King invited his listeners to reclaim the revolutionary spirit that is part of the fabric of this nation. It is Western nations such as the United States that have inspired people all over the modern world to fight for justice and equality. However, he also noted that people in our nation must resist their proneness to adjust to injustice.[44]

King's most famous speech, "I Have a Dream," is a stellar articulation of his conception of the beloved community. In the speech, he critiques the injustices of racism, social leprosy, and poverty and advocates for agape love, freedom, and equality. His belief that all people are created in the image of God is especially conveyed in latter portion of the refrain "I have a dream":

I have a dream that one day this nation will rise up, live out the true meaning of its creed: "We hold these truths to be self-evident, that all men are created equal."....

> I have a dream that one day even the state of Mississippi, a state sweltering with the heat of injustice, sweltering with the heat of oppression, will be transformed into an oasis of freedom and justice....
>
> I have a dream that my four little children will one day live in a nation where they will not be judged by the color of their skin but by the content of their character....
>
> I have a dream that one day in Alabama with its vicious racists, with its governor having his lips dripping with the words of interposition and nullification, one day right there in Alabama little black boys and black girls will be able to join hands with little white boys and white girls as sisters and brothers . . .[45]

When this speech is examined in tandem with his theology, it can be understood as more than an oratorical masterpiece. It can be appreciated as an expression of King's prophetic imagination—an imagination he worked diligently to realize every day of his life as a public theologian, prophet, and preacher.[46] The prophetic imagination is the ability to see through the limited possibilities presented by the status quo to the unlimited possibilities of an omnipotent God.

Implications for Preaching

Issues and concerns stemming from King's life and ministry that raise implications for preaching are many.

Regarding the issue of formation, his upbringing in the racially segregated South prepared him for the social challenges he would face as a pastor, community leader, and racialized human being who intentionally chose to engage in ministry in the segregated South. His education at the universities of Morehouse, Crozer, and Boston provided him with the opportunity to encounter, study, and adapt Gandhi's movement of non-violent resistance for his context. He was able to develop a theological framework and language to communicate his message of liberation to diverse audiences. By the time he and Coretta answered the call to Dexter Avenue Baptist Church in Montgomery, Alabama, he was contextually and theologically prepared to meet the challenges confronting him.

However, it is not only people who lead national movements who can benefit from ministerial formation. It is important for preachers to remind their congregations that all people who claim to be followers of Jesus Christ need to be intentionally formed and taught the will of God through word and deed, theory and praxis. Sunday school, Bible study, workshops, sermons, and other forums for learning are opportunities to impart vital tenets of our faith. Seminaries and divinity schools have an even greater responsibility for forming people who answer a call or make the decision to pursue any number of leadership paths.

Another implication for preaching is the importance of vision for all people of God. It was King's vision of the beloved community—his understanding of what this nation and world could be—that compelled him to spend his life fighting for the rights of the poor, oppressed, marginalized, and socially disenfranchised. His vision transcended seeking justice. It embraced positive peace and existential possibilities that are made possible by all people being treated as though they are created in the image of God. King's vision stimulated the nation's prophetic imagination.[47] Fueled by his prophetic imagination, King's vision of the beloved community served as a catalyst not only for the civil rights movement but also for subsequent movements and campaigns of resistance. Vision has the power to motivate the people of God for change.

From King's life and ministry, preachers glean the importance of a well-developed, well-considered, contextually relevant theology. Though King's theology was informed by European theologians he studied at Crozer and Boston universities, it was also informed by the demands of his lived reality. Preachers should help their congregations think theologically and critically about the world around them. The image of God, (voluntary) redemptive suffering, salvation, agape love, peace, and just war are not just academic considerations for systematic theologians. These are topics for Christian living. Preaching doctrine is not always seen as necessary in our contemporary times. However, King's theology of the beloved community, along with his ability to communicate it by thought, word, and deed, proves that when elements of Christian doctrine are understood and lived out by the people of God, they can change lives and change the world.

In King's day, African Americans were social lepers simply due to the color of their skin. Preachers can help their congregations identify and partner with the social lepers of our day, including people of various races and ethnicities: those with disabilities; those who are severely overweight; those who are lesbian, gay, bisexual, transgendered, or gender nonconforming; those who are poor; and so on. Since all people are created in the image of God, no one should be marginalized and oppressed because of who they are. Preachers can encourage their congregations to foster environments of love and acceptance and serve as advocates when needed.

Preachers can remind their congregations of the consequences of silence in the face of injustice. If the people of God remain silent when they witness injustice, victims will suffer and not be able to live the lives they were created to live. Manifestations of injustice happen in all of our lives. We see injustice in our homes, families, and communities such as child and elder abuse; domestic violence; racial, sexual, or gender discrimination; and police brutality. Victims of injustice need witnesses to speak out against injustice whenever they see it and work to eradicate it.

King's call for a revolution of values is still needed. In 2016 our nation spent more money on defense ($589 billion) than seven other nations combined: China, Saudi Arabia, Russia, United Kingdom, India, France, and Japan.[48] In 2017, 7.8 million families were still living in poverty in the richest nation on earth.[49] King wanted our nation to prioritize people over profits. Preachers can help their congregations understand that a lot of people in this nation and all over the world would benefit greatly from a shift in priorities.

King's contention that it is the agape love of African Americans that could remove the "tensions, insecurities, and fears" of whites puts the burden of the well-being of the oppressor on the oppressed. The tensions, insecurities, and fears of whites exist because of the social construct of race that they have internalized and perpetuated individually and because of their support of racist social structures and practices of discrimination. The oppressed already have enough to worry about without the added burden of thinking about the well-being of the very people making their lives miserable. Preaching should help people understand that while the oppressed should treat their oppressors as they themselves wish to be treated, they, and all people of God, should focus on eradicating oppressive structures and challenging the ideologies that support them. In the case of white racism, white people in general and white Christians in particular have a responsibility to confront and stop the spread of racism and to dismantle racial ideology whenever and wherever they are found.

Voluntary redemptive suffering is another burden that the oppressed should not have to bear. They are already suffering. Voluntary suffering has been used as a strategy in the past to shame opponents into changing their behaviors and ideologies. However, just as with attending to the well-being of the oppressors, preachers should help their people understand that voluntary redemptive suffering should be the work of those who are not already suffering.

King's belief that agape love enables the people of God to love the person who does evil while abhorring the evil they do is an ideal. It is a Christian ideal that was personified by Jesus on the cross. After being beaten and tortured, mocked and belittled, he prayed to God, "Father, forgive them; for they do not know what they are doing" (Luke 23:34). To be like Christ is the aspiration of all Christians (at least in theory). Being able to forgive people who have persecuted us or those we love may not be something we are able to do immediately or within months or even years. Sometimes the actions, words, and their consequences create pain so deep that forgiveness seems to be an impossible act. Sometimes forgiveness may even seem to be an act of betrayal. Preachers need to let their people know that God understands their pain even when they fall short of godly ideals. God will be with them through the pain and will help them to forgive others just as they themselves want to be forgiven.

Questions for Exegesis

1. Are there social lepers in the text? If so, who are they? Why and how are they being oppressed or marginalized, and by whom?

2. Is there evidence of agape love in the text? If so, how is it exemplified?

3. In the face of injustice, are bystanders in the text silent, or are they vocal in their objections and public in their resistance? If they are vocal about or publicly resistant to injustice, what are they saying or doing?

4. Is there evidence of positive or negative peace in the text? If so, which one is evident and how is it maintained?

5. Is the community in the text embroiled in or impacted in any way by war? Is the war just or unjust by King's definition?

6. Hermeneutical Bridge Question: Who are the social lepers of our day? Why and how are they being oppressed or marginalized, and by whom?

Notes

1. Martin Luther King Jr. et al., "The Papers of Martin Luther King, Jr," (Berkeley, CA: University of California Press, 1992), https://king institute.stanford.edu/sites/mlk/files /publications/vol1intro.pdf., 7–8.

2. Ibid., 11.

3. Ibid., 12.

4. Martin Luther King Sr. and Clayton Riley, *Daddy King: An Autobiography* (Boston: Beacon Press, 2016), Kindle Edition.

5. King Jr. et al., 14.

6. Ibid.

7. Ibid.

8. Ibid., 15.

9. King Sr. and Riley, 134.

10. "About Dr. King," The King Center (2014), http://www.thekingcenter.org/about-dr-king.

11. Martin Luther King Jr., "The Drum Major Instinct," *A Testament of Hope: The Essential Writings and Speeches*, ed. James M. Washington (New York: HarperCollins Publishers, 1986), 267.

12. "The King Philosophy," The King Center (2014), http://www.thekingcenter.org /king-philosophy#sub4.

13. Martin Luther King Jr., "The Ethical Demands for Integration," *A Testament of Hope: The Essential Writings and Speeches*, ed. James M. Washington (New York: HarperCollins, 1986), 119.

14. Ibid.

15. Martin Luther King Jr., *Where Do We Go from Here: Chaos or Community?* (Boston: Beacon Press, 2010), 109.

16. Ibid.

17. Ibid., 116–17.

18. King Jr. et al., 12.

19. King Jr., "The Ethical Demands for Integration," 120.

20. Ibid., 121.

21. Ibid.

22. Ibid., 119.

23. Martin Luther King Jr., "The Power of Nonviolence," *A Testament of Hope: The Essential Writings and Speeches*, ed. James M. Washington (New York: HarperCollins Publishers, 1986), 13.

24. Martin Luther King Jr., "An Experiment in Love" *A Testament of Hope: The Essential Writings and Speeches*, ed. James H. Washington (New York: HarperCollins, 1986), 19.

25. Ibid., 20.

26. Martin Luther King Jr., "Pilgrimage to Nonviolence," *A Testament of Hope: The Essential Writings and Speeches*, ed. James M. Washington (New York: HarperCollins 1986), 38.

27. Martin Luther King Jr., "Nonviolence: The Only Road to Freedom," *A Testament of Hope: The Essential Writings and Speeches*, ed. James H. Washington (New York: HarperCollins, 1986), 55.

28. Martin Luther King Jr., "Nonviolence and Racial Justice," *A Testament of Hope: The Essential Writings and Speeches*, ed. James H. Washington (New York: HarperCollins, 1986), 7–8.

29. King Jr., "An Experiment in Love," 18.

30. Martin Luther King Jr., "My Trip to the Land of Gandhi," *A Testament of Hope: The Essential Writings and Speeches*, ed. James M. Washington (New York: HarperCollins, 1986), 26.

31. Martin Luther King Jr., "Stride toward Freedom," *A Testament of Hope: The Essential Writings and Speeches*, ed. James M. Washington (New York: HarperCollins, 1986), 485.

32. King Jr., "Nonviolence: The Only Road to Freedom," 57.

33. Martin Luther King Jr., "Love, Law, and Civil Disobedience," *A Testament of Hope: The Essential Writings and Speeches*, ed. James M. Washington (New York: HarperCollins, 1986), 47.

34. Ibid., 50–51.

35. Ibid.

36. Ibid.

37. Martin Luther King Jr., "Letter from Birmingham City Jail," in *A Testament of Hope: The Essential Writings and Speeches*, ed. James H. Washington (New York: HarperCollins, 1986), 296.

38. Ibid.

39. Martin Luther King Jr., "Remaining Awake through a Great Revolution," *A Testament of Hope: The Essential Writings and Speeches*, ed. James M. Washington (New York: HarperCollins Publishers, 1986), 268–78.

40. Martin Luther King Jr., "A Time to Break the Silence," *A Testament of Hope: The Essential Writings and Speeches*, ed. James M. Washington (New York: HarperCollins, 1986), 235.

41. King Jr., *Where Do We God from Here: Chaos or Community?*, 86.

42. King Jr., "A Time to Break the Silence," 241.

43. Ibid., 240.

44. Ibid., 241.

45. Martin Luther King Jr., "I Have a Dream," *A Testament of Hope: The Essential Writings and Speeches*, ed. James M. Washington (New York: HarperCollins Publishers, 1986), 217–20.

46. The prophetic imagination is a phrase popularized by biblical scholar and theologian Walter Brueggemann. See Walter Brueggemann, *The Prophetic Imagination*, second ed. (Philadelphia: Fortress Press, 2001).

47. Ibid., Kindle Edition.

48. "U.S. Defense Spending Compared to Other Countries," Peter G. Peterson Foundation (2016), http://www.pgpf.org/Chart-Archive/0053_defense-comparison.

49. Kayla Fontenot, Jessica Semega, and Melissa Kollar, "Income and Poverty in the United States: 2017 Current Population Reports, United States Department of Commerce" (Washington, DC: U.S. Census Bureau, 2018), 17.

4
Presentative Eschatology— Creative Discipleship
The Theology of Jürgen Moltmann

A Brief Biography

Jürgen Moltmann was born in the city of Hamburg, Germany, on April 8, 1926. He was the second oldest of five children. (His developmentally disabled older brother died at the age of sixteen and was not forgotten in Moltmann's theology.) Moltmann's father was a teacher who also served in the military. His mother, whom he called his first love, was an avid reader who was unable to complete her grammar school education because of an illness. In 1929, his parents moved to the countryside to escape the housing shortage in Hamburg and build their own home in a communal settlement. The settlement was founded by a group of teachers who longed for the simple life. Child formation was a central element of the community and included academics, music, and physical development through sports (football, volleyball, hockey, and gymnastics). In the settlement, everyone, including the children, contributed to the welfare of the community. Along with the other children, Jürgen worked in the garden planting peas, beans, and other vegetables.

Until the age of twelve, Jürgen was a poor student in school and had an active and vivid imagination. He saw dwarfs and elves when he walked through the woods with his mother and told wild stories. His teachers would often write "could do better" on his grade reports. His failure to do well academically enraged his father, who was very critical and could not understand why Jürgen was not a better student. When he was twelve, his maternal grandmother, who lived in the northern German city of Schwerin, arranged for him to get riding lessons at the royal Schwerin stables. As incentive to do well in school, she gave him a riding lesson for each *A* he earned in school. It was through horseback riding that he learned self-control. His grandmother also taught him proper table manners and how to tend to his personal appearance.

When he was thirteen, his parents sent him to the Jungvolk, a section of Hitler Youth (Hitler-Jugend) for boys ages ten to fourteen. At the age of fourteen he advanced to the mounted section of Hitler Youth. As it relates to the Third Reich, Hitler Youth "was an incubator" in which young people were indoctrinated, mobilized, controlled, and prepared for military duty. In 1943 Moltmann's high school class was conscripted into the air force, and in February 1945 he was taken as a prisoner of war. After spending months sleeping in trenches, suffering from boils, and fighting lice, dirt, and illness, being taken as a POW was partly a relief.[1] While a prisoner in Belgium, he lost hope in the legitimacy of the war. He saw pictures of piles of dead bodies in concentration camps and wondered if it was for the killing of innocent people and the aspirations of one madman for which he and thousands of others fought. He lost hope that he would have a future beyond the end of the war.

Moltmann spent a brief period in a Belgian POW camp before being transported to Scotland. While there, his Scottish overseers treated him and his German comrades with a "simple and warm common humanity" that helped them to begin to live with the shameful past of the German nation.[2] Also while in Scotland, an army chaplain gave him a Bible. Until then, he had never read the Bible. His family was not religious and went to church once a year on Christmas Eve. He found in Psalm 39 "an echo from his own soul"[3]:

> I am dumb and must eat up my suffering within myself.
> My life is as nothing before thee [Martin Luther's
>   translation].
> Hear my prayer, O Lord, and give ear to my cry.
> Hold not thou thy peace at my tears.
> For I am a stranger with thee, and a sojourner, as all
>   my fathers were.

Moltmann read this psalm every evening and experienced his soul being called back to God. When reading the Gospel of Mark, he found in Jesus a "divine brother in need." When he read Jesus' question, "My God, why have you forsaken me?" he believed that Jesus understood him completely. He believed that Jesus understood him because Jesus had been forsaken by God as he had been. Jesus was a fellow sufferer who carried him throughout his suffering. In the passion narrative, Moltmann found hope for a future in Christ.

When he realized that his POW status was going to be prolonged, he applied to study theology at an educational camp so he could become a pastor. He was released from POW camp and returned to Hamburg in 1948. His interest in theology continued, and he attended theological lectures given by church pastors in Hamburg with his father's tutelage. He also prepared for and subsequently passed the requisite Greek exam for entering formal theological study at the University of Gottingen. It was there where he met his future wife, Elisabeth, who was a doctoral student. After completing his doctoral program in 1952, he and Elisabeth married. Moltmann served as a pastor at an evangelical church in Bremen-Wasserhorst for five years. In 1958 he was invited to join the faculty of Wuppertal, a seminary of the Confessing Church, where he began his research on hope and eschatology. The Confessing Church was a group of pastors and theologians who objected to the Civil Service Reconstruction Law that legalized the purging of Jews from civil service. Civil service in Germany during this time included ordained pastors and ecclesiastical officers. He served in Wuppertal until accepting a position at the University of Bonn in 1963, where he published his seminal work, *Theology of Hope*, that same year. In 1967 he accepted the invitation as chair of systematic theology at the Eberhard-Karls University, Tubingen. He remained at Tubingen until his retirement in 1994.

Moltmann traveled extensively throughout his career and received many honors. From 1963 to 1983, he served on the Faith and Order Committee of the World Council of Churches. He was the Robert W. Woodruff Distinguished Visiting Professor of Systematic Theology at Candler School of Theology at Emory University in Atlanta, Georgia, from 1983 to 1993. He was the Gifford Lecturer at the University of Edinburgh in 1984–1985. He won the 2000 Louisville Grawemeyer Award in Religion for his book *The Coming of God: Christian Eschatology*. In April 2017 Moltmann was awarded an honorary doctor of theology degree (*Doctor Divinitatis Honoris Causa*) by the University of Pretoria, South Africa. Moltmann is currently professor emeritus of systematic theology at the University of Tübingen, Germany.

A Theological Overview

Jürgen Moltmann's vision of the reign of God is one of universal redemption, justice, and peace on the earth for all of God's creation (including humanity, animals, and all of nature) in the form of a new heaven and new earth. On the new earth, God brings about justice for the poor and saves them from the power of the wicked.[4] Classism and domination of some humans by others, and of nature by humanity, are a thing of the past.

For Moltmann, hope for a new heaven and new earth did not originate with Jesus. Hope was first found in the form of promise in the Hebrew Bible. He defines *promise* as "a declaration which announces the coming of a reality that does not yet exist."[5] The depth and breadth of future possibilities are limited only by the potential of the "God of the promise" to fulfill God's promises.[6] Faith of the people in the God of the Abrahamic promise is grounded in past relationships in which God demonstrated God's faithfulness by bringing their ancestors through the wilderness to the Promised Land. Through experience, the people of Israel learned that those things that seemed impossible by human standards were possible for the God of the promise. Through experience they also discovered that history that is initiated and shaped by promise trends toward the fulfillment of that promise.

It is by analyzing the experiences of Israel with the God of the promise that Moltmann draws conclusions that apply to all people of God today. Awareness of promise and its potential fulfillment creates a period of tension in which humanity must decide whether or not to obey God. It is the ability to choose obedience or disobedience that distinguishes the consequences of the promise from occurrences of fate. In addition, the history of the promise is not static. When promises of God are fulfilled, they do not pass away or fade from the memory of the community in which they were fulfilled. Quite the opposite is in fact true. Each time a promise is fulfilled, it leaves traces in human hopes and desires that stretch future expectations beyond past experiences or conceptions. As a result, greater hopes are born with each fulfillment of promise. Also, not only does promise expand the realm of the possible, but also, sometimes, the word of promise stands in direct contradiction to the reality in which humans currently live. In this case, the word does not conform to lived reality in the minds of the people of faith. Rather, reality conforms to or expands according to the word.[7]

Since fulfillment of promise is the sole purview of God, how the promise is fulfilled should be left completely to God. God is faithful and free to operate independently of human influence and suasion. Therefore, just because God fulfilled a promise in a particular way in the past does not mean that God is in any way bound to fulfill the promise the same way in the future. God is able to fulfill God's promises in new and surprising ways.

In Christ, the Abrahamic promise becomes universal. What had been promised to Israel is now valid for all Jews and Gentiles who believe. The promise became universal when it was detached from the election of Israel and the confines of the Law. When the crucified Christ was raised from the dead by the power of God, grace usurped the Law—premising grace over works. Those previously deemed by the Law as godless are now given access to God's promise and fulfillment.[8]

For Moltmann, the central event and focus of the Christian faith is the cross. It is through his understanding of the cross that Moltmann's vision of the reign of God is made clear. From the event of the cross, we can understand the Trinity (God the Father, Jesus and his crucifixion, and the Holy Spirit), the relationship between God and humanity, relationships between all people, and relationship between humanity and all of God's creation.

Moltmann developed his conception of the Trinity by introducing the concept of *perichoresis*. While in Christology perichoresis refers to the "interpenetration" of the divine and human natures, for the Trinity it refers to reciprocal indwelling of the Father, Son, and Spirit.[9] It is with perichoresis in mind that Moltmann contends that the Trinity is a non-hierarchical community in which no one person takes precedence over any other. Each person moves with the others, around one another and within one another. The persons of the Trinity become conscious of themselves and come to consciousness of themselves in one another. The persons of the Trinity do not exist independently. Rather, they coexist in a divine life with one another and in one another. No one person of the Trinity is subordinate to another. Though the Father was indeed the origin of the Trinity, in ongoing divine life, the three persons are equal. Perichoresis is not a state experienced only by the persons of the Trinity. Perichoresis also binds together those who are of a different kind. God and humans can indwell each other in mutual love, as Jesus contends in John 17:21:[10] "As you, Father, are in me and I am in you, may they also be in us, so that the world may believe that you have sent me."

Jesus' will for his disciples was for them to dwell in him and in God just as he dwelled in God and God dwelled in him. The Trinity is not closed, as in traditional representations of circles or triangles. Rather, the Trinity is open with an overflow of love which empowers all human beings with space for living and scope for their continuing development. It is through their faith in Jesus Christ that people begin their experiences of the Trinity. It is also through their faith in Jesus that people also experience grace that liberates both the victims of sin and perpetrators of sin from evil powers that would destroy them. Through their experience of Jesus in the Trinity, people become part of the community of God.

The creation process is the work of the Trinity. The Father created heaven and earth through the Son in the power of the Holy Spirit.[11] However, Moltmann believes that God is not the Father because God is the creator of the universe; God is the Father because God has a Son. The Son was not created by the Father but rather proceeded from the substance of the Father. Therefore, God is not a father in the traditional sense of maleness. The God of traditional European religions is a patriarchal God who is father of the church, father of his country, and father of the family. The patriarchal God is a superego who is supposed to be feared. By rejecting patriarchal language and doctrine, Moltmann is rejecting the trinitarian doctrine of early Christianity developed to defend Christianity from accusations of being another polytheistic religion in Greco-Roman society. God, the Father of Jesus, cannot be defined in unisexual and patriarchal terms. God is both a motherly father and a fatherly mother of the Son.[12] By rejecting the patriarchal doctrine of the Trinity, Christians find the ability to overcome sexist language in our language for God. By embracing the Trinity, Christians are able to fellowship with one another without privilege and subordination. When Christians are in fellowship with their "first-born brother," there is no longer male or female. As Paul contends in Galatians 3:28, all are one in Christ and are joint heirs according to the promise.

Moltmann spends a lot of time and effort unpacking relationships using the lens of the cross. Rather than denying or ignoring Jesus' declaration on the cross that he had been forsaken by God, Moltmann embraces it and finds meaning there. At Golgotha, the Holy Spirit emerges from the interactions of God and Jesus. Moltmann turns to Paul's view of the God-Jesus relationship when he contends that it is precisely in the godforsakenness of the crucified Christ that deliverance and liberation for forsaken humanity can be found.[13] The Spirit that creates love for those who are forsaken and enlivens those who have been declared dead emerges from the event of the cross. New possibilities and new life-forces come forth from the grief of the Father and the dying of the Son. On the cross, Jesus suffers as he is forsaken by God the Father. The Father suffers in grief of the death of the Son. Moltmann contends that the grief of the Father is just as important as the death of the Son. While Jesus suffers death, God suffers the death of his Fatherhood. If there were not a mutual suffering and loss between the Father and Son, the Trinity would not exist. Mutuality is also present in that just as God delivered Jesus up to death on the cross, Jesus gave himself up. Jesus willingly surrendered to death. However, the event of the cross is not simply one of mutual suffering. It is also an event of mutual love. From these sufferings, the Holy Spirit emerges, which opens up the future and creates the possibility and force of new life for lost and forsaken humanity.[14] In order to accurately and fully perceive the scope of the implications of the cross of Jesus, one must understand Jesus' death on the cross as a trinitarian event.

As a result of his view of the cross as a trinitarian event, the implications of the crucifixion and the crucified Christ for human existence are many. For example, knowledge of the cross of Christ is a crucifying knowledge that can shatter illusions of grandeur and set people free to love even that which is different and other. We cannot truly know God if we have only "natural" knowledge of God's good creation. Natural knowledge is knowledge of the works that bear witness to God's divinity, power, wisdom, righteousness, and might, such as nature, plants, animals, and the diversity of humanity. In fact, humans can lose their humanity altogether when they seek to replicate God's power and might in our relationships with one another and all of God's creations. Seeking equality with God because of our "natural" understanding of God can create hubris and cause people to deny their own realities. We can become fixated on our need for self-affirmation, praise, and success to such an extent that we are blind to the suffering of others.[15] Through the crucifixion, humanity is able to see another side of God—God's humanity. When people know God only through God's works, they know God's hands. When they know God through the crucified Christ, they know God's heart. Seeking equality with our natural knowledge of God can lead to dehumanization.

Knowledge of God in the weakness and lowliness of the crucified Christ leads to restoration of humanity.

The crucifixion of Christ clarifies God's ability to love. A God who is not capable of suffering is a God who is unaffected by suffering and injustice. A God who is not capable of suffering is insensitive and unshaken by human tragedy and tears. A God who is not capable of suffering is a God who cannot love but is rather preoccupied with being loved. This God is the embodiment of Aristotle's unmoved mover, who is omnipotent while being incapable of feeling and sensing the pain and suffering of creation.[16] On the cross, God and suffering are no longer contradictory terms. God's very being can be found in the suffering of the Son. The suffering of the Son can be found in God's very being because God is love. Those who contend that God is not capable of suffering because God is God do not recognize God's omnipotence. God is capable of suffering because God has the power to voluntarily open up God-self to be affected by the suffering of others.

Love of God that reaches the loveless and unloved in the cross of Christ provides believers with freedom for new possibilities for their lives. Love cannot accept conditions of lovelessness. Love causes believers to grieve contradictions and to take up contradictions through protest.[17] Since Jesus' unconditional love for the rejected made him the enemy of the Pharisees and led to his crucifixion, unconditional love extended to others will lead to enmity and persecution in any world that has social norms, social conditions, and standards for human achievements that are contrary to the will of God.

The relational nature of the Trinity is justification for unity within the church. In a church that embraces trinitarian unity, believers are in fellowship with God and in God. Each person accepts other people in the same way they have been accepted by Christ. Therefore, true trinitarian churches are communities free of authoritarian rule or dominion. Dialogue and consensus replace authority and obedience as ways of being in Christian community.

In many churches and denominations, the Holy Spirit and its role in the Trinity and in the lives of the people of God gets lost or forgotten. However, Moltmann believes all who claim to be followers of Christ must better understand and embrace what following Christ actually means. One role that has been overlooked is that of the work of the Holy Spirit in healing the physical body. Traditional church teachings about the Holy Spirit have been dominated by Platonic and gnostic conceptions that are hostile to the body and detached from all concerns of the world. Moltmann argues that followers of Christ need to adopt the Hebrew understanding of the Spirit that also carries over into the New Testament: Shekinah.[18] Shekinah originated in temple theology in which God dwells simultaneously in the Holy of Holies and in the whole universe.[19] The Holy Spirit is "divine energy, wind, fire, light, side space, inward assurance and mutual love."[20] The Shekinah-like Holy Spirit indwells all of God's creation. Moltmann credits the Shekinah-like nature of the Holy Spirit with the physical and mental healings that are experienced by the people of God. The Holy Spirit is the "divine quickening power of the new creation of all things" and the power that empowers the rebirth of every living thing. Through the Holy Spirit, Jesus fulfilled the Jewish hope that the torture and destruction perpetrated by spirits and demons would disappear. They hoped that people would be able to recover their health and live full lives. Healings were foretastes of the kingdom of God in which God dwelled in all of creation and all of God's creation was filled with vitality. The crucified Christ takes on the breadth of human misery in order to bring healing.

Moltmann highlights the work of the Holy Spirit in healing when he rejects the notion that health and healing are solely about physical or mental cures or restoration of full physical functioning. The work of the Holy Spirit also heals through restoration of relationships. When Jesus healed people with physical or mental illness, he also restored their relationships with God and relationships with other people. People cannot not fully experience healing and health if their relationships with others are somehow disrupted. Healing happens in restored commitments, reestablished trust, and new sociality.[21]

Moltmann invites his readers to embrace the presence of the Holy Spirit in people with disabilities who have often been ostracized and marginalized by society. When Jesus was crucified, he embraced all of humanity, which is whole and beautiful and good. This includes people with disabilities (such as Moltmann's brother). Like all people of God, those with disabilities have callings which they fulfill through their charisma or God-given gifts. He refers to the apostle Paul, who contends that human strength is made perfect in weakness. Paul expects that congregations would be made up of the strong and the weak, wise and foolish, handicapped and non-handicapped. Weak and foolish people have a special charisma among the followers of Christ. People who are handicapped are often deprived of their independence by those protecting and caring for them. He argues that every handicap is an endowment.

Moltmann believes that all of God's creation is interconnected through the power of the Holy Spirit. No strategy to liberate people from economic distress, oppression, and alienation will work if it does not also address human exploitation of nature. Rather than approaching nature as something to be dominated or conquered, humanity should see nature as something to be respected. New models of cooperation that seek a partnership with nature should recognize that as a creation of God, nature has rights that need to be respected. When humans finally exist in peace with nature, they will realize liberation. When all people are free and nature is no longer enslaved, the kingdom of God will have arrived.

In Moltmann's view of the reign of God, the crucified God liberates humanity from idolatry. Humans have the propensity to make idols of ideology and tradition. They worship their own works and bow down to their own gods, such as nationalism, xenophobia, anti-Semitism, racial hatred, class profit, consumption, and anti-social attitudes, thereby becoming neurotic or embroiled in anxiety. These idols produce relative values instead of absolute values. They produce transitory happiness instead of eternal joy. Therefore, when their expectations of joy and happiness do not materialize or are experienced only in the short term, humans resort to ungodly methods to resolve their conflicts. They make their enemies into demons and kill them spiritually. Worship of idols produces a type of slavery that compels humans to act outside of the will of God. The Bible specifically prohibits the worshipping of idols, a prohibition which is intended to protect the image of God and the freedom of God's image in every human being.[22] The crucified God freed humanity from its idols by coming into and existing in the world in weakness and being vulnerable and mortal. Because of Jesus' crucifixion, humans can open themselves to suffering and love. They can embrace people and situations that are new and different and unfamiliar to them. People no longer need idols to protect them. They can open themselves up to love other people.

When the idols humans construct for themselves are threatened, hostility is the likely outcome. Humans who have adopted idols often like only people who believe, think, and love the same things they love. They receive and expect support from people like them to help them suppress their anxiety. People who are different are a source of anxiety for idolaters.

Moltmann cites Sigmund Freud when arguing that the crucified God liberates people from idolatry in particular and spiritual immaturity in general. Freud contended that humans must stop focusing their religious hopes on the world beyond and rather concentrate on implications of their religions to the realities of the world in which they live. Freud saw this refocusing as a type of maturity from living under the guidance of the pleasure principle versus the reality principle. Under the pleasure principle, humans exist in a dream world and seek experiences that offer them the most enjoyment and gratification regardless of the ramifications of their actions. When humans mature to the point of living by the reality principle, they resign themselves to living within the limitations and conditions on earth and give up illusions of "utopianism."[23] Through dreams, humans often hope for freedom and long for better situations and circumstances for themselves and for others. This ground of human hope lies in the situation of the crucified God and understanding of the pathos of a suffering God. Just because some realities are yet unrealized does not mean they are destined to remain that way. Through prayer, people of God can open themselves to the "history of God for the future of God."[24] God has proven to be faithful in the past. God will continue to be faithful in the future. Through prayer, people can remain hopeful for the fulfillment of divine life in the reality of their lives.

Moltmann also contends that there are social, economic, and political implications of the cross for politics as well as psychology. When people of God fully embrace the crucified God, they willingly engage in liberating actions. As followers of the crucified Christ, they realize that the cycles of oppression must be broken and can be broken through Christ. Faith in Jesus Christ avails the people of God with what Moltmann calls a "freedom of faith." A freedom of faith compels people into liberating actions because they become aware of suffering, exploitation, oppression, alienation, and captivity. Moltmann critiques the model of separation of church and state that many churches have taken to politics. When the church separates itself from politics, it can then coexist easily with any form of social or economic oppression. The freedom that people of God experience in faith can become a substitute for the political freedom they cannot experience in the world. People can be at once saved spiritually but in bondage and suffering injustice physically, mentally, and emotionally. For Moltmann, this model does not fully live up to the responsibilities of those who have truly experienced the crucified God.

Moltmann argues that the reign of the crucified God, who was crucified for political reasons, must also include liberation from all forms of oppression. The term "theology of liberation" is a misnomer that should instead be "theology of liberations" because of the vast network of oppressions that work together to keep some people down.[25] Some of these oppressions make up what he terms "vicious circles of poverty" that include racial and cultural alienation, class domination, exploitation, and the industrial pollution of nature. He advocates for people of faith to work to improve the economic dimension of life for all people. The economic dimension of life includes health, food, clothing, and housing. Economic powers need to be redistributed so that all members of society can receive a just share of the products they produce instead of being exploited by the powers that be. People who are economically weak should receive social welfare. Nations that are underdeveloped should receive aid from wealthier, more powerful nations. He contends that the term "socialism" is good if it means the "satisfaction of material needs and social justice in a material democracy."[26]

It is the power of the Holy Spirit that sanctifies or heals the spiritual life of people who repent of their sins and make the decision to follow Christ. Moltmann argues that sanctification has much broader implications than just changing the lives of individuals. Sanctification for the twenty-first century means also rediscovering the sanctity of life and the mystery of divine creation and protecting them from the human propensity to destroy and manipulate them.[27] Understanding the sanctity of life includes having respect for all of human life and the life of all of God's creation. Moltmann believes that the commandment to love should be extended: "You shall love God and this earth and all our fellow creatures with all your heart, and with all your soul, and with all your might." The earth is God's creation and should be treated with reverence and love. With reference to humans, anyone who loves God should respect those who are weaker and vulnerable, including the poor, sick, and defenseless. In the world of nature, weaker plants and animal species must be protected from extinction. Both humans and nature must be protected from exploitation and destruction. On a personal level, people should strive to limit their adoption of consumerism and responsibly dispose of their refuse.

Moltmann also believes that the traditional understanding of salvation that is concerned only with fate of the individual soul fails to recognize the breadth, depth, and magnitude of Christ's work on the cross and the impact and consequences of his resurrection. Salvation also means the realization of justice for all of God's creation, making humans more humane, fellowship and respect among and between all of God's people, and peace for all of God's creation.[28] The power of love that imbues those who have committed to follow Christ should also compel them to realize God's will for justice for all people.

The Holy Spirit inspires people of God to live in the realm of communicative freedom or solidarity. Solidarity exists when people realize that they can truly be free only when they respect others and are respected in return. They are in solidarity when they accept others and are accepted in return. When living in the realm of solidarity, people understand that other people are not a limitation of their freedom but rather an extension of it.

Moltmann quotes Joel 2:28-30 when arguing for equality among men and women in the body of Christ and the wider society. The text from Joel claims that in the last days God will pour out God's Spirit upon all flesh, and both men and women will prophesy. Since all will be endowed by the Spirit, a new fellowship of equality is in order. He argues that the church is thinking in Roman terms versus Christian terms when it declares that men are heads of their households while women are to serve men in subordination to them. He believes that Christianity can learn from the feminist movement that suppression of the gifts of women and their disparagement in general is a sin against the very Spirit that provides gifts for all. When men accept women as equals, they will facilitate their own liberation and only then live into their true humanity.[29]

The church can be considered the body of the crucified and risen Christ only when it engages in acts of service that embody Christ's mission in the world. The church exists for other people. The church is the church of God when it is the church for the world.

As it relates to the gospel mandate to proclaim the gospel to the world in Matthew 28, Moltmann believes the mandate has nothing to do with claiming sovereignty on the part of the church and its officials. Proclaiming the gospel has nothing to do with taking the world or any particular part of it for Baptists, Roman Catholics, Presbyterians, or Methodists. Rather, missions of Christian churches in the world perform their service only when they infect people with hope. The hope of the mission is to spread the gospel and to transform the world from its current state into the reign of God.[30]

Implications for Preaching

One of the most important implications for preaching of Moltmann's eschatological vision is his perpespective about the Trinity. For so long, many preachers have taken one of two approaches to the Trinity: bring it up only when necessary (and then only with fear and trepedation while hoping no one will ask for details) or avoid talking about it altogether. While there may be some who do not agree with all of his teachings on the subject, Moltmann has provided preachers with a new perspective. First, by understanding the relational nature of the persons of the Trinity, preachers can then argue for the correspondingly relational nature of the body of Christ. Each person of the Trinity has different functions but work in cooperation with one another. In like manner, the people of God each have different functions but must find ways to work together to fulfill the will of God.

Moltmann's take on the God-Jesus relationship as it relates to the crucifixion is an important one. By his own admission, Jesus was forsaken by God on the cross. Moltmann contends that this is not a one-sided event. God felt a sense of loss as a father because his son was being tortured and killed. While God's feelings about Jesus' crucifixion are not supported by Scripture, preachers can speculate based on their image of God. Do they and their people believe that God is a God of wrath or a God of compassion? Do they believe it is possible for God to feel emotions at all? If so, would God have emotions about the death of his son?

Moltmann believes that when Christians understand that God is the Father because God has a Son, who came into being because of God's substance rather than the traditional birthing process, they can abandon the use of sexist language for God. Moltmann's characterization of God as a motherly father and a fatherly mother can help preachers encourage their congregations to transcend the boundaries and conceptions of gender in search of equality and respect. Male privilege and female subordination based on patriarchal authority can also be abandoned.

Moltmann can help preachers claim or reclaim the importance of the Holy Spirit for daily Christian life. The Holy Spirit sometimes presents itself in physical healing. The Holy Spirit is holistic in that it not only manifests itself in the form of physical or mental healing but also in the restoration of human relationships that enable human wholeness. In addition, by highlighting the presence of the Holy Spirit in people with disabilities, he helps preachers address concerns about health and healing. Some Christians believe people cannot be whole if they have illnesses, diseases, or disabilities. Moltmann's perespective of the Holy Spirit can help preachers assure their congregations that people can have a sickness, disease, or disability and still be whole if they have healthy relationships with God and other people.

Preachers who are seeking ways to remind their people about the godliness of gender equality will find help in Moltmann's appeal to the prophet Joel and his rejection of the New Testment's hierarchical gender relationships as Roman and nonchristian. When God pours out God's Spirit, God does so without regard to the many ways people divide and separate themselves from one another. Theological terms such as sanctification and salvation have traditionally been defined individualistically and spiritually. Moltmann challenges these traditions while demonstrating that preaching doctrine can be done in a way that is relevant to the lives of the people and that is inclusive.

There is no biblical evidence that God the father grieved the death of the son. With this contention, Moltmann seems to be projecting on God the emotions that a human father would have if his child were to be persecuted. Rather than asserting that his premise is biblical, Moltmann should clarify that this assertion is his own. Moltmann's assertion should remind preachers to make clear to their congregations when their thoughts are biblical and when their thoughts are their own.

In like manner, Moltmann's contention that the Son was not created by the Father but rather proceeded from the substance of the Father seems to contradict his own interpretation of the Trinity, as well as the Bible itself, which states, "When his mother Mary had been engaged to Joseph, but before they lived together, she was found to be with child from the Holy Spirit" (Matthew 1:18). He also contends that the persons of the Trinity do not exist independently. Rather, the persons of the Trinity coexist in a divine life with one another and in one another. By his own admission, the Son was created within the fellowship of the Trinity, which of course includes God. Making inaccurate statements about the Bible can cause confusion and erode the credibility of the preacher. Moltmann's work reminds all preachers of the importance of biblical accuracy.

Moltmann expends a lot of energy and effort finding redemption in the crucifixion. Much of his work is good news for those who are oppressed, marginalized, and forsaken. At the same time, Moltmann does not satisfactorily address the concerns of those who do not find comfort in the crucifixion. There may be those who are still left wondering if they too will be forsaken by God because God has a greater purpose in mind. Can they count on God to be with them in their struggles if God forsook God's own son? How can God simultaneously be a God of love and a God who forsakes? While preachers may comfort some by talking about the sovereignty of God (Psalm 115:3; Isaiah 46:10; Romans 9:19-21; Luke 1:37; Job 42:2) and the faithfulness of God (1 Corinthians 1:9; 2 Thessalonians 3:3; Hebrews 10:23; Psalm 119:90), some of their people may still have unanswered questions and unaddressed doubts.

Questions for Exegesis

1. How do people in the text relate to one another? Are some being oppressed or dominated by others? Is the oppression or domination along lines of gender, class, or ethnicity?

2. Are there people in the text who are suffering from idoloatry? If so, what are their idols? What are some consequences of their idolatry?

3. Are there people in the text suffering from illness or disability? What is the cause or source of their illness or disability? Do they receive healing? If so, are their relationships with other people also impacted by their healing?

4. Are there people in the text who feel they have been forsaken by God? Is God still at work on their behalf even though they cannot see or feel God? If so, what is God doing?

5. What is the image of God being portrayed in the text? Is God the "unmoved mover" of Aristotle who is not affected by the plights of the people? Is God openly concerned about God's people? How does the image of God found in the text affect the people in the text?

6. Hermeneutical Bridge Question: Are we in the twenty-first century suffering from idolatry? If so, what are our idols? What are some of the consequences of our idolatry?

Notes

1. Jürgen Moltmann, *A Broad Place: An Autobiography*, 1st Fortress Press Edition (Minneapolis: Fortress Press, 2008), 26.

2. Ibid., 28–29.

3. Ibid., 30.

4. Jürgen Moltmann, *Sun of Righteousness, Arise! God's Future for Humanity and the Earth*, 1st Fortress Press Edition (Minneapolis: Fortress Press, 2010), 122–23.

5. Jürgen Moltmann, *Theology of Hope: On the Ground and the Implications of a Christian Eschatology* (San Francisco: HarperSanFrancisco, 1991), 103.

6. Ibid.

7. Ibid., 104–6.

8. Ibid., 147.

9. Moltmann, *Sun of Righteousness*, 153.

10. Ibid., 156.

11. Jürgen Moltmann, *The Spirit of Life: A Universal Affirmation*, 1st Fortress Press Edition (Minneapolis: Fortress Press, 1992), 34–35.

12. Jürgen Moltmann, *The Trinity and the Kingdom: The Doctrine of God*, 1st Fortress Press edition. (Minneapolis: Fortress Press, 1993), 165.

13. Jürgen Moltmann, *The Crucified God: The Cross of Christ as the Foundation and Criticism of Christian Theology*, 1st Fortress Press Edition (Minneapolis: Fortress Press, 1993), 357.

14. Ibid., 362.

15. Ibid., 306.

16. Ibid., 324.

17. Ibid., 367.

18. Moltmann, *The Spirit of Life*, 47–48.

19. Moltmann, *Sun of Righteousness*, 103.

20. Moltmann, *The Spirit of Life*, 10.

21. Ibid., 190–91.

22. Moltmann, *The Crucified God*, 429.

23. Ibid., 448.

24. Ibid., 454.

25. Ibid., 480.

26. Ibid., 485.

27. Moltmann, *The Spirit of Life*, 171–72.

28. Moltmann, *Theology of Hope*, 329.

29. Moltmann, *The Spirit of Life*, 239–41.

30. Moltmann, *Theology of Hope*, 328.

5
Feminist Vision
The Theology of Elisabeth Schüssler Fiorenza

The terms *feminist* and *feminism* have been used in relation to culture since the nineteenth century.[1] But feminist theology as a discipline is believed by some theologians and biblical scholars to have begun with white suffragist Elizabeth Cady Stanton and her publication of *The Woman's Bible* in 1895. In that volume, she critiqued the ways in which the Scriptures have been used to characterize negatively (as in voiceless, powerless, conniving, manipulative), to oppress, and to marginalize women. Stanton believed that since the Bible was so influential and instrumental in the formation of societal concepts of gender, women would not achieve social equality until Christianity itself underwent a revision. Revision of Christianity would start with a revision of the core document of the faith, the Bible itself.[2] Stanton agreed with other women in her day that one of the major problems with the Bible was how it was interpreted by male clergy. However, she went even further than her peers by saying that in addition to being misinterpreted, Scripture itself, even before it is interpreted, is androcentric (male-centered) and biased against women.[3]

African American women such as abolitionist and women's rights advocate Sojourner Truth and scholar and educator Anna Julia Cooper also critiqued the way the Bible was used to oppress women and African Americans. Like Stanton, they critiqued the makeup of the Bible itself. For example, Truth believed that the Spirit spoke the truth in Scripture. However, she also believed that "the recorders of those truths had intermingled with them ideas and suppositions of their own."[4] For Cooper, Christ gave the people of God many ideals to live by. Among these ideals is "a rule and guide for the estimation of woman, as an equal, as a helper, as a friend and as a sacred charge to be sheltered and cared for."[5] When using the phrase "sacred charge," Cooper was referring to African American women and girls who worked as domestic laborers in white homes and who were often sexually and physically abused.

In the twentieth century, white feminist theologians such as Mary Daly, Rosemary Radford Ruether, and Elizabeth Schüssler Fiorenza continued Stanton's critique of biblical texts and biblical interpretation. They also critiqued the second-class status of women in the church broadly, and in the Catholic church in particular. Before the emergence of feminist theology, academic theology was the purview of white men under the guise of objective, disinterested scholarship. The perspectives and experiences of women used to develop feminist theology exposes the male-centered bias inherent in traditional theological discourse.[6]

A Brief Biography

Elisabeth Schüssler Fiorenza was born to a working-class Catholic family in Romania in 1938. During World War II she and her family left their home to escape the perils of war. As refugees, they found shelter in barns or beneath trees.[7] It was her experiences as a refugee that would foster concern for those in need and eventually fuel her work as a feminist scholar. Life as a refugee delayed the progression of Elisabeth's primary education by causing her to begin the first grade three times.[8]

After the war, her family moved to a predominantly Lutheran rural village in Germany where life regained a sense of normalcy. Elisabeth proved to be a good student, even qualifying for education at the Gymnasium, a humanistic educational institution dedicated to the study of ancient languages (Latin, Greek, and Hebrew) and ancient literature. The German Gymnasium was also committed to the study of German culture, including literature and grammar, history, geography, mathematics, and nature.

As a teen Elisabeth seriously considered becoming a nun. However, her pastor advised her against that path because he did not believe she had a "vocation to obedience."[9] After completing her studies at the Gymnasium in 1958, she began studying theology at university. She went on to graduate summa cum laude in 1962 with her master of divinity and her licentiate (a degree in a European university that is just below a doctor). In 1964 her licentiate thesis was published as a book focused on the ministries of women in the Roman Catholic Church.[10] Also in 1964, she became the first woman at the University of Wurzburg to "take the full theological degree path" of students for Catholic priesthood.[11] Some of her professors were helpful and supportive of her. Others were openly hostile because she was a female attempting to earn an advanced degree in theology.[12]

Throughout her time as a doctoral student, she encountered sexism. Her adviser, Rudolf Schnackenburg, refused to give her a fellowship even though she had earned degrees with highest honors because he felt he needed "to give them to those who have a future in theology."[13] Because she was a woman, he believed she had no such future. Schnackenburg also believed that laypeople could not teach theology at Wurzburg. Her adviser's dismissal of her academic abilities was devastating for her.

That same year, however, Elisabeth met Josef Schreiner of the University of Munster, who offered her a research position. She thrived there and earned the "best dissertation" award when she graduated in 1970.[14] Throughout her studies, she produced original work that demanded that she develop her own theoretical-theological framework. She wrote about topics that directly affected women, such as the ministry of women in the church and the grace of God at work in women who ministered in the church. Her encounters with biased structures in higher education heightened her awareness of and incentivized her resolve to reform kyriocentric[15] structures of oppression in academia. Though Germany was her home, Elisabeth felt like an outsider in German theological education.

After completing her dissertation, she moved to the United States in 1970 and began a teaching career at the University of Notre Dame.[16] Though she taught at Notre Dame for fourteen years and earned tenure, she experienced sexism and censorship that rendered her unable to truly thrive as a scholar. While at Notre Dame, in 1975 and 1978 she spoke at two women's ordination conferences. Her department chair, who was against women's ordination, called her into his office to object to some of the ideas she espoused during her lectures at the conferences, including those written in "Feminist Theology as a Critical Theology of Liberation."[17] However, the last straw for Schüssler Fiorenza was when she was prevented from using her book *In Memory of Her* in her classes at Notre Dame. After leaving Notre Dame in 1984, Schüssler Fiorenza then taught for four years at the Episcopal Divinity School in Cambridge before assuming her current position as professor of divinity at Harvard Divinity School in 1988. The year before, Schüssler Fiorenza became the first female president of the Society of Biblical Literature.

A Theological Overview

In many of her writings, including *In Memory of Her*, Schüssler Fiorenza envisions the reign of God as a world of justice in which men and women are equals in every sense of the word. For centuries women have been denied ordination, leadership roles in the church, and equality in society based largely on traditions and "malestream"[18] interpretations of biblical texts. It is with gender equality in mind that Schüssler Fiorenza argues that early Christian history needs to be reconstructed to better reflect the roles women actually played.

Schüssler Fiorenza argues for reconstruction rather than solely for better or different biblical interpretation. She agrees with Elizabeth Cady Stanton that the biblical texts included in the Bible do not represent the full extent to which women served as leaders, apostles, preachers, and teachers during the origins of the Christian church. Therefore a critical feminist approach to Scripture not only must critique traditional biased and sexist interpretations of the writings that were selected to be in the canon but also must reclaim those writings that did not make it into the canon. There are writings that more realistically and more fully depict the leadership roles, duties, and functions women served in the beginning of the church that were left out of the canon. Schüssler Fiorenza's biblical reconstruction also includes questioning the agendas of those who were most influential in the canonization process—the church fathers.

As evidence of the mindset of some of the church fathers who influenced the canonization process, Schüssler Fiorenza cites the writings of Origen, Chrysostom, Tertullian, and Jerome, each of whom took one of two strategies when it came to women in leadership in the church: downplaying or denying the significance of the roles women played in the past or characterizing women as unfit for leadership.

Biblical scholar and philosopher Origen (185–254 C.E.) admitted that women had been prophets but stressed that they did not speak publicly and especially did not speak in worship. Chrysostom confirmed that in apostolic times women did travel as missionaries while preaching the gospel. However, he insisted that women could do this only because the early church was in "angelic condition," which referred to the moral state of the world in which the early church was born.[19] The moral state of the world in general, and of women in particular, had changed so much from the days of the early church to Chrystostom's day (349–407 C.E.) that he believed women could no longer be trusted with offices of church leadership.

Tertullian believed that women were the devil's gateway and the root of all sin. He accused women of tempting men and angels and believed they were not permitted to occupy any male function, such as teaching or baptizing. Jerome believed women were not only the origin of sin but also of all heresy.[20] The writings and attitudes of some of the church fathers caused Schüssler Fiorenza to contend that the patriarchal context in which the canon was produced demands that it be approached with a "hermeneutics of suspicion."[21] All interpretation must keep the misogynous and antiwoman context in which the Bible was formed in mind. Information that found its way into the canon is not "value-neutral." As a result, Christian history must be reconstructed in order to determine the roles women actually played in the life of the early church.

With historical reconstruction in mind, Schüssler Fiorenza argues that Christianity experienced a substantive theological, sociological, and ecclesiological shift during the first century. She contends that Christianity started as a radically inclusive reform movement within Judaism, segued into a Christian missionary movement that included the ministry of the apostle Paul, and then emerged divided in the last quarter of the first century into patriarchal communities that espoused an exclusive church hierarchy on the one hand and communities that embraced Jesus' vision of a fully inclusive church on the other.

Schüssler Fiorenza calls Jesus' vision of the kingdom of God the *basileia* of God.[22] She prefers to use words such as "domain" or "commonweal" when translating the Greek *basileia* because those terms underscore how different the Jesus movement was from the Roman Empire in which the movement emerged.[23] To make her case for the inclusive nature of the basileia of God, Schüssler Fiorenza appeals to the writings of the Q[24] biblical source material found in Luke and Matthew and the Jewish Sophia tradition found in writings such as the Wisdom of Solomon.

Schüssler Fiorenza contends that the approach to life and ministry was different for Jesus than that of other Jewish renewal movements. Those who followed Jesus did not perceive of God as a divine warrior or king. Rather, they perceived of God as divine Sophia (wisdom). In the Jewish wisdom tradition, the Sophia goddess language is used to speak about the one God of Israel "whose gracious goodness is divine Sophia."[25] In the Wisdom of Solomon, which is included in the Roman Catholic but not the Protestant canon, Wisdom offers rest, knowledge, salvation, and life for all who accept her. As a result of Jesus' and the movement's very different conception of God, the basileia of God was a radically inclusive reality.

In the basileia of God, all people are welcome, including sinners such as tax collectors and prostitutes. God is on the side of the poor and against all who deny them their basic human rights. Salvation is present in healing moments such as when Jesus cast out demons, healed the sick, and told stories about how the last would be first. In the basileia of God, wholeness and holiness are one and the same.

Thanks to divine Sophia, the basileia of God is a discipleship of equals. Discipleship means serving as a follower of either a great leader or a compelling idea or vision.[26] The discipleship of equals was a vision of a world of justice and love. To be equal did not mean that all people were the same. Being equal meant that in diversity all people had equal standing and dignity before God. Therefore, the discipleship of equals in the basileia of God included people who were marginalized, hopeless, and despised. In the basileia of God, the downtrodden and outcast experienced a new reality in which the shalom of Israel was announced to them and the goodness of God was declared as readily available.

In the basileia of God, Jesus challenged patriarchal beliefs and structures that oppressed and marginalized women. For example, in Mark 10:2-9, when the Pharisees asked Jesus if it was lawful for a man to divorce his wife, Jesus provided a nuanced response. Jesus asked the Pharisees, "What did Moses command you?" The Pharisees accurately stated that Moses permitted a man to divorce his wife. Jesus then informed them Moses wrote that law because human hearts were hard. He also reminded them that the man was supposed to leave his patriarchal household and join with the woman as one flesh in an equal partnership made possible by the creator God.

Immediately after, Jesus rejected the concept of the patriarchal family in which children and slaves occupied the subservient positions. Schüssler Fiorenza believes that when Jesus said in Mark 10:16, that "whoever does not receive the basileia of God like a child shall not enter it," he was admonishing the people to let go of all their claims to power and domination over others, even those in their own households.

As evidence of the role of women in Judaism during the first third of the first century, Schüssler Fiorenza cites the deuterocanonical book of Judith (found in the Catholic Bible). The book is a fictional account of a powerful, intelligent, and beautiful woman whose strategic planning and decisive actions saved the nation of Israel from being annihilated by the Assyrian army. The character of Judith was a devout wealthy widow who used her position and influence to lead the men of Israel to victory in battle. She used her beauty to enthrall her enemies, her intellect to outmaneuver them, and her well-known devotion to God as leverage to establish godly credibility with both her enemies and her own people. As she prepared to embark on her mission to save the Israelites from the Assyrians, Judith offered a prayer that enables readers to understand the image of God held by the Israelites in that period: "For your strength does not depend on numbers, nor your might on the powerful. But you are the God of the lowly, helper of the oppressed, upholder of the weak, protector of the forsaken, savior of those without hope" (Judith 9:11).

Schüssler Fiorenza believes the image of a woman as an influential leader expressed in the book of Judith was not uncommon for Jews in the basileia movement and in the wider society. Schüssler Fiorenza reminds her readers that even though the basileia of God as experienced in the Jesus movement was founded on godly ideals, it was far from perfect. From its beginnings, a variety of conflicts, differences, and divisions existed. These communities were, after all, communities of fallible humans striving to live out the will of God.

After Jesus' crucifixion, death, resurrection, and ascension, shifts in the movement occurred. What had been the Jesus movement became the Christian missionary movement. Whereas the Jesus movement had been centered in the ministry and life of Jesus, the Christian missionary movement was centered in the power of the Holy Spirit. In the Christian missionary movement, those who were in Christ were filled with the Holy Spirit and lived according to the Spirit. In the Christian missionary movement, both men and women received the Holy Spirit.

Whereas the Jesus movement understood Jesus to be a messenger and a prophet of the divine Sophia, the Christian missionary movement believed Jesus was the living embodiment of divine Sophia of God. Jesus was Christ-Sophia who ruled over principalities and powers that enslaved the world before his coming. An example of the Christian missionary movement's concept of Christ-Sophia can be found in Philippians 2:6-11:

> Who, though he was in the form of God, did not regard equality with God as something to be exploited, but emptied himself, taking the form of a slave, being born in human likeness. And being found

in human form, he humbled himself and became obedient to the point of death—even death on a cross. Therefore God also highly exalted him and gave him the name that is above every name, so that at the name of Jesus every knee should bend, in heaven and on earth and under the earth, and every tongue should confess that Jesus Christ is Lord, to the glory of God the Father.

People in the Greco-Roman world believed that the world was being ruled by ungodly powers. Through their belief in Jesus as Christ-Sophia, they sought relief from the powers of this world and anticipated a divine world ruled by the One who now ruled over the principalities and powers of this world. They believed that through baptism they were new creations and were freed from the bondage of death and powers of evil of this world.[27] The gifting of both men and women with the Holy Spirit and the reconception of Jesus as the embodiment of Christ-Sophia rather than the messenger of God were major theological shifts.

The Christian church as we know it today started as house churches. House churches provided spaces for preaching, worship, sharing of the Eucharist, and social interactions. Women played key roles in the movement by not only offering their homes as assembly locations but also by serving as leaders. A businesswoman named Lydia (Acts 16:14-15) was converted to Christianity and opened her home to the Christian mission. Phoebe (Romans 16:1) was a deacon in the church of Cenchreae, as well as a wealthy benefactor of the movement. Schüssler Fiorenza points out that fully one third of the people Paul greeted in Acts 16 as apostles, coworkers, and diligent workers in the movement were women.

On several occasions Paul praises and greets the missionary couple Prisca (or Priscilla) and Aquila in his letters (Acts 18:2,18; Romans 16:3–5a; 1 Corinthians 16:19). Schüssler Fiorenza notes that since Prisca is addressed first she may have been the more important of the two. Like Barnabas and Apollos, Prisca and Aquila were independent missionary workers and Jewish Christians who did not stand under Paul's authority.[28] They traveled to share the gospel and suffered like Paul and other missionaries in that day for their beliefs and activities. Paul was grateful to them because they risked their lives for him (Romans 16:4). Their house churches in Corinth, Ephesus, and Rome were centers of missionary activity. Prisca was Apollos's teacher (Acts 18:26).

When trying to understand Paul's ideas about human relationships in Christian communities, Schüssler Fiorenza considered Paul's letter to the Galatians, which was written sometime between 50 and 55 C.E.[29] In the letter Paul wrote: "There is no longer Jew or Greek, there is no longer slave or free, there is no longer male and female; for all of you are one in Christ Jesus" (Galatians 3:28). Schüssler Fiorenza spends time discerning Paul's intentions with this text. She concludes that on the one hand Paul believed that the old hierarchy associated with men and women, slave and free, Jew and Greek had been overcome. Societal constraints of gender, ethnicity, and class hindered the dissemination of the gospel and threatened the unity of the church. On the other hand, members of the new churches lived their lives in the larger patriarchal Greco-Roman society. The newly acquired egalitarian ethos within their churches conflicted with the dominant ethos of the wider society outside of the church.

Examples of Paul's belief in and commitment to equality can be found not only in his recognition of women as apostles, deacons, and coworkers in Galatians, but also in writings such as Philemon. In this text Paul encouraged Philemon to receive Onesimus, who had been a slave baptized by Paul, back into the community as a beloved brother and no longer a slave (Philemon 1:16). In 1 Corinthians, although Paul encouraged members of the community to remain in the situation in which God called them, he also wrote that if slaves could gain their freedom, they should do so. In Galatians 5:1 Paul wrote that Christ had set them free such that slaves should not submit again to the yoke of slavery. Schüssler Fiorenza contends that when Christian slaves heard the Greek word *eleutheria* or "freedom," they expected more than spiritual liberation. They expected a change of status from slave to free person.[30]

Another writing that exemplifies Paul's commitment to gender equality can be found in the extracanonical book *The Acts of Paul and Thecla*. In this book, Thecla, who is converted by Paul, is persecuted when she refuses to marry. Many attempts were made by Roman officials to have her killed by raging beasts (chapter 9). No efforts to kill her prove to be successful because God delivers her over and over again.[31] On one occasion after she is delivered, Paul instructs her to go and preach the Word. She spent her life teaching and preaching about Jesus Christ.

As it relates to the relationship between Jews and Greeks, Paul chastised Cephas and Barnabas for hypocritical behavior when they ceased their table fellowship with Gentiles because they were not circumcised (Galatians 2:11-13). Paul reminded them that in Christ, circumcision was no longer required for initiation into the community. Baptism was the new rite of initiation for full inclusion (Romans 6:3-6).

Paul's commitment to equality for Gentiles also had ramifications for women. Since circumcision was no longer required, through baptism women became full members with the same rights and duties as the men.

Paul's contention that in Christ believers were no longer male or female also had implications for patriarchal marriage. Women and men were no longer defined by their capacities to procreate or by traditional gender roles. Paul also wrote in 1 Corinthians 7:8, 32-35 that he advised widows and the unmarried to remain single so they could be free from the anxieties associated with marriage, such as pleasing the spouse.

While Paul's teachings were good news for the people in the early Christian communities, they were in direct conflict with the gender roles and societal expectations of the Roman Empire. Roman law in Paul's day mandated marriage and rewarded procreation. In response to concerns about declining Roman populations in the upper classes and immoral behavior, Emperor Augustus instituted marriage laws between 17 and 18 B.C.E. In the laws, men who were not married were forced to pay higher taxes than married men.[32] Women were allowed to be independent or to no longer have male guardians only after they bore three children (if they were freeborn women) and after bearing four children (if they were former slaves). Within one year of the death of a spouse, both genders were expected to remarry.[33]

The only women in Rome who were legally not required to be married were the Vestal Virgins, girls from elite families who were chosen between the ages of six to ten to serve for thirty years as keepers of the perpetual flame of the goddess Vesta. After serving out their term, they were allowed to remain single, if they chose, for the rest of their lives.[34] Though their lives were closely regulated, they were exempt from the state requirements of marriage and not subject to the subjugation they would otherwise experience from husbands.

For Schüssler Fiorenza, although Paul was committed to the discipleship of equals of the Jesus movement, he also recognized the tremendous conflict that nonconformity to the expectations of the Roman government, as it relates to marriage and gender roles, would create. This is why Schüssler

Fiorenza believes the same Paul who wrote Galatians 3:28 also wrote texts such as 1 Corinthians 11:2-16 and 1 Corinthians 14:33-36. In 1 Corinthians 11:2-16 Paul admonished the women to bind up and cover their hair in worship. In 1 Corinthians 14:33-36 he instructed married women not to speak in worship but rather to ask questions of the husbands at home. It is important to remember that many of the leading missionaries in the Christian movement were married, including the women whom he praised and greeted effusively in his letters, such as Prisca and Junia. Instructing these women to be silent in worship and ask questions of their husbands at home was inconsistent with his affirmations of their work, to say the least.

Schüssler Fiorenza believes that with each of these instructions, Paul's ultimate concern was order in worship. Paul was attempting to ensure that worship in Christian communities did not mimic the frenzied worship of the many other cults of his day.[35] At the core of Paul's concern about order were issues of assimilation. How could a movement which had a social and cultural ethos that was so different from that of the dominant culture find ways to blend into the larger culture in some respects? Public worship was one place the Christians could demonstrate that they adopted at least some of the beliefs and practices of the dominant culture. Unfortunately, the attempt of at least partial assimilation came at the expense of women. With his efforts to assimilate, Paul contradicted the very antipatriarchal ethos he purported to support. While Paul espoused the discipleship of equals that the Jesus movement embodied, he simultaneously undermined his own efforts of attaining equality with his attempts to assimilate into Greco-Roman culture and by adopting patriarchal language to relate to his disciples and communities of faith.

Schüssler Fiorenza believes that with his words and actions, Paul opened a door for the post-Pauline and pseudo-Pauline (writings in Paul's name) household codes. Household codes are instructions found in Scripture guiding the behavior of people in private homes and in the wider Greco-Roman society—husbands and wives, parents and children, and masters and slaves. The household codes are found in Colossians, Ephesians, 1 Timothy, Titus, and 1 Peter. These texts were written during the latter part of the first century (Colossians, 60–64 C.E[36]; Ephesians, 60 C.E.[37]; 1 and 2 Timothy and Titus, 95 C.E.[38]; and 1 Peter, 80–100 C.E.).[39]

In the household codes, the basileia vision of God found in the Jesus movement as equality among people of different genders and social status is annihilated. For example, in Colossians, the writer changes Paul's words from Galatians 3:28 to: "In that renewal there is no longer Greek and Jew, circumcised and uncircumcised, barbarian, Scythian, slave and free; but Christ is all and in all!" (Colossians 3:11). In this writing, male and female are not mentioned at all. Words that were liberating in Galatians are now spiritualized.[40] Regarding slaves, the text continues in a similar vein:

> Slaves, obey your earthly masters in everything, not only while being watched and in order to please them, but wholeheartedly, fearing the Lord. Whatever your task, put yourselves into it, as done for the Lord and not for your masters, since you know that from the Lord you will receive the inheritance as your reward; you serve the Lord Christ. For the wrongdoer will be paid back for whatever wrong has been done, and there is no partiality. Masters, treat your slaves justly and fairly, for you know that you also have a Master in heaven. (Colossians 3:22–4:1)

In verse 22 slaves are instructed to obey their earthly masters in everything. Their tasks are to be done for their masters as if they were completing the tasks for God. The "no longer slave or free" of Galatians 3:28 is not interpreted to refer to the physical body. It is now referring to spiritual well-being.

Schüssler Fiorenza has highlighted the reality that the household codes of Colossians and the other four texts reflect Aristotle's influence on the morals of Greco-Roman society. In *Politics*, Aristotle argued that there was a natural order of creation:

> The male is by nature superior and the female inferior, the male ruler and the female subject. And the same must also necessarily apply in the case of mankind as a whole; therefore all men that differ as widely as the soul does from the body and the human being from the lower animal (and this is the condition of those whose function is the use of the body and from whom this is the best that is forthcoming) these are by nature slaves, for whom to be governed by this kind of authority is advantageous, inasmuch as it is advantageous to the subject things already mentioned. For he is by nature a slave who is capable of belonging to another (and that is why he does so

belong), and who participates in reason so far as to apprehend it but not to possess it; for the animals other than man are subservient not to reason, by apprehending it, but to feelings.[41]

For Aristotle, people who were guided by reason, such as men and the elite of society, were natural leaders of those who were guided by feelings (women and slaves). Schüssler Fiorenza believes that the pseudo-Pauline authors of Colossians, Ephesians, 1 Timothy, Titus, and 1 Peter were motivated to prescribe patriarchal hierarchy, by their desire for the Christian community to meet the Aristotelian-inspired patriarchal standards of the larger Greco-Roman society. The household codes directed wealthy women not to serve as leaders of churches the way they had in the Jesus movement and the Christian missionary movement. The codes also made it possible for male and female slaves to be exploited, even in the Christian community.[42]

Schüssler Fiorenza argues that the writings about women in the church advising them to be silent and preventing them from serving as leaders are prescriptive rather than descriptive. In other words, they represented the desires of the men who wrote them. However, just because the instructions were written does not mean they were followed. After all, male clergy were often dependent on the support of wealthy and influential women in their ministries.[43]

While some Christian communities in the latter part of the first century moved far away from the discipleship of equals model (or basileia vision) of ministry found in the Jesus movement, others chose to embrace and embody it. Evidence of this can be found in the Gospels of Mark and John, which are believed to have been written between 68 and 70 C.E.[44] and 95 C.E.[45] respectively. Schüssler Fiorenza highlights the contrasts between the ethos found in the writings of Mark and John and the pastoral epistles. In the Gospels, Jesus stresses the importance of selfless love and service that is demanded not just from the servants, as is found in the pastoral letters, but from all people, including leaders and masters, men and women.[46] In Mark 10:35-40, James and John ask Jesus for seats on his left and right hand in glory. Jesus told them that whoever wants to become great among them must become a servant. Whoever wants to be first must become the servant of all.

For Schüssler Fiorenza it is the dedication to service that separates the women from the men. The male disciples denied even knowing Jesus when he was arrested. The women, however, followed Jesus in Galilee, ministered to him, and went to Jerusalem with him. In Matthew 8:34 Jesus said that those who wanted to be his disciples would have to deny themselves, take up their cross, and follow him. The women left everything behind, took up their cross, and followed Jesus. Therefore, by Jesus' own definition, they were true disciples.

In John, women also occupy leadership positions in Jesus' earthly ministry. The confessions of Martha and Mary after the death of Lazarus express the faith and beliefs of the Johannine community. Martha expressed her belief that Jesus was the Messiah, the Son of God. (Schüssler Fiorenza believes her confession parallels Peter's confession in John 6:68–69.) Mary Magdalene stood at the cross and discovered the empty tomb. She was the first to experience the resurrection. The Gospels of Mark and John present an alternative vision from that of the post-Pauline epistles: women assume leadership and discipleship roles in each.

Implications for Preaching

Schüssler Fiorenza's work reveals the mindset of the church fathers who were instrumental in deciding which books would be included in the biblical canon and which would not. Though the church fathers and the writers of our biblical texts were undoubtedly inspired by their relationships with God, they were flawed and fallible human beings. Schüssler Fiorenza removes the veil that often enshrouds the canonization process by contending that the church fathers had their own agendas: some human and some divine. Their very human agendas included ensuring that women not be allowed to serve as leaders of Christian communities. Because of the actions and agendas of the church fathers, the fullness of the basileia of God cannot be experienced in the Christian Scriptures. This presents an opportunity for preachers to reassert the primacy of the Spirit of God over what is now known as the Word of God.

Though the first of the Ten Commandments in Exodus 20:4 admonishes us not to make an idol of anything, we have throughout Christian history made an idol of the Bible. We have treated the Bible as if it is God. We have used the Bible to teach communities which people, beliefs, and practices Christians should embrace and which they should reject. We have allowed the Bible to be the sole determiner of what is right and what is wrong. For centuries the Bible has been used to not only deny the full participation and inclusion of many of God's people, including women, the differently abled, non-Christians, people of differing ethnicities, and homosexuals. The Bible has also been used to justify slavery, Native American genocide (Manifest Destiny), and wars such as the Crusades. Preachers can remind their congregations of the biblical mandate not to make idols. Nothing, including the Bible, is equal to or more important than God.

By acknowledging that the Bible is not God, preachers can help their people reclaim the importance of the Holy Spirit. The Holy Spirit was sent by God after Jesus' ascension to teach us and remind us of everything Jesus taught during his earthly ministry (John 14:25-26). Also known as the Spirit of truth, the Spirit, Jesus promised, will guide us into all the truth. The Holy Spirit will glorify Jesus because it declares Jesus' words and will to us (John 16:13-14). In Christian practice we have allowed the Bible to supplant the Spirit. Though the Bible, in cooperation with the Holy Spirit, can help us to discern the will of God, the Bible is not God. Preachers can remind their people of the role, purpose, and availability of the Holy Spirit.

Second, by highlighting the differences between the Jewish movement under the leadership of Jesus himself and the Christian missionary movement of the mid-first century and beyond, preachers can help their congregations understand that Christianity as we know it is the result of an evolution. Over the course of one century, what became known as the Christian message shifted from Jesus' vision of the basileia of God in which all were welcome to Paul's double-minded message of social equality and inclusion on the one hand, and gender inequality and class hierarchy and exclusion on the other. The message shifted again with the household codes embodied in the writings of the pastoral epistles in which the social and ecclesial rights of women, children, and slaves were subjugated to men. The evolution of the Christian message over the centuries can be a cautionary tale for Christian communities. With each successive generation, the people who call themselves followers of Christ lost touch with the message and mission of the one whose name they bear. Preachers should help their people understand the original Jesus movement and Jesus' vision of a community of equals.

Using Schüssler Fiorenza's inclusive conception of the basileia of God, preachers can remind their people that the reign of God is both present and yet to come. While many think of the reign or kingdom of God in terms of God's apocalyptic breaking into human history, Fiorenza focuses our attention on the implication of the basileia for daily living. Therefore, while many eagerly await Christ's Second Coming with great anticipation, we are also reminded that as a redeemed people we have responsibilities for the welfare of God's creation in the here and now.

One of the omissions of Schüssler Fiorenza's work is not shedding light on the canonization process itself. She critiques the books that were chosen without clearly stating the particulars of the selection process. What criteria were used to decide which books would be included in the canon and which would not? Was concern about women in leadership part of the stated criteria for selection? Who made the final selection decisions? Over what period of time did the canonization process take place? Did the criteria for making the canon change over time?[47] By helping their people understand how the Bible, the central text of Christianity, came to be, preachers can help them better understand the human influences that shaped the content of their sacred book.

Some of the questions that remain unanswered in Schüssler Fiorenza's work are about Jesus himself. She does not address the ways Jesus may have been influenced by the patriarchal context in which he lived. Was Jesus' choosing of twelve male disciples evidence of his own patriarchal influences? If the Jesus movement was truly inclusive, why were there no women among the twelve? When preachers highlight the ways in which Jesus may have been influenced by his culture, they are reminding their people that each of us is influenced by the cultures in which we live while also being called to be people of God. Throughout our lives we must consciously decide how to live within a culture while be committed to the Christian faith.

Through her selection of particular sections of various books and writings, Schüssler Fiorenza does what many scholars and lay people do—she found in the texts that which she sought. She searched the Scriptures and extra-canonical writings for evidence that women were instrumental in the establishment of Christianity as a world religion and found it. Preachers can help their people become more conscious of the biases they bring to the biblical text in hopes that they begin to approach the texts with a conscious awareness of their own biases and a commitment to lay their biases aside.

Questions for Exegesis

1. Is there evidence of the basileia of God in the text (equal opportunities and valuing of all of God's people)? If so, what is it?

2. What is the role of women in the text? Are they leaders? Are they treated as property? Are their voices and opinions valued?

3. Are there any people in the text living under patriarchal domination or oppression? If so, who?

4. How does Jesus interact with women in the text? Does he honor the practices of his patriarchal culture or defy them?

5. Is the salvation of God evident in the text (through healing, wholeness, holiness, etc.)?

6. Hermeneutical Bridge Question: Is patriarchy present in the lives of people in our churches, communities, and world? If so, how? What should Christians do when they encounter it?

Notes

1. According to the Oxford English Dictionary, the term feminism was first used in 1841 to refer to qualities of females. See "Feminism," *Oxford English Dictionary* (2016), http://www.oed.com.libaccess.sjlibrary.org/view/Entry/69192?redirectedFrom=feminism#eid.; Elisabeth Schüssler Fiorenza, *Transforming Vision: Explorations in Feminist The*logy* (Minneapolis: Fortress Press, 2011). The term was first used in print in reference to gender equality in the British Journal *The Athenaeum* in 1895.

2. Elizabeth Cady Stanton, Carrie Chapman Catt, and National American Woman Suffrage Association Collection (Library of Congress), *The Woman's Bible*, 2 vols. (New York: European Publishing, 1895), 6–7.

3. Elisabeth SchüsslerFiorenza, ed. *Searching the Scriptures: A Feminist Introduction*, vol. 1 (New York: Crossroad Publishing Company, 1993), 4.

4. Karen Baker-Fletcher, "Anna Julia Cooper and Sojourner Truth: Two Nineteenth-Century Black Feminist Interpreters of Scripture," *Searching the Scriptures*, vol. 1 (New York: Crossroad Publishing Company, 1993), 48.

5. Ibid., 43.

6. Phyllis Trible, "The Creation of the Feminist Theology," *The New York Times* (1983), http://www.nytimes.com/1983/05/01/books/the-creation-of-a-feminist-theology.html?pagewanted=all.

7. Glen Enander, *Elisabeth Schüssler Fiorenza (Spiritual Leaders and Thinkers)* (Philadelphia: Chelsea House, 2005), 18.

8. Ibid., 20.

9. Ibid.

10. "Elisabeth Schüssler Fiorenza Facts" on *Your Dictionary* (accessed January 22, 2015), http://biography.yourdictionary.com/elisabeth-Schüssler-Fiorenza. The title of her first book is *The Forgotten Partner: Foundations, Facts and Possibilities of the Professional Ministry of Women in the Church*.

11. Enander, 22.

12. Ibid., 21.

13. Ibid., 22.

14. "Elisabeth Schüssler Fiorenza Facts." The title of her dissertation was *Priest for God: A Study of the Motif of the Kingdom and Priesthood in the Apocalypse, for the Catholic Theological Faculty*.

15. Ibid., 24. *Kyriarchy* is a term that Fiorenza coined from the Greek *kyrios*, meaning "to rule or dominate." She felt she needed a term that included biology as one of the factors of the sociopolitical societal structure. However, the term needed to also include other factors such as social position and wealth. In addition, since *patriarchy* inferred the dominance of all men over all women, it did not account for issues of class and social status.

16. Elisabeth Schüssler married Francis Fiorenza in 1967. They moved to the United States in 1970 to both begin teaching at Notre Dame.

17. Enander, 29. In the article, Fiorenza advocates for the need of a feminist theology to enable women to achieve equality for women as scholars and at every level of church service/employment. She criticizes Pope John Paul VI for demanding legislation to protect women's equal rights in cultural, political, social, and economic life while maintaining that women must not be allowed into church "hierarchical orders" because of inaccurate and antiquated exegesis. She criticizes the "myth of Mary" which she wrote could be liberative but was instrumental in the perpetuation of obedience and submission as desirable and godly virtues for women. She criticized Paul, the Pauline tradition, and the Church Fathers for eliminating women from ecclesial leadership and domesticating women under male authority in their homes and in monasteries. See Elisabeth Schüssler Fiorenza, "Feminist Theology as a Critical Theology of Liberation," *Theological Studies* 36, no. 44 (1975): 605–626.

18. Enander, 3.

19. Elisabeth Schüssler Fiorenza, *In Memory of Her: A Feminist Theological Reconstruction of Christian Origins*, 10th anniversary ed. (New York: Crossroad, 1994), 54.

20. Ibid., 54–56.

21. First used by French philosopher Paul Ricoeur, the term *hermeneutics of suspicion* has been used by biblical scholars as a way of advising those interpreting biblical texts not to take the text at face value. Rather, interpreters should try to understand as much about the context of the texts. See Paul Ricoeur, "Freud and Philosophy: An Essay on Interpretation," *The Terry Lectures* (New Haven, CT: Yale University Press, 1970), 27.

22. Schüssler Fiorenza, *In Memory of Her*, 120.

23. Elisabeth Schüssler Fiorenza, "To Follow the Vision: The Jesus Movement as Basilea Movement," in *Liberating Eschatology: Essays in Honor of Letty M. Russell* Margaret A. Farley and Serena Jones, eds. (Louisville: Westminster John Knox Press, 1999), 134–35.

24. See Paul Foster, "Is Q a 'Jewish Christian' Document?," *Biblica* 94, no. 3 (2013).

25. Schüssler Fiorenza, *In Memory of Her*, 134.

26. Schüssler Fiorenza, *Transforming Vision*, 197–98.

27. Schüssler Fiorenza, *In Memory of Her*, 190.

28. Ibid., 178.

29. Hans Dieter Betz, *Galatians: A Commentary on Paul's Letter to the Churches in Galatia*, Hermeneia—A Critical and Historical Commentary on the Bible (Philadelphia: Fortress Press, 1979), 12.

30. Schüssler Fiorenza, *In Memory of Her*, 210.

31. *The Acts of Paul and Thecla*, Jeremiah Jones, trans. (New York: The St. Pachomius Orthodox Library, Forham University, 1995), https://legacy.fordham.edu/halsall/basis/thecla.asp.

32. Mary R. Lefkowitz and Maureen B. Fant, *Women's Life in Greece and Rome* (Baltimore: Johns Hopkins University Press, 1992), http://www.stoa.org/diotima/anthology/wlgr/wlgr-romanlegal120.shtml.

33. Schüssler Fiorenza, *In Memory of Her*, 225.

34. N. S. Gill, "Six Vestal Virgins: Obligations and Rewards of the Thirty Year Commitment the Vestal Virgins Made," About Education (2016), http://ancienthistory.about.com/cs/rome/a/aa1114001.htm.

35. Schüssler Fiorenza, *In Memory of Her,* 233.

36. W. R. F. Browning, ed., "Paul's Letter to the Colossians," *A Dictionary of the Bible,* http://www.oxfordbiblicalstudies.com/article/opr/t94/e2117.

37. John Muddiman, *A Commentary on the Epistle to the Ephesians* (New York: Continuum, 2001), 34.

38. W. R. F. Browning, ed., "Pastoral Epistles," *A Dictionary of the Bible,* http://www.oxfordbiblicalstudies.com/opr/t94/e1424.

39. Paul J. Achtemeier and Eldon Jay Epp, ed., *1 Peter Hermeneia: A Commentary on First Peter,* Hermeneia—A Critical and Historical Commentary on the Bible (Minneapolis: Fortress Press, 1996), 49.

40. Schüssler Fiorenza, *In Memory of Her,* 253.

41. Aristotle, *Politics* (Medford, MA: Perseus Digital Library Project, 1987), http://www.perseus.tufts.edu/hopper/text?doc=Perseus%3Atext%3A1999.01.0058%3Abook%3D1%3Asection%3D1254b. Aristotle was a Greek philosopher and scientist who lived from 384–322. B.C.E. He was a student of Plato, whose writings widely influenced and shaped Greek culture. See Ben Waggoner, "Aristotle (384–322 B.C.E.)," (1996), http://www.ucmp.berkeley.edu/history/aristotle.html.

42. Schüssler Fiorenza, *In Memory of Her,* 291.

43. Ibid., 310.

44. Adela Yarbro Collins and Harold W. Attridge, *Mark: A Commentary,* Hermeneia—A Critical and Historical Commentary on the Bible (Minneapolis: Fortress Press, 2007), 14–15.

45. "Gospel of John," *A Dictionary of the Bible* (2009), http://www.oxfordbiblicalstudies.com/article/opr/t94/e1018.

46. Schüssler Fiorenza, *In Memory of Her,* 334.

47. See Bart D. Ehrman, *Lost Christianities: The Battle for Scripture and the Faiths We Never Knew* (New York: Oxford University Press, 2003); Robert B. Coote and Mary P. Coote, *Power, Politics, and the Making of the Bible: An Introduction* (Minneapolis: Fortress Press, 1990); Arthur G. Patzia, *The Making of the New Testament: Origin, Collection, Text & Canon,* 2nd ed. (Downers Grove, IL: IVP Academic, 2011).

6
The Vision of the Social Gospel
The Theology of Walter Rauschenbusch

A Brief Biography

Walter Rauschenbusch was born Walther Rauschenbusch in Rochester, New York, in 1861 to August and Caroline Rauschenbusch. Walther was named in keeping with the German prayer "Walt' Herr, ber diesem Kinde" (Rule, Lord, over this child).[1] His father, August, was a sixth-generation Lutheran pastor who hailed from the Westphalia region of northwestern Germany. As a minister, August's passion was to save souls, make members of his congregation aware of their sins, and help them to accept Jesus into their lives.[2] This conviction led him to immigrate to the United States in 1846 to work in the new mission fields of German immigrant communities, first in Missouri, then in New York.[3] Once in the United States, he decided that the Baptist faith, which honored evangelical piety and personal Christian experience, was an excellent fit for his spiritual convictions. After being baptized in the Mississippi River, he became part of the German Baptist Church.[4] He joined the faculty of Rochester Theological Seminary in 1858 as chair of the newly formed German department.

Walter Rauschenbusch spent his early childhood years, ages four through eight, in Germany with his mother and his sisters Frida and Emma while his father remained in the United States. It is to his mother, Caroline, that Rauschenbusch attributes his love for nature and appreciation for beauty in life.[5] While in Germany, they spent time reconnecting with the culture and friends and family, including his paternal grandmother, who happened to be deaf. He completed high school in Rochester, New York, before spending the next four years studying at the Evangelical Gymnasium of Gutersloh in Westphalia. His father believed Walter would receive a better education in Germany than in the United States. Though he struggled to adjust to the German education context in the beginning, he quickly earned the nickname "the energetic American" because of his academic work ethic.[6] On the eve of beginning of his final year, he was granted the honor of Primus Omnium, the top student judged by faculty to have superior intellectual abilities and personal qualities. He mastered Latin, Greek, French, German, and Hebrew. While in Europe, August Rauschenbusch gave Walter money to travel because he believed travel was an invaluable learning experience.[7]

Before returning to the United States in 1883, Rauschenbusch had to decide his next educational path. Though the seminary at Rochester would accept his Gymnasium degree as the equivalent of a bachelor's degree from an American university, he did not want to be the first and only Rauschenbusch not to earn an official bachelor's degree. Therefore, he convinced his father and the administrators of the University of Rochester and the seminary that he could study at both institutions at the same time.[8] He graduated from the University of Rochester in the spring of 1884 and decided to take his first pastoral ministry assignment. He accepted a call to pastor a small German Baptist congregation in Louisville, Kentucky, during the summer. It was during his three months in Louisville that he decided he no longer wanted to be an academic theologian who wrote books. Rather, he felt a very strong call to be a pastor.[9] He was invited back to the Louisville church the following summer.

Like his father, he felt the Baptist faith was a good fit with his convictions. And he believed that the democratic polity of the Baptists best emulated the early Christian church.[10] He graduated from the Rochester Theological Seminary in 1886 and moved to New York City, where he served as pastor of the Second German Baptist Church for eleven years. The church was near a poverty-stricken area known as Hell's Kitchen. While pastoring there, he began to understand the many challenges that American immigrants faced in their daily lives, such as lack of health care, lack of heat in the winter, and persistent hunger.[11]

When Rauschenbusch encountered these conditions, he determined that nothing he had studied in Gutersloh or Rochester had prepared him for it. He had social questions but no tools with which to analyze and remedy the problems.[12] The development of Rauschenbusch's version of the social gospel began after he encountered social activists and read some of the writings of British socialists, German social economists, and American social commentators such as Josiah Strong and Washington Gladden, who each wrote about the importance of the kingdom of God in the pursuit of social transformation.[13]

In 1893 Rauschenbusch joined several pastors to found a group called the Brotherhood of the Kingdom. The purpose of the group was to meet at least once a year to strategize about religious and social reform. He also served as co-collaborator and translator in a German hymnal project that resulted in the publication of two hymnals in 1891 and 1895. He believed that the social gospel needed hymns that embodied the quality and character of other traditions such as nineteenth-century evangelical revivalism.[14] Like others in his family, he experienced hearing loss. Though he never lost his hearing completely, hearing loss did present challenges during his pastorate, in lectures, and in the seminary classroom. After eleven years serving as a pastor in Hell's Kitchen, he became professor of church history at the Rochester Theological Seminary.[15] Though he had declared he had no desire to write books when he experienced his call to pastoral ministry, he did in fact write great books, including his seminal works *Christianity and the Social Crisis* and *A Theology for the Social Gospel*.

Rauschenbusch died of colon cancer in Rochester, New York, on July 25, 1918.

A Theological Overview

Walter Rauschenbusch's vision of the kingdom of God is one in which every facet of society—family, church, educational systems, government, and businesses—is guided by Christian principles so that all people have an opportunity to live good and productive lives. Under his vision, Christian people would fight for the rights of all people to have good wages, sanitary living conditions, and access to good education and health care. He believed that for far too long, Christians have been concerned only with people's souls and not with the social conditions in which they lived. His vision for a Christianized society or the kingdom of God on earth became a priority for him while serving as pastor of a church near Hell's Kitchen. His congregation was made up of 125 working-class German immigrants.[16] Members of his church were employed as carpenters, shoemakers, butchers, grocers, and many types of skilled and unskilled laborers.[17] Though a small number had indeed done very well financially, many of them experienced severe poverty and unemployment, malnutrition, and sickness and disease.[18]

Rauschenbusch was doing ministry during the throes of the Industrial Revolution. This was a period in world history in which the economy was radically changing from one based on agriculture to one based on commerce and industry. Establishment of manufacturing technologies such as the cotton mill, which was imported from Britain, brought an influx of jobs into the Northeast. People migrated from rural communities as well as from other countries, such as Germany, in hopes of finding employment and prosperity. Railroads and canals were soon developed to support and expand industries. Other inventions, such as airplanes, internal combustion engines, automobiles, the telegraph, the telephone, and electricity, completely transformed business and the ways people lived their daily lives. On the one hand, the standard of living went up. There were some who were making great fortunes, such as the Vanderbilts and the Rockefellers. The middle class was also expanding. Technological advances brought with them new amenities and extravagances that also offered opportunities for investments.

On the other hand, there existed debilitating poverty. Some of the working class found themselves living in appalling conditions in urban slums with open sewers and contaminated water supplies, which led to illness and disease. Some worked in dangerous conditions for substandard wages. Child labor was being used and exploited in large industries. Rauschenbusch believed that the individualistic orientation of theology left the social aspect of theology completely undeveloped. Therefore, he developed a theology for the social gospel. With his theology of the social gospel, he attempted to reclaim the theology embodied in the life of Jesus Christ.

For Rauschenbusch, Jesus was a revolutionary force sent by God to realize a revolutionary program, commonly known as the kingdom of God.[19] The term *revolutionary* is typically associated with violence and destruction. In Jesus' case, *revolutionary* referred to his commitment to overturning the existing social order in pursuit of the will of God. In the kingdom of God there was a reversal of values. The first would be last and the last would be first (Mark 10:31). Values esteemed by society were instead an abomination before God (Luke 16:15). In the kingdom of God, the poor and the hungry were not sad but comforted and satisfied. The meek would inherit the earth (Matthew 5:1-12). Rather than acquiescing to the powers and principalities of his day, Jesus called out the hypocritical behaviors of religious leaders by critiquing their piety and interpretations of the Law. Even while he was calling out the ungodly behaviors of the religious leaders, he lived and ministered among the people. He worked as a carpenter. He owned no land or property. When he spoke, the common people resonated with him because he lived as one of them.[20]

From the beginning of Jesus' earthly ministry, Jesus preached the kingdom of God, which was central to all his teaching. Though the term *kingdom of God* was familiar to his listeners, the meaning of the term was very different for Jesus than for many of the people of his day. Some believed the kingdom of God meant the reign of an earthly king brought about through violent revolution. Others believed the kingdom would be a period of human history brought about through some sort of divine catastrophe. Instead, Jesus rejected violence of all forms and declared that the kingdom of God was already among them. He used approaches such as parables to highlight manifestations of the kingdom that were already in the midst of the people. The healing power of God at work in him was evidence that there was a power higher than the power of this world. Jesus lived in hope: hope that the national, social, and religious lives of those around him could be transformed.

Rauschenbusch believed Jesus to be a Hebrew prophet who was preparing humanity for a righteous social order. A righteous social order had to be populated with humans filled with goodness that compelled them to live right and good social lives with other humans. It is with the righteous social order in mind that he declared Jesus' most fundamental virtue: love. Love creates fellowship and bonds humans to one another. Love for Jesus was not a fickle emotion. Rather, love for Jesus was "the highest and most steadfast energy of a will bent on creating fellowship."[21] Love creates a sense of worth for those receiving it, pride when those we love advance, pain when they suffer, joy in their happiness and realization of solidarity.[22]

It is with love in mind that Rauschenbusch revisited the definitions and conceptions of traditional theological doctrine, beginning with sin and sin consciousness. Traditional religion focused most of its attention on personal sins. Rauschenbusch believed that in order to propagate the importance of the social gospel, Christians also needed to develop a sin consciousness that includes social sins. He cited an example of a Mennonite farmer who swore out loud when his milk was rejected at the markets because it contained cow dung. He was expelled from his church not because he endangered the lives of babies and young children who drank his product but because he swore. Perhaps, Rauschenbusch suggested, the church should encourage the farmer to take up the issue of swearing with God. The church should also encourage the farmer to repent for his sin of violating the trust of the public to which he is accountable as a supplier of dairy.

Rauschenbusch identifies the individualistic teaching of the fall, and the doctrine of total depravity that evolved from it, as part of the reason Christian theology was devoid of a social ministry component. Total depravity is the belief that when humans were originally created by God, they were righteous, holy, good, and upright in the eyes of God. However, when Adam and Eve sinned in the Garden of Eden, they not only corrupted their own existence but also defiled all of humankind. As a result, all of humanity is morally evil and unable to live good and godly lives. If Christ had not died for our sins, all of humanity would have been cast away by God.[23]

The church fathers and theologians through the centuries have claimed Paul as the source of validation for their theologies based on the Fall, as told in Genesis 3. Though Paul does cite Genesis 3 in his letters to the Romans and the Corinthians, Rauschenbusch felt that the biblical story of the fall could not bear the tremendous theological weight historically placed on it. Rauschenbusch understood the religious motive of the doctrine: to bring all people under the conviction of sin and condemnation so that they would realize the need for grace and salvation. However, because total depravity fails to address corporate or social sins, he rejected this doctrine.

He believed that theologians expanded the doctrine of the fall far beyond the words contained in the Bible by using exegetical inference, allegory, and typology. For example, the writer of Genesis used the term *serpent* when referring to the being that led Eve to eat of the forbidden fruit rather than *Satan*. Yet many theologians equated the serpent with Satan. Rauschenbusch therefore argued that the term *sin* needed to be revisited. He defined sin as selfishness. Selfishness has personal (ethical) and social implications that render it very different than the conceptions of sin of the Greek fathers.[24] The Greek fathers viewed sin as sensuousness and materiality. He believed that clarifying the definition of sin and declaring the doctrine of total depravity unbiblical cleared the way for a gospel that better reflects the biblical texts and the life and teachings of Jesus.

According to Rauschenbusch, Jesus was not concerned with the origin of sin. Rather, Jesus was concerned with the sources of sin at work in his immediate environment, which included human hearts out of which evil actions proceeded, social stumbling blocks that caused the weak to fall, and the kingdom of evil. Rauschenbusch clarified that Jesus' interests were "practical and not speculative, religious and ethical and not philosophical."[25] He reminds his readers that for centuries the Hebrew prophets were able to understand and combat sin without having the doctrine of original sin as their theological foundation.

Therefore, Rauschenbusch contends that the question of the origin of evil is best left to God. Humanity should concentrate instead on present, active sources of evil. The key to being able to identify current sources of evil is an expansion of sin consciousness. Traditional theology has acclimated people to the wrongness of personal sins while ignoring social sins. Traditional theologians watched in silence while the poor and working class were "sucked dry by the parasitic classes of society and war was damming poor humanity." They offered no critique. In addition to personal sins, attention needed to be focused on issues of public morality—wrongs done by whole classes or professions of people. For example, Rauschenbusch found it problematic that churches that were against war before World War I allowed themselves to be convinced that war was good and necessary with arguments such as "as a nation we are soft and flabby, without training in order and obedience"; "young boys and men need to be under military discipline and drill" in order to "improve American character"; "war is essentially noble, the supreme test of manhood and of the worth of a nation were made to justify war in Rauschenbusch's day."[26] People who continued to contend publicly that war was a contradiction to Christianity were labeled extremists.

Inhibition, which he believed was a good faculty, goes wrong when evil becomes part of society's moral standards, as happens when the social and religious authorities are corrupted.[27] Sin is emboldened when supported and protected by societal authorities. He cites the example of alcohol. Alcoholism is deemed intolerable to scientific and moral minds. Yet production of wine and liquor not only persisted in his day but also acquired social acceptance and justification. While local governments wanted to control public drunkenness, political and religious authorities with investments in breweries and distilleries passed laws to pad their own pockets.

Having revisited traditional individualistic conceptions of sin and sin consciousness, Rauschenbusch also addressed the doctrine of salvation. He affirmed the need of all to experience forgiveness for personal salvation and the opportunity it presents to enter into voluntary obedience and the higher freedom found in Christ. He also contended that some who become saved do not improve in worth, or, in the worst case, may grow worse by getting saved because they become self-righteous, opinionated, more devoted to emotions, and less responsive to actual duties.[28]

In the kingdom of God, salvation is a change that turns people from self to God and humanity. "Salvation is the voluntary socializing of the soul."[29] Selfish people believe they are the centers of the universe, and God and all of humanity exist to serve their pleasures. Rauschenbusch believed that the person who experiences salvation in the kingdom of God should undergo a reorientation to the common life and good of all humankind. Conversion in the kingdom becomes more than a break with one's own sinful past. Rather, it is also a break with the sinful past of a social group. Regeneration is the creation of new life within us that allows us to see the kingdom of God as is found in the story of Nicodemus in John 3:1-21. Through regeneration, the light of Christ is able to shine and create a new religious identity.[30] The term *faith* also assumes a broader meaning: "faith is an energetic act of the will, affirming our fellowship with God and man, declaring our solidarity with the Kingdom of God, and repudiating selfish isolation."[31]

Rauschenbusch believed that the church failed to teach followers of Christ about social sin because leaders overlooked the doctrine of the kingdom of God. He defines the kingdom of God as the realm of love and the commonwealth of labor. He contends that Jesus made love the distinctive characteristic of God by superimposing himself on previous conceptions of God. Therefore, the reign of God is the reign of love. The kingdom of God is also the commonwealth of cooperative labor because each person is given particular abilities by God that are to be used to serve others. We cannot be fully who we were created to be without employing these abilities in the service of others through labor.

A community that is divinely ordered provides opportunities for education and enjoyment for all its people while also expecting all to contribute their labor. With this in mind, idleness is a sin. Productive labor is a condition of salvation. In addition, to overburden some classes of people with labor while others contribute no productive labor is a sin. To live off the labor of others and contribute nothing in return is the sin of parasitism. When wrestling with the ways sin is transmitted and perpetuated, he identified the most potent motive as profit. Ordinarily sin is an act of weakness followed by shame of the perpetrators. However, when the sin is "fed with money, sin grows wings and claws."[32]

Rauschenbusch believed that one of the most important and needed functions of the social gospel was to reclaim the image of God developed for and by those on the margins or those in solidarity with those on the margins. The image of God needed to be reclaimed because throughout the history of Christianity the images of kings, governors, and others who were the greatest purveyors of earthly powers were superimposed on God. He cited an example of Anselm, a Benedictine monk and archbishop of Canterbury in the Middle Ages. Anselm developed his "theory of satisfaction" in which humans had to pay for their sins. God, he taught, is under no obligation to show humans any favor when they sinned. Rather, God had to exact satisfaction for the violation of God's honor. Satisfaction could be achieved through some work or deed performed over and above the legal requirements of God. Since it is impossible for humans to render the appropriate deed, Christ was needed. This theory of satisfaction is the basis of his theory of atonement. Rauschenbusch contended that one of the key influences in the development of his theory was the law and custom of autocratic power in his day. Anselm lived in a society ruled by monarchs who rated offence against members of the royal family or governing class to be more heinous than other crimes. The honor of the king was thought to be important enough to violation of the initiate war over.

The image of God as an unmerciful tyrant was sometimes the result of the psychological trauma inflicted upon the masses by parents, school masters, priests, and officials. God has been a great terror. Gifts have been given to churches by the wealthy and influential over the years in hopes that God would not inflict them in any way. For some in the feudal system, God was a feudal lord who held tenants without hope of escape until he got from them the payments due to God. God would put people in a prison hotter than the holds beneath the duke's castle as punishment for sin, just like the civil authorities.

As a result of these images of God, which were directly related to their conception of social relationships in their contexts, some church and civil authorities distorted the image of God. Rauschenbusch contended that one of the most vital acts that Christ performed while here on earth was taking God by the hand and calling him "our Father," thereby democratizing the concept of God. Christ's words separated God from the "coercive and predatory state" and instead associated God with family life, solidarity, and love. He believed that Christ not only saved humanity; he saved God by giving God an opportunity to be loved.

Therefore, people who are committed to the social gospel recognize that images of God that emulate the powerful make autocratic social conditions seem necessary, tolerable, and desirable. The social gospel is a means of revealing that God loves righteousness and hates iniquity. The development of a Christian social order in the form of the kingdom of God would be proof of God's power to save. Failure of the social movement would "impugn God's existence."[33] Rauschenbusch offered critique on doctrines of suffering that attempted to mask responsibility of those in power for their actions. One approach to explaining the existence of suffering is to deny the existence of unjust suffering. In the book of Job, his friends searched for the secret sin that Job must have committed to merit his suffering. This secret sin explanation could not be maintained within the facts of Job's situation.

A dualistic explanation of suffering posits that the good God has nothing to do with suffering. Rather, the evil god who is the lord of this world is the source of all suffering. Hope for vindication of the righteous who suffer would be experienced in heaven. Rauschenbusch pointed out that when purgatory was debunked during the Reformation, this particular conception lost some of its appeal. The final explanation for suffering is one in which God is actually the source and distributor of suffering. God allocates suffering with intentionality according to individual strength, relieves it in response to prayer, and uses it as a deterrent for excessive pride or to prevent humanity from conforming too closely with the ways of the world. God uses suffering lovingly to keep humans in check.

The problem with these views of suffering is that the injustices perpetrated by humanity go unaddressed. The social gospel recognizes that when one person sins, others suffer. When one social class sins, other classes suffer. The more powerful the sinful individual or class, the more widespread the suffering. However, when the social body comes to the aid of those who are suffering, the body is preserved. If oppressive forces succeed in suppressing actions against injustice, the suffering continues and the community is "kept in suicidal evil."[34] Rauschenbusch surmises that bourgeois theologians have misrepresented God who has proven God's self to be revolutionary. Suffering of the innocent is not tolerated in the kingdom of God.

The image of God has also been tainted by the use of Christianity to colonize world populations. Rauschenbusch cited the proliferation of the myth that Negroes are not descended from Adam but rather from African jungle beasts, to place Negroes outside of the protection of moral law. Rauschenbusch believed that God has shown God's self to be a barrier breaker. The social gospel emphasizes God's barrier-breaking ability and commitments and seeks to make them part of Christian consciousness.

As it relates to the sacraments of baptism and the Eucharist, Rauschenbusch believed that the social gospel could build on the traditions already present. For example, the meaning and significance of baptism have changed throughout church history. In the apostle John's day, baptism was a sign of consent to being part of a messianic community that was a revolutionary movement within Judaism. Later in the early church, it became an act of obedience and faith in anticipation of the messianic kingdom at Christ's return. When Christianity assimilated into the Greek religious and social environment, it became an act of cancelling the guilt of past sins or regeneration. The newly regenerated individual was leaving an old pagan life behind and embracing the fellowship of the Christian community. Therefore since baptism has always been an exit and an entrance, why can it not become an exit from the kingdom of evil into the kingdom of God? This reorientation would also help baptism escape its individualistic focus, thereby restoring its ethical and spiritual purity.

The Eucharist has also undergone changes in the kingdom of God. Jesus' original purpose was to keep memory and faithfulness alive among his disciples until he returned. Paul admonished the Corinthians for allowing class divisions wherein the rich gathered to eat in abundance while leaving the poor neglected, hungry, and ashamed. In the early church people who had enmity with other believers were barred from Communion until they reconciled. Prior to the Reformation, the Eucharist evolved into the Mass with a performative element, meaning that the priest partook of the bread and wine while the people watched. In this case there were no social implications. During the Protestant Reformation, it became solely an act of reflection on the death of Jesus.

Rauschenbusch believed that the Eucharist should be an act of fellowship while also being connected to the social hope of the kingdom of God. Here is some of the language he suggests be used for the Eucharist itself:

> In the Lord's Supper we re-affirm our supreme allegiance to our Lord who taught us to know God as our common father and to realize

that all men are our brethren. In the midst of a world full of divisive selfishness we thereby accept brotherhood as the ruling principle of our life and undertake to put it into practice in our private and public activities. We abjure the selfish use of power and wealth for the exploitation of our fellows. We dedicate our lives to establishing the kingdom of God and to winning mankind to its laws. In contemplation of the death of our Lord we accept the possibility of risk and loss as our share of service. We link ourselves to his death and accept the obligation of the cross.[35]

In this statement, Rauschenbusch admonished Christians to work with all people to realize the kingdom of God while eschewing the selfish use of power and money for personal gain.

As it relates to eschatology, Rauschenbusch was very critical of "the premillennial scheme" in which adherents root for the defeat of humanity and social collapse because these are signs of the imminent return of Christ. Those who hold this position believe that working for the salvation of society is vain activity and against the will of God. For Rauschenbusch, this perspective defeats the Christian imperative of righteousness and salvation as it relates to the social order.

He contended that the individualistic aspects of eschatology which espoused immortality and a profound sense of sin and sadness about this earthly life were derived from Greek life and Greek religion. Social conditions in the immense power of the Roman state benefitted the aristocracy on the backs of the people and created a sense of futility. Escaping from this life was the only way to be free. These religious desires contributed to the otherworldly orientation of Christianity. Protestant theology denied the existence of purgatory and taught that the fate of the human soul is sealed at death. It is the saved who enter into heaven. He believed that the doctrine of hell may have originated under adverse social conditions in which despotic governments publicly executed and imprisoned their citizens. Jewish people developed their eschatology under social and political oppression.

The social orientation of eschatology necessitates that determination of future eschatological beliefs contend with the sources (social, biblical, and theological) of traditional eschatology. With that in mind Rauschenbusch submits several propositions for moving forward: the future development of humanity should have a larger place in practical Christian teaching, all Christian discussions of the past and future must be religious and filled with the consciousness of God in human affairs, millennial hope needs to be restored, there needs to be a shift from emphasis on catastrophe to development, all constructive and educational forces must be employed to uplift all of humanity, the kingdom of God will encounter conflict, and eschatology has no final consummation.

Rauschenbusch ended his work on theology by wrestling with the place of the doctrine of atonement in the social gospel. As with his other doctrines, he examines the doctrine historically. The early church used the terminology of sacrifice when referring to the work of Jesus. God offered Christ as a ransom in exchange for the lives of the rest of humanity. Though Satan believed Satan would get Christ in exchange for humanity, in actuality he got nothing because he could not hold Christ. In essence, according to this theory, God tricked Satan. It was Anselm who offered an alternative to this theory that is still widely accepted today: substitutionary atonement. Human sin robbed God of honor due. Equivalent honor had to be offered to God in order for God to forgive sin. Only God can render satisfaction to God for human sin. Therefore, God became human in the form of Jesus Christ.

Rauschenbusch thinks this theory raises more questions than it answers. How can God pay an equivalent to God? How can the death of an innocent being satisfy justice of the guilty? If the debt for all sin has been paid, why is it an act of grace for God to remit sin? This theory obfuscates the love and mercy of God. He contended that the Reformation made no great advancements in this theory. Rather than believing that Jesus bore the sins of humanity by imputation, Rauschenbusch suggested solidarity as a better explanation. Jesus was influenced by the historical life of Jewish people who lived in Palestine, which was governed by the Roman Empire. These real-life experiences enabled Jesus to understand the lives of ordinary people in his day. While espousing the kingdom of God, Jesus lived amidst the kingdom of evil. It was the kingdom of evil that killed him. Jesus' life is evidence that when evil is organized, prophets suffer.

It is with solidarity in mind that Rauschenbusch enumerated six sins that combined to kill Jesus: religious bigotry, the combination of financial corruption and political power, corruption of justice, mob spirit and mob action, militarism, and class contempt. It is with these sins in mind that

Rauschenbusch contended that focus on Christ must shift from his death to his life. It is in his life that humanity finds the answers we need to move into the future of the kingdom of God. He believed that the only clear interpretation of Jesus' death was that his sufferings were commensurate with the suffering of prophets throughout the ages.

Implications for Preaching

Implications for preaching can be drawn from both Rauschenbusch's life and his writings. From his life, we find the importance of solidarity. He was privileged in many ways: his family valued and had financial means for education, he was educated in the United States and Germany, and he was acculturated through extensive travel. Yet he still managed to form solidarity with German immigrants who lived in one of the poorest and marginalized neighborhoods of New York City. He lived where they lived. He ate what they ate. By living among them he was able to understand their daily struggles and challenges. It was solidarity with them that compelled him to develop a theology that met their needs. Perhaps his own experiences of solidarity allowed him to identify the solidarity of Jesus with the poor and marginalized of his day. People of God who claim to follow Christ today also need to be in solidarity with the poor and marginalized. By understanding the challenges and struggles of others, we can better work and walk beside them in the struggle for justice.

Rauschenbusch's critique of Anselm's theory of atonement challenges communities of faith to emphasize the solidarity with which Christ lived his life rather than the traditional doctrine. The language of sacrifice is so ingrained into many church cultures that there may be tremendous resistance to introducing new language. Perhaps the key to implementation is the word "emphasis." Spending more time in the pulpit communicating about the life of Christ and his ministry with the least and lost rather than his death could go a long way to helping the congregation embrace the social gospel.

The critique of total depravity is an important one in all communities. It is especially important in marginalized communities who may already lack a sense of self-worth and value for a myriad of reasons. Some are told by society that they have less, little, or no value because of race, ethnicity, gender, color, or sexual orientation. To add to that, the teaching that they are worthless without Jesus Christ may add insult to injury.

Rauschenbusch's conception of salvation as the "voluntary socializing of the soul" helps people of God understand that the purpose of salvation is not just to secure their own relationship with God. Salvation is intended to have social consequences so that people who were once focused on themselves begin to care about other people. Conversion as a break from sin of a social group highlights the reality that some sins are reinforced by the consensus of social groups. When people have truly been converted, they should be compelled to change not only their individual behavior and actions to better reflect the will of God but also their associations. Once converted, people can no longer deny their personal culpability and responsibility in actions taken by groups with which they associate.

For Rauschenbusch, the potential impact of suffering multiplies with the availability of power. By the same token, when social groups choose to aid those who are suffering, they too can have the impact of preserving humanity in the image of God they are created to embody.

Rauschenbusch contends that productive labor is a condition of salvation. While this idea has a lot of merit, it is not biblical. Instead we read throughout the New Testament that salvation is a gift of God which we receive by faith. For example, in Romans 10:9 we read: "Because if you confess with your lips that Jesus is Lord and believe in your heart that God raised him from the dead, you will be saved. For one believes with the heart and so is justified, and one confesses with the mouth and so is saved." Those who are idle and live off of the labor of other people must answer ultimately to God and to their families and communities. It should be the hope of God's people that all the who claim to follow Christ have the will to do everything they can to contribute to the welfare of all people. This includes developing their God-given gifts and talents and working to help others.

Rauschenbusch contended that one of the most vital acts that Christ performed while here on earth was taking God by the hand and calling God "our Father," thereby democratizing the conception of God. He believed that calling God Father wrestled the image of God away from the hands of earthly rulers like kings and religious leaders who sought to cast God in their own image. However, calling God Father casts God in the male image and has historically been cited as justification for discriminating against women and excluding them from positions of authority and leadership inside and outside of the church. Preachers can remind their people that God is Spirit (John 4:24)—neither male nor female. If it is our desire to truly democratize God, we should refrain from using gendered language or use diverse language when referring to God. Language such as God, Creator, Jehovah, and Holy One identifies God without assigning gender.

Rauschenbusch believed that the existing social order should be Christianized. While he put forth a theology of a Christianized social order, he did not acknowledge the difficulty of deciding what flavor of Christianity will be followed in the new order. There are many different Christian denominations, traditions, and ways of being under the large rubric of Christianity. In addition, he did not address how Christians attempting to Christianize the social order will relate to people who profess other faiths or no faith. Do they have a say in the new order, or are only Christians allowed to exercise leadership? If this is the case, does not Christianity become the new Rome—oppressors of all who do not follow the state religion? Preachers can remind their people that Christianity is a "whosoever will" kind of faith. Jesus never mandated that people follow him. People followed him willingly. The charge of Christians is not to force people to live according to their interpretation of Christian faith. Rather, the charge is to live godly lives and use prayer, their powers of persuasion, and their Christian witness to convince people to follow the way of Christ.

Questions for Exegesis

1. Is there evidence of the love of God in the text? If so, through whom and by whom is it being shared?

2. Are social sins being perpetrated in the text? If so, what sins are they? If so, are the people of God confronting or ignoring the perpetrators? Or are the people of God the actual perpetrators?

3. Who wields social and political power in the text? Who are the powerless? Are the people with the power understood as godly or sinners?

4. Are all of the people in the text engaged in some form of labor that contributes to the welfare of their family or community? If so, what do they do?

5. What is the image of Jesus being projected in the text? Is Jesus loving and compassionate? Is Jesus confrontational and combative? How does he relate to the poor or the rich in the text? How do the poor and the rich people in the text relate to Jesus?

6. Hermeneutical Bridge Question: What image(s) of Christ do we project in the world? How do we relate to the poor and the rich in our world? How do the poor and the rich in the world relate to us?

Notes

1. Paul M. Minus, *Walter Rauschenbusch, American Reformer* (New York: Macmillan, 1988), 1.

2. Christopher Hodge Evans, *The Kingdom Is Always but Coming: A Life of Walter Rauschenbusch*, Library of Religious Biography (Grand Rapids: William B. Eerdmans Pub., 2004), 6.

3. Ibid.

4. Ibid., 8.

5. Dores Robinson Sharpe, *Walter Rauschenbusch* (New York: The Macmillan Company, 1942), 42.

6. Minus, 21.

7. Sharpe, 42.

8. Evans, 30–32.

9. Sharpe, 54.

10. Evans, 155.

11. Walter Rauschenbusch, *Christianity and the Social Crisis in the 21st Century: The Classic That Woke Up the Church*, Paul B. Rauschenbusch, ed. (New York: HarperOne, 2007), xi.

12. Minus, 61.

13. Evans, 106.

14. Ibid., 83.

15. Ibid., xii.

16. Ibid., 57.

17. Ibid., 58.

18. Sharpe, 61.

19. Walter Rauschenbusch, *The Righteousness of the Kingdom* (Nashville: Abingdon Press, 1968), 118.

20. Rauschenbusch, *Christianity and the Social Crisis*, 66–68.

21. Ibid., 55–57.

22. Walter Rauschenbusch, *Dare We Be Christians?* The William Bradford Collection from the Pilgrim Press (Cleveland: Pilgrim Press, 1993), 25.

23. Ibid.

24. Walter Rauschenbusch, *A Theology for the Social Gospel* (New York: The Macmillan Company, 1917), 47.

25. Ibid., 40.

26. Ibid., 65.

27. Ibid., 62.

28. Ibid., 96.

29. Ibid., 99.

30. Ibid., 100.

31. Ibid., 102.

32. Ibid., 66.

33. Ibid., 178.

34. Ibid., 183–84.

35. Ibid., 206–7.

7
Black Liberation Vision
The Theology of James Cone

A Brief Biography

James Hal Cone was born to Lucy and Charlie Cone on August 5, 1938, in Fordyce, Arkansas.[1] When he was one, his family moved to Bearden, Arkansas, a small community of eight hundred whites and four hundred blacks. In Bearden the blacks experienced social and political oppression at the hands of the whites. Oppression included being beaten by police and spending long periods in jail, attending "separate but equal" schools, watching movies from the balcony of movie theaters (rather than on the main floor with the whites), and drinking from water fountains labeled "colored only."[2] His parents were members of the Macedonia African Methodist Episcopal (A.M.E.) Church. Like other churches in that day, Macedonia served as source of identity and survival, as well as a source of empowerment in the struggle for freedom.[3] Lucy Cone was a pillar of the church who also believed in the justice of God. Charlie Cone joined the church at Lucy's insistence before their marriage.

James Cone joined the church at the age of ten and became a minister at the age of sixteen. He preached his first sermon in 1954. Resisting injustice and oppression was in his genes. It was the courage and integrity of his father that inspired him to resistance. His father refused to work for white people or allow his wife to work as a maid. Charlie Cone also filed a lawsuit against the Bearden School Board after the Supreme Court decision of 1954 to integrate the public schools and refused to remove his name from the suit even when rumors of his being lynched began to spread.[4]

After graduating from high school, James Cone traveled eighty miles from home to attend Shorter College, a small, two-year, unaccredited A.M.E. college, before transferring to Philander Smith, an accredited Methodist college. Both were in Little Rock. While at Philander Smith, he began to hear about Martin Luther King Jr. and the Montgomery bus boycott. His time there also coincided with the integration of Central High

School by the Little Rock Nine in 1957. It was while watching the resistance of white people and the advocacy of black people to integration that he began to raise questions about theology. How could both black and white churches be Christian if they took opposite positions on integration? After all, each claimed to base their positions on the Bible and Christ. How could the whites who harassed the nine black children also be Christians? He had begun to read about black history while at Philander, and though he had been introduced to it before, he was able to dive deeply into it and understand how important knowledge of black history was for the formation of black racial identity.

After graduating with a BA from Philander Smith College in 1958, he and his brother Cecil went to Evanston, Illinois, to attend Garrett Biblical Institute (now Garrett Evangelical Theological Seminary) together.[5] They believed that they would experience racial equality and racial fairness in the North. Their naiveté was shattered when James was refused service at a white barbershop. He was told, "We don't cut niggers' hair in this place."[6] Many of the professors at Garrett treated African American students as if they lacked intelligence. The professor of Christian ethics at the time told racist jokes regularly. Cone had been accustomed to earning all A's at Philander. He was told by three Garrett professors that black students rarely earned more than a C in their classes. However, he worked hard and focused on improving his writing. He bought a ninth-grade English book and taught himself how to write. In his second quarter he earned two B's. By the time he reached his senior year, he was a straight-A student. He earned his master of divinity degree in 1961.

With encouragement from two professors, he decided to apply to the PhD program. Even after proving his academic aptitude for advanced work, the graduate student advisor at Garrett tried to discourage him from applying to the PhD program by telling him that several straight-A white students from Harvard and Yale were being rejected from admission, so what chance did he have? When he conveyed this conversation to William Hordern, who was professor of systematic theology, Hordern told Cone that if Cone was not accepted into the program, he would resign as professor of systematic theology. Cone got in, becoming the first African American PhD student at Garrett. He received no financial assistance, though it was rumored that all PhD students automatically received major scholarships.

After earning his MA but before completing his dissertation, he accepted a teaching position at Philander Smith College in January 1964. He worked diligently to complete his dissertation in spite of his teaching responsibilities and successfully defended his dissertation in the fall of 1964. After his successful completion of the program, one professor refused to shake his hand at the graduation.

Cone began his teaching at Philander Smith with great enthusiasm. However, he soon discovered that the white theology he studied at Garrett, including the theologies of Barth, Tillich, and Brunner, had very little to do with the lives and experiences of black girls and boys who came to his classroom from the cotton fields of Arkansas, Mississippi, and Tennessee. The black students he taught refused to accept his responses to their theological questions that were framed solely from white, Western, male perspectives. They challenged him and caused him to go back to the basics and ask questions such as "Who is God?" while relating his classical education to his own black experiences of growing up in Bearden. His interactions with the black students coincided with social upheavals such as the black power movement.

Cone left Philander Smith in 1966. While there he had become so involved in the politics of the school and responsibilities of being a new teacher that he had almost no time to think. He accepted a position at predominantly white Adrian College in predominantly white Adrian, Michigan. At Adrian College he had time to write and develop his black theology of liberation because he was no longer involved in the black community and its struggles. From his reflections on black life in conversation with classical theology, Cone developed black liberation theology. In black liberation theology, Jesus Christ is a liberator and God is a God of justice with a penchant for the marginalized and oppressed.

Cone wrote *Black Theology and Black Power* in the summer of 1968, just months after Martin Luther King Jr.'s assassination. He used his pent-up anger over King's assassination and white racism in general to fuel his writing. It was a liberating experience for him. When writing that book, he discovered that when his writing was defined and controlled by black history and culture rather than by standards set by white seminaries, he could write with energy and passion.

He received several job offers after publishing his first book. He accepted a position at Union Theological Seminary in New York because it was located near Harlem, the largest black community in the United States. Union also symbolized major intellectual forces of white theology, having been the academic home of Reinhold Niebuhr and Paul Tillich. He wanted to try to make the case for black theology among some of the most well-respected white theologians in the country.

James Hal Cone served as the Bill and Judith Moyers Distinguished Professor of Systematic Theology at Union Theological Seminary in New York. He published twelve books and more than 150 articles[7] and was awarded thirteen honorary degrees. He lectured throughout the United States, Asia, Africa, Europe, the Caribbean, and Latin America. In 2018, he received the Grawemeyer Award in Religion for his book *The Cross and the Lynching Tree*. He died on April 28, 2018.

A Theological Overview

James Cone's vision of the reign of God is one in which black people are fully liberated from all forms of white oppression. The eschatological perspective of black liberation theology challenges the current structures that support black oppression while encouraging black people to resist injustice because the "present humiliation is inconsistent with its promised future."[8] In other words, it is not the will of God that they be oppressed. And black people do not have to wait until they get to heaven to experience lives free from the daily struggles instituted by racism and its many manifestations.

Cone's black liberation theology cannot be fully understood apart from the social and political context in which it was written in 1968. The 1960s in the United States were turbulent political times. The Vietnam War continued to inspire tremendous opposition in the form of organized protests. Marginalized populations, including disabled Americans, women, and LGBT people, were vying for civil rights. African Americans had experienced significant legal progress in the form of major legislative victories: the Civil Rights Act was passed in 1964 and the Voting Rights Act was passed in 1965. However, after the signing of this legislation, the civil rights movement began to lose steam. The societal gains that should have resulted from new legislation did not materialize because of white resistance to black progress and the refusal of white people to follow the law. Poverty, lack of educational opportunities, unemployment, and underemployment were still daily realities in the lives of the black masses.[9] African Americans were still experiencing abuse and mistreatment from civil authorities. Frustrated African Americans in cities such as Rochester, Philadelphia, New York, Chicago, and Los Angeles rioted in protest over untenable social conditions and continued oppression. Many African Americans agreed with Malcolm X that for them, America was a nightmare rather than a dream. In response to the lack of meaningful progress in the social, economic, and political order, black people adopted the new attitude of black power, a means by which black people affirmed their essential worth. Black power means "complete emancipation of black people from white oppression by whatever means black people deem necessary."[10] The term *black power* was first used in June 1966 during the civil rights movement by Stokely Carmichael, a leader in the Student Nonviolent Coordinating Committee (SNCC) and later a leader within the Black Panther Party as a more appropriate response to white racism than calls for integration.[11] Possible methods of emancipation included boycotting, marching, selective buying, and rebellion. The black power movement was a social movement to achieve power for black people to determine their own destinies.[12]

Another key inspiration for Cone was the publication of Joseph Washington's *Black Religion* in 1964.[13] *Black Religion* made an academic argument that contrary to prevailing assumptions of white Christians and some blacks as well, there did exist a distinctive black religion that can be understood alongside Protestantism, Catholicism, and Judaism. While arguing for black religion's existence, Washington blamed white Christians for its evolution. He wrote that when blacks were excluded from white churches because of racism, they were forced to form their own. Washington argued that since black churches were excluded from white churches, black churches were not genuine Christian churches. Instead, they are religious societies. There can therefore be no genuine Christian theology in black churches. While white churches agreed with Washington's argument, black churches rejected his assumption that white people had a monopoly on the true church and the theology that derives from it. They argued that in reality it is black religion that is truly Christian because it is directly related to the gospel and the struggle for justice in society. White churches are hypocritical because they preach love and neglect justice. Black clergy created black theology to correct two misconceptions: that black religion is not Christian and has no theology, and that the Christian gospel has nothing to do with the struggle for justice in society.[14]

The response of white Christians to "black power," along with the publication of *Black Religion*, inspired the convening of a group of African American clergy to form the National Committee of Negro Churchmen (NCNC, which later became the National Committee of Black Churchmen, NCBC). The phrase "black power," instead of being seen as godly cries for integration during the civil rights movement, created alarm for white Christians who contended that black power was un-Christian. These same white Christians, many of whom were clergy, called upon black Christians to denounce the slogan. However, rather than denouncing it, the NCNC published a black power statement in the *New York Times* on July 31, 1966. In a full-page statement, this group of forty-eight clergy justified the need for black power in the struggle for racial justice and racial equality in the United States. The significance of the statement makes it worth quoting at length:

> We realize that neither the term "power" nor the term "Christian Conscience" are easy matters to talk about, and especially in the context of race relations in America. The fundamental distortion facing us in the controversy about "black power" is rooted in the gross imbalance of power and conscience between Negroes and white Americans. It is this distortion mainly which is responsible for the widespread, though often inarticulate, assumption that white people are justified in getting what they want through the use of power, but that Negro Americans must, either by nature or by circumstances, make their appeal only through conscience. As a result, the power of white men and the conscience of black men have both been corrupted. The power of white men is corrupted because it meets little meaningful resistance from Negroes to temper it and keep white men from aping God. The conscience of black men is corrupted because, having no power to implement the demands of conscience, the concern for justice is transmuted into a distorted form of love, which, in the absence of justice, becomes chaotic self-surrender. Powerlessness breeds a race of beggars. We are faced now with a situation where conscience-less power meets powerless conscience, threatening the very foundations of our nation.[15]

The publication of the statement was the beginning of the intentional development of theology wherein black clergy separated their understanding of the Christian faith from that of white Christianity. In this statement, the black clergy suggested that white Christianity and its underlying theology were bankrupt. They also wanted to connect black faith to the African heritage of their congregants and with the ensuing struggle for justice.

Another inspiration for Cone in developing a black liberation theology was Malcolm X. Malcolm X critiqued black people's acceptance of the white man's Jesus:

> Brothers and sisters, the white man has brainwashed us black people to fasten our gaze upon a blond-haired, blue-eyed Jesus! We're worshiping a Jesus that doesn't even look like us! Oh, yes! . . . Now just think of this. The blond-haired, blue-eyed white man has taught you and me to worship a white Jesus, and to shout and sing and pray to this God that's his God, the white man's God. The white man has taught us to shout and sing and pray until we die, to wait until death, for some dreamy heaven-in-the-hereafter, when we're dead, while this white man has his milk and honey in the streets paved with golden dollars here on this earth![16]

For some time, Cone tried to ignore Malcolm X's critique of the Christianity Cone was taught and that was widely practiced in black and white churches. He was a follower of Martin Luther King Jr. and the philosophy of nonviolence. However, Malcolm X's stinging critique weighed heavily on his conscience.

Though the civil rights movement, the publication of and response to *Black Religion*, the rise of the black power movement, and Malcom X's critique were motivating for Cone, it may have been the response of his students at Philander Smith College that served as the precipitating event to the development of black liberation theology. From the confluence of these events, Cone's black liberation theology was born.

Another key to understanding Cone's black liberation theology is his understanding of ideology and social determination. Ideology is deformed thought that contains ideas that serve the interest of an individual or group. Truth becomes what the individual or group wants it to be. Ideological thinking can be total or partial, meaning that the individual or group can have ideas or thoughts that affect some of their thinking. Or, ideological thinking can be so influential that it shapes their *Weltanschauung* or entire worldview. In the case of total ideological thinking, particular ideas or concepts grow and develop from the life one is living. In this way, ideas can be a distortion of the circumstances in which the ideological people are living, thus rendering them incapable of comprehending truth. Therefore, social determination of thought directly addresses how thought is formed. Cone acknowledges that some sociologists of knowledge believe that social reality precedes thinking and that determination is a natural outcome of existing ideologies.[17]

As it relates to the Bible, Cone contended that ideology is any interpretation of biblical texts that contradicts God's will to liberate the poor and oppressed. In order to develop nonliberative interpretations, one has to ignore God's liberating acts in the Bible, such as the Exodus, the covenant between God and Israel, and the proclamation of the prophets. Biblical ideology is a way of thinking that excludes the experiential truth of the biblical story. People who think ideologically about the Bible interpret truth legalistically and philosophically. They glean from the text information about God without comprehending fully what God is about.

Ideological thinking has been the hallmark of white theology and ethics throughout Christian history. While Christian theology informs people who God is, Christian ethics informs people of what they should do. Cone believed that white Christian theology throughout the centuries has been errant because rather than being centered in the liberation ethic found in biblical texts, it is founded in Greek philosophy. As a result, Christian ethics has traditionally reflected the values of the status quo rather than the God of the Bible. For example, Cone believed that the ethics of the Church Fathers in the fourth century reflected the values of the Roman state more than the values found in the Bible. To Augustine, people were enslaved because of their own sin. He admonished slaves to be obedient to their masters instead of resisting their enslavement or fighting for their liberation. Thomas Aquinas believed that slavery was part of the natural order of human creation and there existed a special right to domination between a master and the slave. Martin Luther, who proclaimed *sola Scriptura* during the Reformation to call attention to the abuses of the Catholic Church, did not affirm the cries of the poor and oppressed in his society because he was not a victim.[18] More contemporary white theologians also identify with the status quo. For example, Reinhold Niebuhr characterized black people in terms of "cultural backwardness" and contended that the Founding Fathers should not be considered immoral because they owned slaves. This perspective reveals that Niebuhr developed his ethics from the white dominant culture of his day rather than biblical revelation. Ethicist Paul Ramsey spent more time in *Christian Ethics and the Sit-in* admonishing black people about their lack of respect for law and order than for the ungodly nature of Jim Crow laws.[19] Through the centuries white theologians and ethicists have suffered from theological blindness caused by prioritizing their interpretations from their fellow theologians rather than the Bible, which clearly affirms that God is a liberator of the oppressed.

Cone believed that God is about liberation. Therefore, Christian theology in general is a theology of liberation. He defined Christian theology as "a rational study of the being of God in the world in light of the existential situation of an oppressed community, relating the forces of liberation to the essence of the gospel which is Jesus Christ."[20] Since he believed that the focus of Christian theology is on the work of God in oppressed communities, it follows that there was a pressing need for a fully developed black theology that shed light on the gospel of Jesus Christ in light of the oppressed conditions of blacks. Blacks needed to understand that the gospel provides them with the power they need to break the chains of racism and its many manifestations. Therefore, Cone focuses black liberation theology on the central figure of any Christian gospel, Jesus Christ.

Cone contended that in the Gospels, the nature of Jesus' ministry is made clear in Mark 1:15: "The time is fulfilled, and the kingdom of God has come near; repent, and believe in the good news."[21] The announcement of the presence of the kingdom is an in-breaking of a new age of liberation in human history. In this new age "the blind receive their sight, the lame walk, the lepers are cleansed, the deaf hear, the dead are raised, the poor have good news brought to them."[22] God's ultimate kingdom is in the future with the Second Coming of Christ. However, the kingdom is also present now—releasing humanity from all manifestations of human evil that seek to hold them captive. In the kingdom of God, God takes the side of the oppressed through a reordering of society in which "the last will be first, and the first will be last."[23] God is on the side of the oppressed because they are utterly dependent on God for their continued existence while the rich are confident in their own strength and power. Cone believed that the kingdom is the rule of God breaking into human existence, overthrowing the powers that enslave human lives. While poverty is not a precondition for entering into the kingdom of God, it is the poor who are most likely to recognize their need for God.

Cone argued that if the gospel is truly a gospel of liberation, then Jesus must be where the oppressed are. Jesus is not locked up in the first century. Rather, Jesus is in our world, including in urban ghettos, proclaiming release to the captives and fighting injustice. That being the case, Christianity is not alien to black power. Christianity is black power. The black rebellion against injustice that occurred during the black power movement was a "manifestation of God himself actively involved in the present-day affairs of men for the purpose of liberating a people."[24]

Christ is the source of the power that enables black people to say no to dehumanization and oppression. Black people marched, picketed, and boycotted so that they could have the freedom to become like Christ. As long as humans are enslaved to other humans, they are not free to live out their destinies in Christ. Christ power is black power.

In a society where people suffer because of the color of their skin, Cone believed there is no place for a colorless God. He therefore asserted that Jesus is black. Cone realized that historically and anthropologically Jesus was a Jew. Jesus' Jewishness locates him in the Israelite tradition of the Exodus. He is the fulfillment of God's covenant with Israel. Jews were the black people of their day—poor, oppressed, and marginalized. God chose to be their God and liberate them from their oppressors. The fact that God chose a poor and oppressed people to be God's people reflects God's commitment to liberation.

It was through the cross of Jesus that God broke into human history. Jesus was the Elected One who took the place of Israel as the Suffering Servant. Jesus' willingness to suffer liberated all of humanity. Through Jesus' resurrection, oppression and injustice were conquered. The divine freedom that had previously been available to the people of Israel was now available to all. Jesus is as willing to take the pain of the poor and the oppressed upon himself and bear it today as he was when he was on the cross. Therefore, if Jesus' presence is real and he is faithful to the divine promise to bear the suffering of the poor, then he must inhabit the pain of the people who were most oppressed in the United States in the sixties (and in the twenty-first century)—black people.[25] Therefore, Jesus is black.

Cone made the case that if blacks are to achieve full emancipation from white oppression, they must achieve liberation from all the ungodly influences of white religion, including white theology's interpretation of who God is. American white theology sanctioned the genocide of Native Americans and the enslavement of Africans and African Americans. In the 1960s, many white theologians chose not to engage in the struggle for black liberation. White theological thought has been more patriotic than biblical because it either defines Christianity as compatible with white racism or defines Christianity as being completely unrelated to black suffering. In either case, white theology has become a servant of the state.

When those in power perform heinous acts in the name of God, the oppressed must decide: either they reject the God of their oppressor outright or they form opinions of God based on their own experiences. Cone chose the latter course.

In black liberation theology, one finds two hermeneutical principles. First, the Christian understanding of God evolves from the revelation of God experienced by the people of Israel in the Bible. The revelation of God is completed in Jesus Christ. There are many sources through which people can recognize God's activity in the world. However, the Bible can never be ignored by those who speak of the Holy One of Israel. Second, the doctrine of black theology must reflect the participation of God in the liberation of the oppressed. God is revealed in the activities of oppressed Israel. God is also revealed in Jesus Christ. Other approaches to biblical interpretation, for Cone, risk denying biblical revelation.[26]

For Cone, freedom and liberation are integrally linked. People who are free determine their own destinies by making their own choices in all aspects of their lives. People who are free also will not be content in the world until all people in society are treated humanely. Free people choose between submitting to the wrongs being perpetrated in society or risking everything they have to oppose wrongs. By opposing wrongs, people actively choose to participate in God's liberating activities. However, they may suffer at the hands of oppressors for their opposition. People in power may seek to silence dissent by cutting off access to life-sustaining resources and ostracizing those who dare to rebel. If these tactics do not work, those in power may seek political solutions to open rebellion. These and other tactics have been perpetrated against African Americans for simply being black. Christians who see the suffering of others are called to suffer with them in pursuit of freedom for all.[27]

Sin for Cone is a way of life in which people cease to be human because of their willingness to participate in the oppression and misery of others. When people live in sin, they live according to their own personal values in pursuit of their personal interests. For the people of Israel, sin was divergence from the covenants God made with Israel. Cone critiqued white Christian fundamentalists in general and evangelist Billy Graham in particular for teaching that the trouble with the world is that humankind needs God to help us turn from our wicked ways. Graham defined wicked ways narrowly as failing to live by the rules of white society. Other whites define sin as broken relationships with God without taking the time to define what "broken relationships" means. Cone argued that further explanation of the meaning of broken relationships is likely not coming because oppressors do not want to know what is wrong.

By contrast, the oppressed know what is wrong. The sin of white people from the perspective of black people is the act of living comfortably within the structures of whiteness. Whiteness is "the desire of whites to play God in the realm of human affairs."[28] Sins of whites include accepting conditions responsible for Native American reservations, the ravaging of Vietnam, and the existence of urban ghettos, just to name a few. Perhaps one of the greatest sins even for those whites who do fight to make the Constitution a reality for all is believing that whiteness and humanity can coexist. This nation was founded by and for whites. Structures such as the Constitution, the Emancipation Proclamation, the government, and unions are white. Whiteness, as a social construction which privileges white people over all other people, is sin. Sins such as whiteness cause whites to believe they are chosen by God to receive special privileges in the world. Sins such as whiteness permeate human beings and render them incapable of even recognizing some structures and conditions as sin. What is needed is a confrontation of whiteness or white racism with blacks in Jesus Christ. For too long, blacks have allowed whites to shape the future of our nation. Blacks have reinforced white values by uncritically accepting white values.[29]

One impetus for participating in God's liberating activity is recognition of the image of God. Cone differs from other theologians who contend that all people are made in the image of God as an unchanging existential reality. While all humans are created in the image of God, they do not always reflect the image of God in their interactions with others. To be the image of God means being human. Being human means having the freedom to be creative, treat others humanely, and oppose acts of inhumanity. Anyone who oppresses others ceases to be human and therefore ceases to be the image of God.[30]

The theological conception of God as Creator has particular significance in black liberation theology. The reality that all humans are created by God means that the meaning and purpose for the existence of each human is not found in the oppressors but rather in God. God is the source of all being. This means that God, not whiteness and how whiteness is perpetuated and embodied in the world, dictates how humans should behave. Humans who claim to follow Christ owe obedience only to God. Black people who are minorities in a world defined by whiteness must resist behavioral dictates that are contrary to the will of God. This is why Cone insisted that the term *black revolution* was more apropos than *reformation*. Reformation assumes that the system needs only to be cleaned up a bit, but the system of whiteness needs to be abolished, not reformed. God as Creator means that the oppressed are free to revolutionize society.[31]

Cone stressed the immanence of God—God's activity in concrete historical situations of human existence. Rather than conceiving of God as a pious feeling in human hearts or believing that God is way up in heaven, Cone contended that God can be found in the world wherever liberation from suffering is occurring. As a result, God has taken on blackness and is part of the black struggle for liberation.

The transcendence of God is eloquently highlighted in Ephesians 3:20: "Now to him who by the power at work within us is able to accomplish abundantly far more than all we can ask or imagine." God is more than our finite experiences. Truth is not limited to what humans can and cannot do. For the black liberation struggle, God's transcendence means that the humanity of black people is not dependent on winning against the forces of evil. In fact, white oppressors often use the threat of force to keep blacks from even attempting to change the status quo. The good news of the transcendent God is that physical life is not the ultimate reality.

Transcendence of God and transcendence of the people of God can be found in the resurrection of Jesus. The resurrection frees the oppressed from concerns about their physical existence. Christ's crucifixion manifested the many contradictions the oppressed experience in their lives. The Savior of the world was executed by a method reserved for rebels and insurrectionists. Black people have been publicly shamed and tortured simply because of the color of their skin. Jesus' death was a public spectacle in which he was tortured and shamed. Black people have been crucified through lynchings, which were often public spectacles used by whites to keep black people in their place. If God resurrected Jesus from such perilous circumstances—if God gave Jesus victory over death, hell, and the grave—then surely God will do the same for black people. Since Christ conquered death, humans should no longer be afraid of dying. Remembering and living into God's transcendence can liberate black people to struggle for liberation without reserve.[32]

Eschatology for Cone did not include traditional images of the Promised Land found in many hymns sung in church and in apocalyptic novels or books, or preached in otherworldly sermons about pearly gates, streets paved with gold, long white robes, and a golden throne. Instead he asked what good are golden crowns, slippers, and long white robes if in our earthly lives we have turned our backs on the plights of our children. He cited Rudolf Bultmann, who rejected the traditional apocalyptic views as being mythological or having no foundation in reality. Instead, Bultmann contended that the future of humanity cannot be separated from the present and that eschatology must be founded in the historical day-to-day realities of human existence. What happens in the future is integrally linked to the present. Though Cone lauded Bultmann for his perspective, he believed Bultmann did not go far enough. Bultmann did not include the significance of pursuing issues of justice for an oppressed community. God's future belongs to the poor, who will experience the glory of God in their struggles against injustice.

Cone was clear that the focus by African Americans on heaven in the past was directly caused by their belief that little or nothing could be done to change the state of their earthly existence. During periods such as slavery and Jim Crow, the power to define African American day-to-day existence was in the hands of whites who were determined to deny social, political, and economic equality to people of African descent because of the color of their skin. The evolution of black power changed the power dynamic. With the rise of the black power movement, black people began to believe that something could be done about the world in which they live. Achieving the goal of reaching heaven after death no longer had to come at the expense of ignoring injustice on earth. There is work to be done on earth by those who "refuse to accept hell on earth."[33]

While Cone asserted that people of God must be engaged in work on earth for the elimination of oppression, they must also know that when they die in the struggle for freedom and equality they will have a future in Christ. Otherwise, they would have died in vain. At the core of the meaning of the resurrection of Christ is that those who fight against the odds stacked against them through earthly principalities and powers will experience the future of God.

As it relates to black liberation theology, Cone believed the church has three primary responsibilities. First, the church must preach a liberating gospel in the world. The liberating gospel informs black people that slavery and oppression have come to an end. They no longer have to live according to white rules. They do not have to live a ghetto existence. In their new lives their loyalty is not with white people but with the God of their salvation. Since they have been redeemed, they can live like the free people they have become in Christ. This liberating gospel must also be preached to white people. The message preached to whites must be to let go of the chains they have used to bind black people. White privilege and whiteness must be deconstructed. Whites must be made aware of their complicity in systems and structures that hold black people down.

Second, the church must share in the liberation struggle. Worldly powers are still attempting to enforce old orders. It is the responsibility of the church to remind those in the old orders that they are no longer in power. It is the responsibility of the church to make the gospel a reality in all of its manifestations (social, economic, and political). The church must be reminded that it is called to counter the oppressive cultures of the world as it pursues freedom for all.

Every day, the church has to manifest visibly the gospel that it preaches. In its structure, politics, worship, and interactions with members and with surrounding communities, the church must represent the kingdom of God as it was preached and embodied by Jesus. If the church refuses to change or resorts to the old order, then no one will believe the liberating gospel it preaches. Cone warned the churches that retreating from the troubles of the world into postures of piety is not an option. Prayer is always good. However, actions speak louder than words. Prayer in churches where the gospel of liberation is preached is a spirit of determination found in oppressed communities. Prayer is communication with God that emboldens the oppressed to fight against various and sundry evils.

Third, churches cannot embrace the world. The history of Christianity is replete with churches that chose the traditions of the world as their gospel rather than the liberating message of Jesus Christ. Some churches have combined the gospel with nationalism or capitalism to such an extent that they oppress the weak rather than liberate them. The church must visibly represent the lordship of Jesus. Cone also takes to task black churches that are guilty of prostituting the name of the church of God. Some black churches are content with things the way they are. Some are growing wealthy on the backs of those for whom they should be fighting. Instead of seeking to realize a black revolution, some churches employ white solutions to injustice that do not meet the needs of the people they serve.

Implications for Preaching

Cone's admonitions to churches about the message they preach and about their work in the world as it relates to the biblical mandate of liberating the oppressed has already been conveyed above and does not need to be repeated here. But some particulars of black liberation theology do call for elaboration. Cone's illumination of ideology and social determination have profound implications for preaching. In the United States, we live in a racialized society wherein the distortions of racial ideology impact every aspect of our daily human existence. Racial ideology that was developed to justify and maintain the institution of slavery has been in the past, and continues to be in the present, supported and maintained by systems and structures deeply rooted in white privilege such as laws and government administration, educational curriculum, the media, sports, and entertainment entities. The degree to which racialized ideology is woven into the fabric of our society renders it difficult, if not impossible, for some of those who have gained their understanding of racial ideology through social determination or experience to understand the truth—that racial ideology is a myth.

Therefore, it is incumbent on preachers to expose the insidiousness of racial ideology by using aspects of black liberation theology to nullify and ultimately exterminate the myth of white supremacy. It is important for people to understand that white privilege and the systems that support and sustain it are sin. If all people are created in the image of God by the one and same Creator God, it is not God's will for some to oppress and marginalize others for their own benefit.

Preachers should adopt and employ the hermeneutical principles of black theology by first highlighting whenever possible God's liberating activity in the Bible. By doing so, the people may better understand not only who God is and what God is about, but also who God wills them to be and what they should be about as people of God. By understanding the hermeneutical principles of black theology, the people of God can recognize and reject interpretations that seek to marginalize and oppress others as inconsistent with the will of God.

While the immanence of God has been debated in academic theology, its validity is affirmed repeatedly in the biblical texts. God is continually involved in the affairs of humanity. Those who are people of faith must believe that the God they serve did not create and then forsake them. Rather, like with the people of Israel, God hears God's people when they call and delivers them from hurt, harm, and danger. It is this faith in God's presence and will for their well-being that provides hope for the oppressed that their tomorrows can be better than their today.

Black liberation theology broadens the definition of sin beyond the realm of individual sins such as lying, stealing, fornication, and adultery. Cone indicted whiteness and white privilege, as well as the systems and structures that support it, as sin. Preaching against white privilege in congregations filled with privileged whites is not an easy task. Yet the systems and structures that support white privilege will never fall unless and until people with privilege actively participate in its decimation. Reminding the privileged that it is the will of God that all people have the same opportunities to fulfill the will of God for their lives is crucial.

Cone's argument that the people of God can find liberation by believing in the transcendence of God requires confronting the topic of death. Death is not something that people like to talk about. Though Christians often talk about heaven and "going home to be with God," they often do not deal with death as a fact of life. Often death, especially if it is associated with accidents, violence, sickness, or disease, is seen as punishment or as something that is not to be desired. While we say we want to be with God, we simultaneously try to hold on to life at any cost. Preaching about God's transcendence can be an opportunity to begin conversations about death in contexts other than funerals.

Cone believed that the core of the meaning of the resurrection of Christ is that those who fight against the odds stacked against them through earthly principalities and powers will experience the future of God when they die in the struggle for freedom. The problem for preachers is that even the most committed Christians may not want to die. While many battles for justice are life-threatening, many are not. Preachers should encourage their people to engage in the battles for justice to which they feel most called. Cone's call as a theologian was fighting for justice. He lived a long and fruitful life. For those who feel called to lay down their lives for the cause of justice, they not only experience eternal life in Christ but also cause the resurrection hope of Christ to be present in the lives of those they leave behind.

Cone's theological framework was thoroughly dualistic, casting the white oppressors against the poor oppressed blacks. While many on both sides embody these characterizations, many others do not. Some whites are poor for a host of reasons, including lack of educational opportunities and access to health care, environmental toxicity, and generational poverty. Some black people are middle class or wealthy and live comfortable lives. There are poor whites who oppress other poor whites, and blacks who oppress other blacks. While social structures of power are still overwhelmingly in the hands of white people in the United States and other parts of the world that were colonized by Europeans, by framing the issues dualistically Cone risked overlooking oppressions that occur within oppressed communities. In Cone's theology, anyone who oppresses other people ceases to be human and therefore ceases to be the image of God. Preachers can remind their people that anyone of any race, class, gender, gender identity, sexual orientation, socioeconomic status, or ethnicity can cease to be the image of God. Rather than only preaching that all people are created in the image of God, preachers can also add that while we are all created in the image of God, we can all cease to be the image of God by ways we treat other people.

Cone's insistence on the immanence of God fails to help preachers explain to their people the absence of God in human oppression of all forms. Cone contends that God can be found in the world wherever liberation from suffering is occurring. Does this mean that God is absent wherever oppression and marginalization continue to occur? If so, is the immanence of God solely dependent on the willingness of humanity to embody the will of God in the world? What does this view of the immanence of God say about the omnipotence of God or lack thereof? In Cone's view the immanence of God and issues of theodicy—why God allows evil to exist in the world—go unaddressed. Rather than preaching about the immanence of God, preachers can talk about human free will that allows us to do good and evil and the sovereignty of God that allows God to intervene when God chooses.

Questions for Exegesis

1. Are people in the text being oppressed in any way? If so, how and by whom?

2. Are there ideologies at work in the text? If so, who is enforcing them? Who is being victimized by them?

3. Is God's will for the liberation of God's people being experienced in the text? If so, how?

4. Are there people in the text who are willing to sacrifice themselves for the well-being of others? If so, who is making the sacrifice? Who is benefitting from the sacrifice?

5. Is there sin present in the text—people living according to their own values instead of according to the will of God? If so, who is sinning, and what is the sin?

6. Hermeneutical Bridge Question: In what manifestations is the sin of racism evident in our world today? Who are the perpetrators and who are the victims?

Notes

1. Melissa Turner, "James Hal Cone," *Blackpast*, http://www.blackpast.org/contact.

2. James H. Cone, *God of the Oppressed*, Rev. ed. (Maryknoll, NY: Orbis Books, 1997), 2.

3. James H. Cone, *My Soul Looks Back* (Nashville: Abingdon Press, 1982).

4. Ibid.

5. Turner.

6. Cone, *My Soul Looks Back*.

7. "James H. Cone," (2017), https://utsnyc.edu/faculty/james-h-cone/.

8. James H. Cone, *A Black Theology of Liberation*, 20th anniversary ed. (Maryknoll, NY: Orbis Books, 1990), 137.

9. Martin Luther King Jr., *A Testament of Hope: The Essential Writings of Martin Luther King, Jr,*. James Melvin Washington, ed. (San Francisco: Harper & Row, 1986), 557–60.

10. James H. Cone, *Black Theology and Black Power* (Maryknoll, NY: Orbis Books, 1997), Chapter 1.

11. James H. Cone, *For My People: Black Theology and the Black Church* (Maryknoll, NY: Orbis Books, 1984), 10.

12. The Black Panther Party, "What We Want, What We Believe," *The Digital Public Library of America* (1966), https://dp.la/primary-source-sets/sources/388.

13. Joseph R. Washington, *Black Religion: The Negro and Christianity in the United States* (Boston: Beacon Press, 1964).

14. Cone, *For My People: Black Theology and the Black Church*, 9.

15. National Council of Negro Churchmen, "'Black Power': Statement by the National Committee of Negro Churchmen," *The New York Times*, Sunday, July 31, 1966, https://www.episcopalarchives.org/Afro-Anglican_history/exhibit/pdf/blackpowerstatement.pdf.

16. Malcolm X, *The Autobiography of Malcolm X As Told to Alex Haley*, 1st Ballantine Books hardcover ed. (New York: Ballantine Books, 1992), Chapter 13, Kindle Edition.

17. Cone, *God of the Oppressed*. 83–84.

18. Ibid., 182.

19. Paul Ramsey, *Christian Ethics and the Sit-In* (New York: Association Press, 1961).

20. Cone, *A Black Theology of Liberation*, 1.

21. Mark 1:15.

22. Luke 7:22.

23. Matthew 20:16.

24. Cone, *Black Theology and Black Power*, Chapter 2, Kindle Edition.

25. Cone, *God of the Oppressed*, 124–25.

26. Cone, *A Black Theology of Liberation*, 60–61.

27. Ibid., 101.

28. Ibid., 107–108.

29. Ibid., 109.

30. Ibid., 90–94.

31. Ibid., 74–76.

32. James H. Cone, *The Cross and the Lynching Tree* (Maryknoll, NY: Orbis Books, 2011).

33. Cone, *A Black Theology of Liberation*, 141.

8
Womanist Vision
The Theology of Emilie Townes

A Brief Biography

Womanist ethicist and theologian Emilie Townes was born on August 1, 1955, in Durham, North Carolina. While in her predominantly African American elementary school in Durham, the teachers lined the classroom walls with pictures of famous African Americans.[1] The pictures were at once aspirational and inspirational. They were aspirational in that they served as role models. Just as the famous African Americans had done great things in the world, so the students could, too. They were inspirational in that teachers used the famous people to inspire the students when they became unruly or decided not to do their homework by asking questions like, "Do you know how hard Harriet Tubman worked so we could be free? And here you are wasting that freedom."[2]

Though the academic trajectory that her life would assume was undoubtedly influenced by her elementary school teachers, Townes had two other influencers whose life work and daily examples helped to seal her fate as an educator: her parents. Townes is the daughter of two college professors, Dr. Mary McLean Townes and Dr. Ross E. Townes.[3] Her father, a native of Scottsdale, Pennsylvania, earned a PhD through the GI Bill after serving in the military in World War II.[4] Her mother, a native of West Southern Pines, North Carolina, earned a scholarship to North Carolina Central College (now North Carolina Central University), where she went on to teach, taking some time away to earn a PhD in zoology from the University of Michigan. Townes parents met when they were both teaching at North Carolina Central. Her mother went on to become department chair and retired as dean of the College of Arts and Sciences. Her father retired as professor emeritus of physical education.[5]

Townes describes herself as the personification of Alice Walker's definition of "womanist" when she was growing up.[6] She drove her parents and teachers crazy with all of her questions. She believes that this kind of inquisitiveness pointed her in the direction of Christian social ethics. She is fascinated with structures and social phenomena and how they are created and maintained, which is a significant part of social ethics.

As she grew up, Townes realized that most of the pictures on the walls of her elementary classroom were of men.[7] Therefore, she assumed, like many other African American girls, that men were the leaders of African American communities, so when women became leaders, they were the exception rather than the rule. The civil rights movement and women's liberation movement challenged her assumptions and compelled her to read biographies and autobiographies of African American women.

After graduating with a Doctor of Ministry degree from the University of Chicago Divinity School, she was working as a bookstore manager when she received an invitation to teach at Garrett Evangelical Seminary. Garrett was experiencing an influx of African American women students, and the students were asking why the school did not have more African American female professors. She worked with the administration to develop a course on black women in the church. When she began lecturing on her first day, she realized that teaching, rather than preaching, was her calling. It meant, to her chagrin, that she would have to earn a PhD and then get into the family business. She went on to earn a PhD in religion in society and personality from Northwestern University. She has served on the faculty at St. Paul School of Theology, Union Theological Seminary, and Yale Divinity School. Townes has served as president of the Society for the Study of Black Religion, was the first African American woman elected to the presidential line of the American Academy of Religion in 2008, and she was inducted as a fellow in the American Academy of Arts and Sciences in 2009. In 2010 she received a Doctor of Humane Letters from the Garrett-Evangelical Theological Seminary. She has also received honorary doctorates from Washington and Jefferson College and Franklin College. She currently serves as dean of the Vanderbilt University Divinity School and E. Rhodes and Leona B. Carpenter Professor of Womanist Ethics and Society.

A Theological Overview

Womanist eschatology is a worldview gleaned from the lived experiences of African American women. The ultimate hope of womanist eschatology is the realization of a new heaven and a new earth in which all of God's creation is held together by justice and love and all oppressions are annihilated.

The term *womanist* originated from the word *womanish*. In African American communities, "womanish" is an adjective describing black girls who are "precocious, inquisitive, stubborn, ornery or some combination thereof."[8] Womanish girls do not usually adhere to cultural and socioeconomic boundaries drawn by the dominant society. Therefore, womanists are first and foremost threats to homogenizing forces at work in the larger society. In addition, womanists are communal. They have an in-depth understanding of the contemporary and historical lived experiences of African Americans that recognizes interdependency. No segment of African Americans can separate itself from the larger group without damaging the future of African Americans as a whole; therefore, womanists must locate and inhabit their spaces within African American communities. As individuals, womanists are grounded in love—love of self, community, the worlds of black women, and the Spirit. Womanist love points toward wholeness and hope. Womanists recognize and reject the tendency of feminists to highlight gender inequities while failing to recognize the intersections of race, gender, and class oppression. As a result, womanists seek to work together with all people to help to realize wholeness for all.

Emilie Townes's womanist vision of the reign of God mandates a radical change in the current social order so that all people are able to live healthy, productive, and fulfilling lives. Social structures, beliefs, and practices that enforce gender, race, and class inequality impede the ability of millions to experience the just existence they were created to live. Since womanists believe that God made all people not just to survive in the world but to thrive, access to health care and redefining of health as cultural production (meaning, the state of an individual's health is a product of the culture and environment in which they live) is a vital part of the vision. Townes developed her vision of the reign of God throughout her career using a praxeological approach (reflection and action) oriented in the experiences of African American women and African American communities. For her analysis and recommendations, she employed the tools of social ethics, social history, philosophy, and public health.

In *Womanist Justice, Womanist Hope,* Townes gleans her womanist eschatology from the lived experiences of Ida B. Wells-Barnett (1862–1931). Wells-Barnett was a journalist, activist, and dedicated church-woman who took seriously her commitment to Jesus Christ. She believed that her Christian faith mandated that she live a life free of personal sin (as much as possible). Realizing her shortcomings, she prayed that God would help her to control her temper when she was working with others.[9] Though she believed that being a Christian mandated a life of personal piety, she also believed that being a Christian conferred upon her social responsibility. Salvation was both individualistic and communal for Wells-Barnett. For example, after boarding a train from Memphis to Woodstock, Tennessee, to visit her family in 1884, she was asked by the conductor to give up her seat in the ladies' car and join the other African Americans in the smoking car.[10] She refused and was forcibly thrown off the train by three men when the train stopped at the next station. That was not the end of the matter. Wells-Barnett hired an attorney and sued the Chesapeake, Ohio and Southern Railroad. She won her case and collected five hundred dollars in damages. However, the decision was later reversed on appeal by the Tennessee Supreme Court.

In her unwavering commitment to justice, Wells-Barnett was often unable to work well with others. She was impatient with prolonged processes, lengthy debates, and long meetings. She sometimes acted impulsively and independently of groups to get things done and, in an effort to accomplish particular tasks, ignored the benefits of dialogue.[11]

Wells-Barnett is best known for her public activism around the issue of lynching. In her day, lynching was used as a way of arresting the social aspirations and progress of African Americans. Blacks were legally, systematically, and regularly lynched thanks to a lynching law put in place in 1877.[12] Wells-Barnett used her platform as a journalist and eventually the owner of the newspaper *The Memphis Free Speech* to share the truth about the lynching of African Americans occurring throughout the United States. She used her place as a churchwoman to advocate for justice among Christians and Christian organizations in the United States and Great Britain.

Lynching of African American men was most often perpetrated under the guise of protecting the honor of white women. African American men were publicly characterized as beasts on the prowl. Wells-Barnett exposed not only the untruth of this contention but also the hypocrisy of its purveyors. She published details about the lynching of Thomas Moss, a Memphis grocery store owner who was lynched along with his business partners for the crime of being successful—more successful than some white business owners.[13] She published stories of white women who willingly entered into relationships with African American men but cried rape when their relationships were discovered.[14] She also highlighted the hypocrisy of white men acting to protect white womanhood who simultaneously raped African American women with impunity. Wells-Barnett's unwavering dedication to realizing justice on behalf of all people, but especially African Americans, reflected her belief that God is a God of justice.

In her analysis of Wells-Barnett's life and work, Emilie Townes develops ethical and theological themes that can be helpful to all who seek to live out their Christian faith and realize the reign of God on earth. Townes contends that Wells-Barnett chose from two paradigms of authority when engaged in her work: authority as domination and authority as partnership.[15] Authority as domination is the model based on obedience and submission. In this scenario, some have power over others. Wells-Barnett challenged the domination paradigm whenever and wherever she found it. Townes contends that "power over" is dysfunctional because it impedes diversity and growth for all involved. The power over paradigm is imposed. The better paradigm is authority as partnership or "power with" because it invites participation and interaction. "Power with" encourages communal listening, which results in a more nurturing and empathetic environment.

Wells-Barnett's social justice work reflected her belief that she was accountable to God through Jesus Christ first of all. This accountability necessitated mutual accountability with the communities with whom she worked to bring about the reign of God. Though she challenged systems of domination that wielded power over some, she did not take advantage of the breadth of communal possibilities that could evolve from power with. She sometimes ignored the merits of authority as partnership as a tool for dialogue. Authority as partnership or power with enables all people to be "co-creator[s] of God's Kingdom on earth."[16]

According to Townes, Wells-Barnett and other social activists of her day reshaped the evangelical understanding of obedience to address their concerns for social justice and personal virtue. Townes therefore chose from one of two models of obedience available to her: authoritarian and discerning. The authoritarian model of obedience is the embodiment of the power over paradigm in which the dominated do not ask questions and divest themselves of any responsibility to engage in the work of freedom.

People who subject themselves to authoritarian obedience are subject to manipulation. In these cases, the Bible, tradition, and experience can be used to repress rather than to grow and guide. In this scenario, groups and individuals do not engage in their own interpretations or critically reflect on the world in which they live and the circumstances in which they find themselves. They do what they are told.

The discerning model of obedience is an exercise of the power with paradigm. This paradigm is a process that seeks interaction and values the interconnectedness of human existence. In the discerning model, the people of God accept responsibility to first discover the will of God and then decide how best to respond. Townes believes that the discerning obedience model best exemplifies "God's will for justice and truth."[17]

As it relates to the authority of Scripture, Wells-Barnett believed that the Bible reveals how to live faithfully as people of God in the world. However, the Bible is not the only source of truth. When conducting her research about the truth of the circumstances in which African Americans found themselves embroiled, she discovered the truths of discrimination, oppression, physical abuse, and murder through sociology, political science, history, psychology, communication, and biology.[18] She used the lenses of her faith that were grounded in the Bible through which to interpret the living texts of her life and the lives of African Americans of her day. She recognized that humanity lives in a place of tension between the revelation of God found in the Bible and the revelation of God found in the world. It is the Bible that helps the people of God see and understand what God is doing in the world.

Wells-Barnett rejected the notion that human suffering is the will of God. Therefore, the belief that human suffering in relation to God is redemptive or punitive was problematic for her. Townes cites the work of liberation theologian Dorothee Sölle and James Cone to illuminate the womanist understanding of suffering espoused by Wells-Barnett. In *Suffering*, Sölle wrote that the misguided belief that God allows suffering in order to thwart human pride, highlight human powerlessness, or somehow exploit dependency on God equates to Christian masochism.[19] This view of suffering becomes an endurance test while also desensitizing people to the suffering of others.

When people view human suffering as punitive or punishment for wrong behavior, their God is in danger of becoming sadistic. If indeed suffering is a test that people must pass in order to prove their worthiness of God's love, then love of God becomes conditional rather than unconditional. If people do not pass God's test, are they then not worthy of the love of God?

Sölle reminds Christians that Jesus volunteered to suffer. It is when Christians volunteer to suffer in pursuit of justice that they are following in the footsteps of Christ. Those who claim to follow Christ but do not accept the cross of Christ are attempting to embody a "suffering free Christianity." As a result, those seeking to live in the image of Christ volunteer to suffer to demonstrate their opposition to oppression as they choose to stand with the oppressed. In this manner, the suffering of Christ is no longer symbolic but very real.[20]

In addition, Sölle contends that it is precisely because Jesus suffered that humans have the assurance that God understands and relates to the depths of human suffering. This point is very important for people on the margins who are struggling for basic human rights or even basic human dignity.

In *God of the Oppressed* Cone develops his understanding of human suffering as a way of reconciling the dilemma of the existence of an omnipotent and good God with the presence of evil. For Cone, Jesus' earthly ministry and death on the cross set free those previously oppressed by sin to struggle against the injustice of earthly rulers. Cone deems those willing to suffer in the struggle "liberated sufferers." Like Sölle, he believes that following Christ means answering the call to suffer with God in the fight against evil.

Townes also believes that the distinction made by Audre Lorde, womanist poet and writer, between suffering and pain is directly reflective of Wells-Barnett's understanding of her charge as a Christian. For Lorde, pain is an event that should be recognized, named, and then transformed into strength, knowledge, or action. Suffering happens when one relives "unscrutinized and unmetabolized pain."[21] If we live through pain without recognizing it, we rob ourselves of the ability to use our pain to energize movement beyond it. Suffering becomes an "inescapable cycle" when we don't attend to our pain. Townes then couches Lorde's premise in theological terms by contending that the resurrection has moved humanity past suffering to pain and struggle.[22] The suffering of Christ set free the oppressed from their suffering so they can struggle against injustice out of their pain. From this perspective, while suffering can be debilitating, pain can be energizing.

Townes contends that Wells-Barnett realized that suffering is a reactive position to oppression while pain is a transformative position. Therefore, "she [Wells-Barnett] lived her life through the critical stance of pain" by refusing to accept the status quo, using her critical thinking and investigative skills to unearth the truths fueling the injustices of lynching.[23]

Townes argues that Wells-Barnett exemplified how to live liberation ethics by giving of her gifts and talents to make freedom a reality for others. Using the work of Cone, Townes distinguished between liberation and freedom. Liberation is a process, while freedom is a state of being. Liberation is made manifest through the salvific work of God through Jesus Christ. Liberation yields transformation of individuals and communities as they struggle together to bring about freedom for all. Liberation affects not only external conditions but also internal terror or the societally imposed weight of double consciousness or only seeing oneself through the eyes of others.[24] Double consciousness destroys the spirit as well as the body.

Townes also believes that Wells-Barnett participated in the subjective realm of reconciliation all her life. The subjective realm of reconciliation is the place humans inhabit when they are being faithful to their newfound gift of freedom in Christ. Humans inhabit the subjective realm when they decide to live their lives like Wells-Barnett by working to bring into being America's highest ideal of liberty and justice for all.[25] The objective realm of reconciliation is where God works. In this realm, God creates new relationships with God's people through their faith. In this new relationship, the love and grace of God abound.

From Wells-Barnett's life, Townes gleans some womanist wisdom about leadership. Townes differentiates between the pastoral voice and the prophetic voice as models of leadership that are not mutually exclusive. A person with a pastoral voice is able to work well with others by providing comfort, accepting people with their shortcomings, considering all of the relevant information, and encouraging others to grow and change. A leader with a pastoral voice is also one who is able to accept criticism. After all, if she encourages others to grow and change, she should be willing to as well.

A person with a prophetic voice is one who is able to discern the will of God, willing to expose the oppressive nature of society, able to motivate people to act while also sharing consequences of inaction, confront people with dignity and respect, and create a community of faith, partnership, justice, and unity.[26]

Through a womanist ethical and theological analysis of the Alice Walker novel *The Color Purple*, Townes contends that Walker conveys a clear message to African Americans: concepts of God either support the oppression of blacks as it relates to gender, race, sexuality, and class or serve as companions in the fight for liberation. Townes takes the time to analyze the lives of three women in the novel whose characterizations are familiar in African American communities: Celie, Sofia, and Shug Avery. Celie lives a life of abuse at the hands of her husband, Mr.____. Mr.____, who marries Celie so he will have someone to take care of his kids, describes Celie as "black, poor, ugly, a woman, nothing at all."

Throughout the novel, Celie reveals her image of God through letters she writes to God and to her sister, Nettie, who was forced out of her own home by Celie's husband. Writing letters to God helps Celie bear her abuse, pain, and suffering. While her God is kind, her God is also silent in her suffering. As a result of God's silence in the midst of her pain, Celie's low self-esteem is only reinforced. Even with all her issues with God, Celie believes church is still a place in which she needs to prove herself worthy of God's love. When Celie finds out about the truth about her family, "lynched daddy, crazy mamma, lowdown dog of a step pa and a sister [she] probably won't ever see again," she begins to equate the God she has been taught is male with the men she knows who are "trifling, forgitful and lowdown."[27]

Townes quotes Delores Williams, who contends that Celie's understanding of God resembles theological views and ecclesiastical practices that have been part of African American communities for years. Celie's eschatology is like that expressed by black slaves in some spirituals who claim one's relief from the life of oppression is death and going to heaven.

Shug Avery is a lounge singer, Celie's friend, mentor, and lover. Though Shug's father is a preacher, she has managed to embrace an image of God that is radically different from the one she grew up with. For Shug, God doesn't look like anything because God is spirit—neither male nor female. Shug's God is never found in church but is a God that people bring with them to church to share with others. Shug believes that people come into the world with God. Only those who search for God inside find it. Thanks to Shug, Celie begins to believe in a God who is beyond gender.

Sofia is a large, feisty woman who marries Mr. ____'s son Harpo. Sofia refuses to be beaten, though Harpo tries numerous times to do so. When the mayor slaps Sofia after she refuses to be his maid, she slaps him back. She is sent to jail and physically brutalized before she is eventually forced to serve as a maid by the mayor.

In her analysis, Townes calls upon African Americans to have a spiritual awakening to a loving God who wants people of faith to celebrate life and foster loving relationships. Reconceptualizing God means replacing Celie's image of a kind God who is silent while people suffer with a God who cares and desires all God's people to be free and loved. By conceiving of God as neither male nor female, African Americans can let go of the dominant paradigm of male superiority and embrace a paradigm of mutuality and equality of all people regardless of gender. By acknowledging the positive loving relationship of Celie and Shug, African Americans can begin to understand that love is love even when it is between people of the same gender.

The people of God do not have to wait until they die to be happy. They can experience peace and happiness on earth. Sofia's refusal to be abused demonstrates her recognition that it was not God's will that she be unhappy. Subsequently, she stood up to those who tried to abuse and control her. However, in a world in which various forms of domination are woven into the social fabric, Sofia's commitment to embodying liberation came with its own risks. She suffered physically for her resistance to oppression. From Sofia we learn that resisting requires not just a new heaven but also a new earth in which the religious and social orders are radically transformed.

For Townes, transforming our world into a new heaven and a new earth includes exploring and dismantling evil as cultural production. There are narratives that have been intentionally constructed to support and perpetuate structural inequities and various forms of social oppression. She explores cultural productions of black womanhood that have shaped the public image of African Americans for decades, such as Aunt Jemima. Aunt Jemima evolved from the Mammy image that was constructed during the years of slavery to counter rumors that slave owners sexually exploited female slaves. Slave owners were especially attracted to light-skinned female slaves. As a result, the Mammy image of a fat, dark-skinned, unattractive, old, desexualized black woman provided cover for the "idealized patriarchal White family structure."[28] The Mammy was supposedly proof that white men did not find black women attractive. The fictional Mammy was loyal to such an extent that she put the welfare of the white family above the welfare of her own-and waited on them hand and foot. This Mammy was a complete fiction. However, with the Mammy in place, white men could continue to rape black female slaves with impunity.

Aunt Jemima was invented in 1889 when two white men who had developed a pancake mix saw a blackface minstrel show in St. Joseph, Missouri, being performed to the tune of a song called "Old Aunt Jemima." They decided to adopt the name Aunt Jemima while using the image of a Southern Mammy as part of a minstrel act in which one of the two men dressed up as the Mammy.[29] "Aunt Jemima began when a White man decided that he could be Black and a woman, and so he dressed in drag, put on blackface, and became a part of the minstrel tradition that helped to sing the White man's cares away."[30]

Real black women were hired to play Aunt Jemima in national marketing campaigns all around the country. They were forced to speak in broken dialect. They told inoffensive tales of slavery as they served pancakes at fairs and grocery stores. Many legends were created about Aunt Jemima. The image of a fat, dark-skinned, black woman with thick red lips and white pearly teeth was commodified and sold as rag dolls, salt and pepper shakers, cookie jars, and syrup pitchers.

The version of the Mammy gone bad who is blamed for all the social ills of the African American community is the Black Matriarch, also known as the Welfare Queen. She was first introduced in 1976 by Ronald Reagan at a Republican campaign rally in Chicago to help make his case for welfare reform.[31] Reagan pointed to an example of one woman in Chicago who committed welfare fraud by bilking the system out of hundreds of thousands of dollars. Even today, Reagan's story is thought by some to be a complete myth. Subsequent investigations have found that the woman upon which the image of the Welfare Queen is loosely based did exist. However, she was a racially ambiguous (sometimes claiming to be white and other times claiming to be black) career criminal whose crimes included kidnapping and perhaps even murder. While she did indeed commit welfare fraud, her story was in no way indicative of widespread welfare fraud by recipients of public aid.[32]

The Welfare Queen was also a cultural production. The culturally produced narrative is of a single woman who is head of her household. She works full-time and has several children whom she cannot properly supervise because she is away from home for large periods of time working to support them. She is single because of her attitude and aggressiveness that her male friends and husbands find emasculating. Her black children fail in school and in life because of her failure to embody good moral values that would translate into better social status and conditions were they fully embraced. From a white, male, epistemological worldview, white upper- and middle-class children succeed because of the care and nurture they receive at home. Black children could succeed as well if they received similar attention. This single black mother/Black Matriarch/Welfare Queen is thus set up to take the blame for the plight of the entire race.

The cultural production of the Welfare Queen is a symbol for women of every race and ethnicity of the lengths to which white patriarchal power will go to secure its cultural dominance. Women who do not conform to the ideal narratives of womanhood will be castigated in the public square. Black women who refuse to be passive, play by their own rules, and control their own sexuality and fertility are threatening to the racist, sexist, classist social order constructed and maintained by elite white males.

The compounding evil of this cultural production of the Welfare Queen, as if public demonization is not enough, is perpetrated when it is used to shape and make public policy that impacts the lives of black people in particular, and poor people in general, for decades. The Welfare Queen was key in helping to craft welfare reform policies in 1996.[33] The cultural production of evil takes many different forms and uses many different strategies to accomplish its mission.

Townes argues that dismantling the cultural production of evil can be accomplished through solidarity with an ultimate vision of justice and peace for all.[34] She contends that truth telling and culturally produced mythologies cannot coexist. "If we can hold on to digging up the truth when it gets buried in geopolitical, sociocultural, and theoretical cat fights and mud-wrestling contests, then we will be able to bring together justice-making and peacekeeping to dismantle evil."[35]

Another form of cultural production critiqued by Townes is health. Health is a cultural production dependent on many different factors. Oppression resulting from sexism, racism, and classism can result in a higher likelihood of poor health outcomes because of its many consequences, including poverty, lack of educational opportunities, poor working and living/environmental conditions, lack of access to healthy food, low wages, and limited promotional opportunities. Other factors that impact heath include biology, environment, and social networks.[36] Attending to matters of health ensures that all people are able to experience wholeness (physical, mental, emotional, and spiritual well-being). Human wholeness is facilitated by access to affordable, comprehensive health care, including mental health treatment.

Townes is clear that when she writes about health she is not referring to the curative model that seeks to diagnose illness and find cures. Townes's critique of the health care system, long before the advent of the Affordable Care Act, concludes that providers were more interested in increasing the profit margins than in providing health care for all. Trust between African American communities and health care providers needs to be rebuilt because of a history of medical experimentation and exploitation. The Tuskegee syphilis study initiated in the 1930s is a case in point. The United States Public Health Service, in cooperation with the Tuskegee Institute, agreed to treat four hundred African American men who had unknowingly contracted syphilis. The men were never told they had syphilis. They were told they were being treated for bad blood.[37] "Bad blood" is a colloquialism that encompasses a number of different illnesses. Even after penicillin was available in 1940, researchers did not make the cure available. Researchers wanted to monitor the progression of the disease throughout the men's lives, so they watched as the men died, went blind or insane, or experienced other severe health problems due to their untreated syphilis. As a result of not being informed that they had a communicable venereal disease, many of the men passed the disease on to their spouses. Some of their children were born with birth defects. The legacy of the Tuskegee study continues to reverberate in African American communities.

Working-class and poor people all over the nation have problems accessing quality, appropriate, and affordable health care. Those living in urban and rural communities find it particularly challenging to find care. In May 2018, the uninsured rate among working-age people—that is, those who are between nineteen and sixty-four—was at 44 percent for non-Hispanic whites, 12 percent for blacks, and 36 percent for Latinos and Latinas. The overall uninsured rate increased up from 12.7 percent in 2016 to 15.5 percent in 2018, meaning an estimated 4 million people lost coverage in that short period.[38]

Having defined health as cultural production, Townes argues that comprehensive approaches to insuring the good health of all people are needed. In addition to ensuring that access to affordable, comprehensive health care is available for all, preventive-health programs should be developed to meet unique cultural experiences and needs. For example, when prevention programs are developed based on the Westernized nuclear family (traditional father, mother, and children), other cultural models such as African kinship structures are overlooked. In this case, the influence and importance of extended families must also be factored into all models. Townes highlights programs and actions that contribute to overall health, including those that build self-esteem and skills and promote positive behavior changes. Some African American community groups successfully thwarted cigarette ad campaigns targeted at African Americans. Another community group whitewashed billboards in their neighborhoods that advertised alcohol. One community in Kansas developed groups for teenage girls to learn how to prevent HIV/AIDS. Another developed a Working Girl Luncheon to help prostitutes avoid contracting HIV. In San Francisco, The Grandparents Who Care Support Network was developed to provide support for poor, working-class, middle-aged, and predominantly African American women who are raising their grandchildren. The network provides emotional, informational, and practical aid for its members. In Kansas City, school-based full-service health clinics provide nutritionists, social workers, nurse practitioners (who can prescribe medications), mental health counseling, and doctors on call. The clinics meet the needs of students whose parents are not willing or able take them to a doctor.[39]

Implications for Preaching

Townes's womanist vision of the reign of God provides preachers an opportunity to help their people understand the difference between "power over" and "power with." Wells-Barnett understood that shared power has the potential to change the world in some very positive ways. However, shared powered is not a practice that needs to be adopted only by the powerful. By not embracing shared power,

Wells-Barnett prevented her ministry from being as effective and far-reaching as it might have been. Her impatience and inability to work with others was a detriment to her ministry. Shared power is a practice that must be embraced even by the oppressed as they live their daily lives.

Womanist critique of the cultural production of evil can help preachers understand that the reality of the lives of all people is impacted not only by who they are (race, ethnicity, education, age) and their individual decisions and actions. The reality is also impacted by the myriad of influences that shape the world in which they live (such as faith community, family, local and national political climates of the day). By informing their people of the intentional strategies put in place to give privilege to the few while disenfranchising the many, preachers can help their communities think of creative ways they can work in solidarity to improve the lives of people in their communities.

Preachers should help their congregations understand Wells-Barnett's view of suffering. Wells-Barnett rejected the notion that God wants any of God's people to suffer. For that reason, when she saw African American men being lynched and African American communities being torn apart, she got to work. She understood that she had skills and gifts that could impact the practice of lynching. She used her influence to convince others to take up the cause. Some traditional views of suffering contend that God employs or uses suffering for redemptive or punitive purposes. Womanists do not believe that God uses suffering to somehow redeem or punish God's people. God loves God's people completely and unconditionally and wishes them no harm.

Townes gives preachers tools to help their congregations develop a more inclusive understanding of God. Through her approach, Townes informs her readers that the language we use for God and the images we have about God (God's temperament and way of being) influence our relationships with one another and the ways we look at the world. Therefore, the language we use for God matters. The way we interpret biblical texts and the stories we hold sacred about God matter. *The Color Purple's* Shug's God is loving, without gender, and okay with gay. By understanding that God is neither male nor female, people can begin to understand that everyone is equal in God's eyes. God values all relationships, even romantic relationships between people of the same gender. For many people, conceptualizing God differently is a challenge. However, Townes believes that the dividends for making such an investment of time and effort will pay off in substantive ways.

Townes's womanist vision of the reign of God challenges the belief that Scripture is the sole authority for godly living. There are other sources of truth in history, sociology, political science, psychology, communication, and biology that, when embraced, can inform and empower previously disempowered and misinformed people. Preachers can share the importance of knowledge in seeking to realize the reign of God.

Preachers can also help their congregations understand that health is a cultural production, meaning there are many factors that contribute to human health.

Access to affordable, quality, and comprehensive health care is necessary. However, other types of programs that provide resources, incentives, and information to improve their physical, emotional, economic, or mental health are also needed.

The womanist ethical strategy of using the lived experiences of African American women as the basis of social, theological, and ethical critique risks diverting attention away from the larger issues onto the particular characteristics of individuals. For example, Wells-Barnett had a difficult time working with others. At the same time, her anti-lynching campaign helped to bring an end to a heinous and shameful chapter of American history. Preachers can highlight the reality of the fallibility of all humanity. Even with our flaws and shortcomings, we can be used by God for God's good purposes.

The cultural production of evil that morphed into Aunt Jemima could not have flourished without the cooperation of African American women who posed for the pictures and embodied the character at fairs and grocery stores. While Townes included an account of the complicity, preachers can more fully critique the ways in which oppressed people sometimes cooperate with the powers-that-be to their own detriment. By highlighting in their preaching the strategies used by some to denigrate others, preachers may be able to help their people avoid becoming pawns of the powerful.

Townes quotes Dorothee Sölle, who critiques those who want their Christianity to be free of suffering. Townes makes the point that many people, if not most, do not want to suffer in their lives. Preachers can help their people understand the need for voluntary suffering by sharing the ultimate vision that voluntary suffering can help bring about a world in which justice and peace are experienced by all.

Questions for Exegesis

1. Are there issues of authority in the text? If so, what are they, and how do issues of authority affect relationships between people in the text or between the people and God?

2. Is there redemptive or punitive suffering in the text? If so, what is its source (God or human)?

3. What are the many forces at work in the text and in the lives of the people in the text that prevent them from fully experiencing the unconditional love of God?

4. Are there situations, circumstances, or other factors in the text that are negatively impacting the health of the people in the text? If so, what are they?

5. Are there cultural productions of evil in the text? If so, what are they, and who produced them?

6. Hermeneutical Bridge Question: In what ways can people in our communities be impacted by an image of God who is genderless and kind, who cares about people and desires for all to be loved?

Notes

1. Emilie Maureen Townes, *Womanist Justice, Womanist Hope*, American Academy of Religion Academy Series (Atlanta: Scholars Press, 1993), ix.

2. Ibid.

3. Patricia E. LaRosa, *Finding Aid for Emilie M. Townes Papers*, 1971–2005, New York: Union Theological Seminary, 2006, http://library.columbia.edu/content/dam/library-web/locations/burke/fa/awts/ldpd_5907200.pdf.

4. Emilie M. Townes, "A Conversation with AAR President Emile Townes" (Religious Studies News, March 2008), 9.

5. LaRosa, *Finding Aid*.

6. Townes, "A Conversation," 9–10.

7. Ibid., 1.

8. Emilie M. Townes, *In a Blaze of Glory: Womanist Spirituality as Social Witness* (Nashville: Abingdon Press, 1995), 9–10.

9. Townes, *Womanist Justice, Womanist Hope*, 109. In her diary entries at the age of twenty-five, Ida B. Wells-Barnett asks God for help as she attempted to do more good works. She began teaching a Sunday school class of young men that included her brother. Part of her prayer to control her temper was aimed at controlling her emotions toward

her brother, who was not yet saved. She realized that she "alternated between harshness, indifference, and repulsion in his regard." Therefore, she needed help from God.

10. Ibid., 8.

11. Ibid., 182.

12. Ibid., 136. Lynching can be defined as "an extra-legal trial—the lynchers professing to represent for a time society itself, freed from artificial restraint which hampers its proper action—on the alleged ground of offenses recognized as felonies by the very law which they supplant, though not perhaps chargeable with the same penalties."

13. Ibid., 140. Thomas Moss was a close friend of Wells-Barnett. The lynching was particularly devastating for her and the African American community of Memphis. Moss and his business partners sold their goods at prices competitive with those of a white grocery store owner across the street. The identities of those in the lynching party were known. However, they were never held accountable for their actions.

14. Ibid., 141.

15. Ibid., 179–80. Townes borrows these paradigms of power from Letty M. Russell, *Household of Freedom: Authority in Feminist Theology*, 1st ed., The 1986 Annie Kinkead Warfield Lectures (Philadelphia: Westminster Press, 1987).

16. Ibid., 183.

17. Ibid., 184.

18. Ibid., 187.

19. Sölle, Dorothee. *Suffering* (Philadelphia: Fortress Press, 1975), 18–22. When expounding on her point about Christian masochism, Sölle uses an example of a woman in a marriage in which she is physically and emotionally abused but stays in the marriage because she believes it is God's will. She also stays because of the social stigma she would encounter from her church community and neighbors if she were to seek divorce. Sölle writes that Christian masochism places a low value on human strength, venerates a God who is powerful rather than good or logical, understands suffering as a matter of endurance, and demonstrates no sensitivity to the suffering of others.

20. *Womanist Justice*, 193.

21. Audre Lorde, *Sister Outsider: Essays and Speeches*, The Crossing Press Feminist Series (Trumansburg, NY: Crossing Press, 1984), 171–72. Throughout this essay, Lorde laments the tendency of African American women to lash out at each other due to the unrecognized and unprocessed internal pain inflicted on them by racism and oppression. Townes posits Lorde's premise in theological terms.

22. Townes, *Womanist Justice*, 195.

23. Ibid., 196.

24. W. E. B. DuBois, *The Souls of Black Folk* (Greenwich, CT: Fawcett Books, 1961), 16–17. DuBois contends that when one measures her or his value by the tape of the world, it is difficult if not impossible to ever see oneself clearly.

25. James H. Cone, *God of the Oppressed* (Maryknoll, NY: Orbis Books, 1975), 213–14.

26. Townes, *Womanist Justice*, 205–10.

27. Alice Walker, *The Color Purple* (New York: Harcourt Brace Jovanovich, 1970).

28. Emilie Maureen Townes, *Womanist Ethics and the Cultural Production of Evil, A Dictionary of the Bible* (New York: Palgrave Macmillan, 2006), 32.

29. Ibid., 36–8.

30. Ibid., 38.

31. Dahleen Glanton, "The Myth of the 'Welfare Queen' Endures, and Children Pay

the Price," Chicago Tribune (2018), http://www.chicagotribune.com/news/columnists/glanton/ct-met-dahleen-glanton-welfare-queen-20180516-story.html.

32. Gene Demby, "The Truth Behind the Lies of the Original 'Welfare Queen'," All Things Considered (2013), https://www.npr.org/sections/codeswitch/2013/12/20/ 2558 19681/the-truth-behind-the-lies-of-the-original-welfare-queen.

33. Townes, *Womanist Ethics and the Cultural Production of Evil*, 124–26.

34. Ibid., 159.

35. Ibid., 162.

36. Emilie Maureen Townes, *Breaking the Fine Rain of Death: African American Health Issues and a Womanist Ethic of Care* (New York: Continuum, 1998), 2.

37. Elizabeth Nix, "Tuskegee Experiment: The Infamous Syphilis Study," *History* (2017), https://www.history.com/news/the-infamous-40-year-tuskegee-study.

38. Sara R. Collins et al., "First Look at Health Insurance Coverage in 2018 Finds ACA Gains Beginning to Reverse," *To The Point: Quick Takes on Health Care Policy and Practice* (2018), https://www.commonwealthfund.org/blog/2018/first-look-health-insurance-coverage-2018-finds-aca-gains-beginning-reverse?redirect_source=/publications/blog/2018/apr/health-coverage-erosion.

39. Townes, *Breaking the Fine Rain of Death: African American Health Issues and a Womanist Ethic of Care*, 153–64.

9
Mujerista Vision
The Theology of Ada María Isasi-Díaz

A Brief Biography

Ada María Isasi-Díaz was born in La Habana, Cuba, on March 22, 1943, the third of six girls and two boys born to Josefina Díaz de Isasi and Domingo G. Isasi-Battle, a civil engineer. Her father worked at sugar mills in three different provinces of Cuba. Ada María received her primary and secondary education at Merici Academy, a school run by nuns of the Order of St. Ursula.[1] It was at home as a member of a family of practicing Catholics that she gained concern for the poor and oppressed and a love of the religious practices of her faith. From her mother she learned the importance of the struggle (*la lucha*) for what she believed.

The family left Cuba in 1960 as political refugees just after Fidel Castro became prime minister. The family settled in Baton Rouge, Louisiana, where Domingo Isasi-Battle found work as an engineer in sugar refineries. After arriving in the United States, Ada María became a novitiate in the Ursuline order, the first group of Roman Catholic nuns organized in the United States. The Ursuline order sent her to the College of New Rochelle for undergraduate studies and in 1967 dispatched her to work as a missionary in Peru.

It was while serving in Peru that she learned the real meaning of religion from the poor. They taught her that if religious beliefs are not the basis for the struggle for liberation, they can indeed become the "opium of the people." They taught her that God stands for the poor.[2] She left the order before taking her final vows in 1969 and returned to the United States. She taught high school in Louisiana for several years and lived in Spain for sixteen months. When she returned to the United States she settled in Rochester, New York. The years that followed were difficult for her because she was not sure what to do with her life. She understood that she still had a vocation in ministry but was uncertain about what her vocation was. During this period she worked as a salesperson at Sears and began studies for a master's in medieval history. It was also during this time that she signed up to receive a newsletter from Mary Walden, an Ursuline sister, who went on to organize the first Women's Ordination Conference (WOC), a movement working for the ordination of women into the priesthood of the Roman Catholic Church.[3]

Isasi-Díaz often stated that on Thanksgiving weekend in 1975 she was born a feminist at the WOC in Detroit. A friend who was in charge of religious education for the diocese invited her to attend the conference. However, she had no money for travel or for a hotel. She rode with and roomed with friends and volunteered to facilitate a small group to waive the cost for the registration. During that weekend, the excitement of possibility permeated the many different caucuses that were organized around common interests. Her birth as a feminist came at the end of the conference when women were asked to stand if they believed they were called to ordination. She hesitated to stand because she was tired of battles. However, at that moment she found herself surround by a mighty cloud of witnesses letting her know that she would not be alone in the fight. That day she signed a paper declaring her willingness to work for the ordination of women in the Roman Catholic Church.[4]

She received a call a few months after the conference to join the ongoing effort to achieve ordination for women. She worked as a volunteer for several years before becoming a paid staff member. It was while working for the WOC that she began to think critically about gender oppression and the interconnections between gender, race, and class. It was also while working at the WOC that she began to take courses in a master of divinity program at St. Bernard's Seminary in Rochester, New York. Eventually she became very vocal about racial and ethnic prejudice within the movement and began to disagree with movement leaders about priorities and styles of leadership. She also confessed that she had some personal shortcomings that made her continued employment difficult. As a result, she was asked to resign her job that she had held for seven years.

As she tried to figure out the course of her life after the WOC, Isasi-Díaz knew for certain that her future would involve the struggle for justice with grassroots Latinas. In the fall of 1983 she began studies and temporary work at Union Theological Seminary in New York. She met women such as Yolanda Tarango and Katie Cannon, with whom she began to work out a Latina theology. She earned a master of divinity degree and completed a PhD in theology with a concentration in Christian ethics in 1990.[5]

Isasi-Díaz served on the faculty at Drew University Theological School, Graduate Division of Religion, from 1991 to 2012. She is the author or editor of eight books and had the opportunity to speak to women throughout the United States, Africa, Asia, Europe, and Latin America. She died of cancer in 2012.

A Theological Overview

The eschatological vision of Mujerista theology, the "kin-dom of God," is grounded in the lived experiences of grassroots Latinas (Latin American women) and in traditional understandings of the term *familia* (family). The kin-dom is the embodiment of a new world order of realized justice in which all exploitation and abuse has passed away. All people feel safe and are able to develop a healthy self-identity and sense of self-worth. In the kin-dom, people are brought together through bonds of friendship, love, care, and community. The kin-dom is a lived reality in which all people, especially grassroots Latinas, experience *shalom* or the fullness of life. Jesus' command to love one's neighbor as one loves oneself is the guiding principle with which all people live their lives.[6] Since love for Mujeristas is communal rather than individualistic, the kin-dom of God is based on interdependence in which people work and live together in such a way that all people can be whom they are created to be.

Isasi-Díaz developed Mujerista theology through years of research with Hispanic women. She conducted ethnographic research interviews with women from Cuba, Mexico, and Puerto Rico, who are the people to whom Isasi-Díaz refers when she uses the term "Hispanic."[7] Ethnographic research is qualitative research conducted by observing people in their own settings and speaking their own languages. The research is done on the terms dictated by participants. Some of the women were interviewed during weekend retreats during which they challenged each other to continually share more deeply and reflectively. Some women were interviewed in their homes or other places of their choosing. The approaches ranged from focused and free story to case studies and life histories. Ongoing relationships with the women yielded life histories, processes of socialization, motivations, and religious understandings.[8] She used their experiences, motivations, and themes to develop Mujerista theology.

She believed the cultural modifications and innovations that emerged from the mingling of these three cultures would result in the creation of a new culture designated by the term *mestizaje,* racially or culturally mixed people.[9] People included in this new group live between their home countries and the United States. They are marginalized in the United States—not able to participate fully in all aspects of the wider society. In addition, they are not able to go back to their countries of origin because they have experienced some level of transformation in the United States that makes returning almost impossible. The coming together of races represented by *mestizaje* prevents the subordination of one group to another, as well as the exclusion of some groups by groups that control society.

One of the major causes for the necessity of a theology for Hispanic women is their socioeconomic reality in the United States. The period during which Isasi-Díaz began to formally develop her Mujerista theology was just after the Reagan era. President Ronald Reagan's supply-side economics (also known as Reaganomics) had a devastating impact on the poor and working classes in general and on Hispanic populations in particular. The premise of Reaganomics was that by cutting the tax rates of corporations and the wealthiest Americans, more jobs would be created, thereby increasing production. After-tax income would increase. The tax cuts would result in people working more, saving more (because of higher net income), and investing more (due to high net income and increased corporate profits). However, cutting taxes actually resulted in a decrease in federal revenue. In order to compensate for decreased revenues, social programs were restructured. Aid to Families with Dependent Children (AFDC) denied eligibility to four-hundred-and-eight thousand families and reduced aid to two-hundred-and-seventy-nine thousand families. By lowering the income limit for families of four, one million people lost eligibility for food stamps.[10] Cuts were also made to job training, nutrition, health, and social service programs.

Another cause for the necessity of a theology for Hispanic women is their lack of agency. Hispanic women, who have always been present in history, have been erased from the histories of their countries of origin and from the history of the United States. Not only are Latinas erased from history, but also their voices and contributions continue to be ignored in the present. Mujerista theology uses the phrase *permítanme hablar* (allow me to speak) to insist on having a woman's past made known and on being agents of their present and future. With the phrase, Latinas are requesting that those in power be quiet long enough to hear their denunciations of oppression and injustice and understand their vision of a just society.[11] Also, when they say "Permítanme hablar," they are asserting their right to think, defend their rights, and have a say in what is normative for humanity.[12]

Isasi-Díaz wrote that "to name oneself is one of the most powerful acts any person can do."[13] When Isasi-Díaz and other grassroots Latinas with whom she was collaborating were deciding what to name themselves and their new theology, they considered the term *feministas hispanas*. However, many in the Hispanic community rejected any association with the term "feminism" for several different reasons: feminism does not deal effectively with difference; does not share power well among all involved in the movement; fails to pay attention to the intersections of race or ethnicity, class, and gender; and seems to reject liberation as a goal in favor of limited benefits for a limited number of women. In other words, feminism is content when some women and men are oppressed as long as some other women benefit. The women settled on the term *Mujerista*. Unlike feminists, Mujeristas refuse to participate in or benefit from oppressive structures.[14] Rather, the goal of Mujeristas is to transform structures to eliminate oppression for Latinas in particular and all people in general.

A Mujerista is an Hispanic woman who gathers the hopes and aspirations of her people with the ultimate goal of freeing them (and herself) from systems and structures that oppress them, such as racism, ethnic bias, sexism, and capitalism. The ultimate goal is liberation from, rather than equality within, oppressive systems.[15] Mujeristas build bridges among the different segments of their communities as communities seek justice within the larger society. Isasi-Díaz admits that the term "Hispanic" is imposed upon Spanish-speaking people by the white dominant culture in the United States in an attempt to control and assimilate peoples of many different races and cultures. By choosing to use the term "Hispanic," Isasi-Díaz is not denying the many differences that exist among the different cultures. Diversity is to be acknowledged and celebrated.

Isasi-Díaz argues that using the term "kin-dom" is a better and more inclusive alternative than kingdom when referring to Jesus' work and mission. The term "kingdom" is packed with gendered language that supports systemic oppression through hierarchical and patriarchal structures.

The term also refers to a time and sociopolitical configuration with which few people in the twenty-first century can relate. The metaphor of kin-dom, however, suggests that the people of God are a family that transcend blood relationships and embrace friendships, love, care, and community. Kin-dom also displaces the primacy of the traditional nuclear family in which the man is the head and chief decision maker for an individualized, inwardly focused, self-contained unit. The metaphor of kin-dom is modeled after the familia, which is the most important institution in the lives of many people of Hispanic descent. It is within the familia that people get a healthy sense of identify and self-worth. Familia is a support system that carries with it a sense of duty to its members. It is within the familia that Latinas learn that people are more important than ideas and that relationships are important enough to warrant time, care, and cultivation.[16]

In the kin-dom of God, Jesus' mandate for the people of God to love their neighbors is embodied through solidarity. Solidarity for Isasi-Díaz exists when people are bound together through "common responsibilities and interests, as between classes, peoples, or groups."[17] She believes that for far too long people have equated solidarity with charity. Charity is making a donation to people or a cause out of abundance. Solidarity means participating in the liberation of God's people out of compassion.[18] Solidarity, which leads to action toward a common cause, is exemplified in Matthew 25:34-46. When the people of God meet the needs of the "least of these" (the hungry, the thirsty, the naked, the sick, and those in prison), then they are truly in solidarity. Mujeristas believe that the people of God must have a preferential option for the poor. Isasi-Díaz argues that social progress for Latinas can be positively impacted if people who have privilege use their privilege to effect radical change instead of denying the reality of their privilege. Mujeristas welcome others who are committed to the well-being of Latinas into their communities.

Solidarity seeks the liberation of God's people from all forms of oppression. Isasi-Díaz defines liberation as the participation of the people of God in the process of salvation. Liberation has three different aspects: freedom from social oppression, freedom from psychological oppression, and freedom from sin. Liberation destroys the roots of oppression and exploitation that humans perpetrate upon one another. Liberation is the means through which the kin-dom of God unfolds and grows on earth. While liberating events are indeed salvific, they do not represent salvation in its entirety.

Salvation is a gift of God; it is not earned or won through struggle. Salvation occurs within the realm of human history through God's actions that break into and shape human history, including creation, incarnation, and redemption.[19] For Latinas, experiencing the salvation of God means having a relationship with God that requires them also to love their neighbors. Mujeristas believe that their relationships with God impact every aspect of their lives. As a result, they reject any conception of salvation that does not affect their present and future reality.[20] The state of salvation is contingent not only upon the degree to which people love God but also the degree to which they love their neighbors, which is expressed through solidarity. Neighbors are the poor and oppressed. Therefore, salvation is experienced not just between God and each person but also among human beings. God's salvation is initiated and sustained by love. Human participation in salvation is called liberation. There can be no salvation without liberation. Liberation is the work of God's people to transform the world.

It is the socioeconomic reality of many Hispanic women, combined with their lack of agency, that makes *la lucha* (the struggle) a necessary part of their daily lives in the United States. The poverty, oppression, and marginalization they experience produce immense suffering and threaten them with anthropological poverty. Anthropological poverty is insufficiency of material resources and complete deficiency of social and political power that threatens to rob Hispanic women of their very being.[21] In the midst of their suffering they must decide, consciously or unconsciously, how they will deal with it without allowing themselves to be defined by it. Since suffering is both part of their daily lives and a central tenet of their Christian faith, Isasi-Díaz clarified the difference between suffering and struggle. In the cases of Hispanic women, suffering is pain, agony, or distress inflicted on them because of their race or ethnicity and/or gender by the powerful in order to control and manipulate them. *La lucha*, the struggle, is Hispanic women's response to suffering. One informal act of resistance to suffering is the *fiesta*. Fiestas are festivities that can celebrate many different occasions. As it relates to suffering, fiestas don't celebrate suffering. Fiestas celebrate the struggle against suffering. Hispanic women use fiestas as opportunities for solidarity. During fiestas they may encourage one another and offer and receive advice on how to approach different situations and circumstances that seem beyond their control. They may find the strength to continue to resist oppression through verbal support. They may also use the fiesta as a brief chance to forget about their suffering even for a little while.[22]

Isasi-Díaz unapologetically rejects the idealization and romanticization of suffering that has made it a core tenet of the Christian faith because of Jesus' suffering during his crucifixion. While she has no doubt that Jesus suffered incredible pain through no fault of his own, she refuses to believe that God demanded Jesus' suffering to fulfill a godly mission. It is because suffering has been idealized as a virtue that the powerful use suffering as an ideological tool to control and manipulate the poor and the marginalized. Suffering of any sort must be rejected as being against the will of a merciful and loving God.

Lo cotidiano (everyday reality) is the phrase that encompasses the fullness of the daily realities of the lives of Hispanic women. It includes how Latinas see themselves and the ways they speak and interact within families and among friends and neighbors. It also includes social systems and structures, habits, gender roles, expectations, routines, and other cultural norms. Since *lo cotidiano* is the lens through which grassroots Latinas experience and see the world, it can be empowering. No one knows the full substance of any situation better than the people who live it. Therefore, when Latinas apply a hermeneutic of suspicion to their lives, they undoubtedly experience conscientization. Conscientization is the awareness of the oppressed that "there is something suspicious about one's oppressed condition."[23] Through conscientization, people move from naiveté or uncritically accepting shallow or even illogical explanations to critical awareness that compels them to dig deeply into issues, ask penetrating questions, and find root causes when possible. It is through conscientization that the oppressed begin to envision a different reality and work to realize it in solidarity with others.

Mujeristas use the phrase *proyecto histórico* (historical project) to refer to the articulation of and the strategy to realize their preferred future of liberation. The proyecto histórico challenges the legitimacy of systems embraced and sustained by the rich and powerful as "ultimate, fundamental, and permanent."[24] It offers a vision of what can and should be that inspires commitment and action. Rather than attempting to make large structural changes in society, Mujeristas target small structural changes on many different levels that honor diversity and particularity while also positively affecting everyday reality. The poor, who are accustomed to having their voices silenced in society, are given life and agency through norms, values, virtues, and understandings of God given by Mujerista theology. Examples of small structural changes that can substantially benefit Latinas include changes in the family dynamics that allow marriages to have more balance between work and family for women and men; achieving better political representation by holding political office; and expanding public education so that Hispanic culture and Spanish language are taught in public schools. Proyecto histórico is a vision for the future for which Latinas are willing to struggle daily.

Mujeristas have a unique relationship with the Bible. While there are Latinas who are members of evangelical churches and believe the Bible is the Word of God, most Latinas believe that the *palabra de Dios* (word of God) is not necessarily what is written in the Bible. Rather, the word of God for them is when God shows up in their lived experiences and struggles. Even within the Christianity that became an integral part of Latino culture, the Bible is used in a limited way. The conquistadores or conquerors of Latin America in the sixteenth century imposed their culture, including their Christianity, upon the masses of people. The masses were not able to make the Christianity of the conquerors personal because they were not provided education. As a result, Christianity for the masses became a cultural expression composed of the Spanish culture of the conquerors and the indigenous culture of the conquered. Their new Christian culture, which became an important part of Latino culture, uses the Bible in a very limited way. It emphasizes traditions and customs of the Spanish church rather than the primacy of the biblical text.[25] The Bible and biblical truth are not considered by most Latinas to be very important. Therefore, many Latinas use their experiences and struggles as the source of their theology and do not consult the Bible. Rather than going to the Bible when they need help, they tap into resources to which they believe they have direct access: God, the saints, and/or Mary.

The Christianity of many Latinas includes religious traditions of African slaves who were brought to Latin America and the Caribbean during the slave trade. Latin American Christianity is also influenced by Amerindian traditions of the Aztecs, Mayans, and Incas. This synthesis of cultures and traditions form Latino popular religiosity, which stands in stark contrast to more organized or official Christianity. Popular religiosity pertains to the religious practices and understandings of the masses. Through popular religiosity, Latinas and Latinos find access to God and salvation using rituals, beliefs, and experiences.[26]

Another factor that has influenced the way Mujeristas view the Bible is the fact that within current church/religious structures, they have little or no input into the ways the Bible is interpreted. They feel they do not have direct access to the Bible because its needs interpretation. They have been forced to accept interpretations of priests and pastors that do not include ongoing revelation of God that is relevant to their lived experiences.

When Mujeristas do use the Bible, it is to meet a particular need. They are most drawn to people in the biblical texts who have struggled with adversity, marginalization, or oppression like they do. For example, when Isasi-Díaz was asked to facilitate a Bible study for four thousand women at the Tenth International Christian Women's Fellowship Quadrennial Assembly at Purdue University in 1994, she chose to use a Mujerista lens through which to conduct it. She chose the narratives of four women who had overcome adversity in some way: Eve (Genesis 1:26–2:3), the persistent widow (Luke 18:1-8), the woman with the flow of blood (Matthew 9:20-22; Mark 5:25-34; Luke 8:43-48), and Mary, the mother of Jesus (Luke 1:46-55).[27] By reading and hearing about other people and communities who have struggled for justice and against adversity for centuries, they gain hope—hope that, like the people in the biblical texts, they too will realize transformations of conditions and circumstances of the world in which they live if they resist injustice. These and other biblical stories encourage Latinas to believe in themselves and in the power of their communities.

Mujeristas reject the practice of appropriating biblical texts solely to achieve and maintain a sense of personal piety or personal salvation. It is easy for individualistic interpretations to become oppressive by demonizing personal behaviors deemed sinful while allowing systems and structures of oppression to remain unchecked. They contend that even though interpretation of the Bible should be communally focused, the ultimate source of moral values is the struggle for liberation because the Bible cannot be directly applied to their everyday lives.[28] Mujeristas believe that God is present and involved in their daily lives through human conscience. They understand conscience to be the word of Christ (as spoken in creation, in the incarnation, and through the influence of grace) that enables the people of God to receive guidance of the eternal law of God. Guidance of the conscience is not the imputation of divine revelation. Rather, guidance of conscience is the voice of God that compels individuals to act according to rational insights.[29] Isasi-Díaz argues that each person has the right to moral agency or the freedom to never act against her, his, or their own consciences. This is especially important in relation to the authority of the church, which has attempted to restrict dissent paternalistically through canon law (as it relates to the Catholic Church) or through interpretation of biblical texts. The moral agency of Hispanic women in particular is jeopardized when acting in contradiction to canon law or dominant biblical interpretations results in being labeled disobedient or sinful. As a result, conscience should not be understood as a faculty or power but rather as awareness of oneself as someone with the ability to think, decide, and judge.

Therefore, rather than focusing interpretations on individuals, Mujeristas focus on community. They believe that interpretation of texts should focus on the goals, values, norms, attitudes, decisions, and dispositions that people who claim to be Christians should adopt. The Bible itself should implore communities of faith to strive for the kin-dom of God by struggling for justice.

A key element of liberation is the *comunidades de fe* (communities of faith), which are praxis-oriented communities guided by religious understandings to provide personal support and community action. Latinas believe that people who claim to be in relationship with God must relate to God on a daily basis. They must have an intimate relationship with God. An intimate relationship with God for Mujeristas means expressing gratefulness for all God has done and is doing while also arguing, bartering, and getting upset with God. *Communidades de fe* are organized with the realization that Latinas cannot depend on church structures to develop their communities. They can only depend on themselves and other Latina organizations that are committed to the liberation of their people. *Comunidades de fe* must be ecumenical to allow common cause and commitment to the struggle to outweigh denominational allegiance.

Comunidades de fe are necessary to help Latinas confront and overcome the myth of the American dream. Many Latinas who live under some of the most oppressive conditions believe that if they work hard and sacrifice their own well-being, their children will be the beneficiaries and therefore acquire the material rewards and other privileges that America offers. Isasi-Díaz contends that belief in the American myth hampers the ability to understand the reality of systemic oppression. If Latinas succeed in the current system, other people will take their place at the bottom of the socioeconomic ladder. Belief in the American dream presents the temptation of looking out for themselves or embracing individuality instead of striving for communal liberation.[30]

The primary obstacle to the unfolding of the kin-dom of God is alienation from God—also known as sin. Sin for Mujeristas is not simply disobedience to God. People sin when they are not available for other people. For example, not going to church is not a sin. Not caring for children in the community is. Sin is both personal and structural. Though sin can be personal, it is not private.[31] Personal behavior impacts human relationships with God and with one another. Sin also impacts society-at-large through systems and structures that support and sustain sin. Ultimately, sin is the cause of poverty, injustice, and oppression.[32]

Implications for Preaching

The impetus for what turned out to be a significant part of Isasi-Díaz's life's work grew out of her being in touch with the socioeconomic reality of Hispanic women. She was in touch with their reality because she talked to them. She spent time with them. She interviewed them. But most of all she listened to them. She listened to their narratives and believed that even though they did not have advanced theological degrees, they had relationships with God from which they learn. As a result she was able to develop a theology that empowers Hispanic women and provides people of faith with a theological perspective that challenges many of their long-held assumptions and helps them to think differently about God, Jesus, and the Bible. Preachers can learn from Isasi-Díaz the importance of truly listening to people in the pews and on the streets who may not have theological degrees but know something about God and their relationship with and to God. Our preaching can be greatly enhanced if we allow the voices and experiences of the people to inform and positively influence it.

Anthropological poverty is insufficiency of material resources and complete deficiency of social and political power that threaten to rob people of their very being. Much of the insufficiency and deficiency is caused by racial or ethnic and gender bias perpetrated by those in power who benefit most from inequitable social arrangements. Preachers can highlight the existence of anthropological poverty by highlighting the Mujerista vision of the kin-dom of God. In the kin-dom, anthropological poverty no longer exists. In the kin-dom, people work in solidarity to resist all oppression that denies people the resources, self-worth, and self-sufficiency to live the lives God created them to live.

Despite the fact that the word *charity* in the New Testament is often translated from the Greek term *agape*, meaning "love," Isasi-Díaz rightly highlights how charity has been degraded to refer to the act of giving by those who have much to those who don't. Charity or love has been reduced to a single act of generosity rather than a lifetime commitment to solidarity. She argues that being in solidarity with oppressed communities is more important and effective than giving material goods. Giving material goods is good and often necessary. However, sustained progress that leads to liberation most likely occurs through solidarity. Preachers can help their people understand that when Jesus mandated in Matthew 22:39 that we love our neighbors as we love ourselves, he intended the people of God to have a lifetime commitment of solidarity with other people. Having a lifetime commitment of standing in solidarity means working together to ensure all people have what they need to thrive.

In some congregations, the word *sin* is not often uttered. Isasi-Díaz's description of sin as alienation from God provides preachers with language to revive the use of the term. The language of alienation advances the characterization of sin as not just wrong behavior by offering a reason for ungodly behavior. When people are out of touch with God, they are more apt to behave in ways with which God is not pleased. As a result, preachers can preach not only about the results of alienation but also about the causes and solutions. Actions typically classified as sin can be seen as causes that do not necessarily have to be acted on. For example, greed can be the cause of the sin of theft. Learning to be content with material goods through Bible study and prayer can be a solution. Sexual attraction can be the cause of the sin of adultery. Being reminded that we should love our neighbors as we love ourselves could be motivation not to inflict the pain of broken expectations and betrayal on others.

Isasi-Díaz highlights the centrality of suffering to the Christian faith. Christ suffered physically and emotionally when he was crucified. Suffering was God's will for Christ, according to the common Christian doctrine of atonement. Isasi-Díaz was concerned that when people uncritically

accept suffering as a virtue, they become less likely to resist their own oppression and the oppression of others. They may believe they it is God's
will for them to be poor, marginalized, and unfulfilled. Preachers have an
opportunity to revisit the doctrine of the atonement and the concept of
suffering by highlighting the pros and cons of atonement theory and offering some alternatives. For example, by focusing on the life of Christ,
his ministry, and his message instead of his death, preachers are able to
shift the focus from death to life.

Isasi-Díaz believed that salvation is a gift of God that comes with a responsibility. One cannot fully experience salvation unless one loves one's
neighbors. She also believed there could be no salvation without liberation. In other words, a person who is being oppressed is unable to fully
experience salvation. Liberation for her is the participation of humans in
God's salvation. Preachers can take the time to broaden the conceptions
of salvation held by many of their parishioners. Her definition links the
importance of salvation directly to God's justice. Her expanded definition
of salvation demonstrates that God is a holistic God who is not just concerned about the human soul; God is concerned about the whole person.

Mujerista theology demonstrates the importance of vision. The vision
of the kin-dom is modeled after la familia, where people care for one another and all people have an opportunity to thrive. Vision in Mujerista
theology also includes the *proyecto histórico* that targets small practical
changes that positively affect the daily lives of all the people. Proyecto
histórico provides a vision for which the people strive every day. Preachers
can emphasize the importance of vision for fulfilling the will of God. With
vision, people have an ultimate goal for which to aim.

Isasi-Díaz admitted that while the term *kin-dom* is much more inclusive
and less hierarchical than *kingdom,* it is not without its own challenges.
The kin-dom is based on la familia. La familia can be a support system in
which positive identities and senses of self-worth are formed. La familia
can be a community of supportive relationships of nurture where people
can truly be themselves while knowing that they can always count on the
love and support of people they care about the most. But la familia can
also be patriarchal, abusive, and emotionally taxing, depending on the
people and relationships that are part of it. When preachers use the term
kin-dom of God, they should do so with full knowledge of its strengths
and limitations.

Largely because of a lack of education in the past and the patriarchal and racist ways the Bible has been and continues to be interpreted in the present, Mujeristas have written off the importance of Bible for their lives and faith. While this is understandable and they can certainly find, understand, and commune with God quite well without the Bible, not cultivating a relationship with the Bible cedes its interpretation to people likely to continue their toxic interpretations of it. The Bible is the central document of the Christian faith. By reading and interpreting the Bible for themselves or as part of a faith community, people can broaden their understanding of God and learn about the life and ministry of the central figure of their faith: Jesus Christ. They can also participate in forums where some are seeking to use their toxic interpretations to justify discrimination and oppression of various forms. Knowledge of the Bible can strengthen their public theological voices. Therefore, it would be an act of love for those with knowledge of the Bible to share their knowledge in collaborative, inclusive, and nonpatriarchal ways.

For Mujeristas, the guidance of the conscience is the voice of God that compels individuals to act according to rational insights. They understand conscience to be the word of Christ (as spoken in creation, in the incarnation, and through the influence of grace) that enables the people of God to receive guidance of the eternal law of God. However, if that conscience was formed in a faith community that is patriarchal, sexist, and racist, can that conscience be an effective guide? Preachers can help their people understand that the human conscience is only as reliable as the tenets that shape and form it.

Questions for Exegesis

1. Are people in the text being oppressed in any way? If so, how and by whom? What is the social status of women in the text?

2. Are the people in the biblical text living under the governmental structure of a kingdom or some other form of government? If they are living in a kingdom, how are their lives being impacted? (For instance, do they have to pay taxes or some other form of payment to support the kingdom? Are they forced to do public obeisance to the king even if their faith forbids worship of anyone other than Yahweh?)

3. Is solidarity (participation of people in the liberation of others out of love and compassion) being experienced in the text? If so, how?

4. Are there people in the text who experience conscientization? If so, who? How does conscientization come about?

5. Is there suffering in the text? If so, who or what is the cause of it? Are there any actions being taken to alleviate it?

6. Hermeneutical Bridge Question: How do our beliefs, practices, and traditions contribute to the suffering of other people? How can we form solidarity with the very people we (at least partially) cause to suffer?

Notes
1. Ada María Isasi-Díaz, "Biographical Information" Drew University Theological School Graduate Division of Religion, https://users.drew.edu/aisasidi/bioInfo.htm.
2. Ada María Isasi-Díaz, *La Lucha Continues: Mujerista Theology* (Maryknoll, NY: Orbis Books, 2004), 13.
3. Ibid.
4. Ibid.
5. Paul Vitello, "Ada María Isasi-Díaz, Dissident Catholic Theologian, Dies at 69," *The New York Times* (2012), https://www.nytimes.com/2012/06/06/nyregion/ada-maria-isasi-diaz-dissident-catholic-theologian-dies-at-69.html.
6. Isasi-Díaz, *La Lucha Continues: Mujerista Theology*, 243–51.
7. Ada María Isasi-Díaz, *En La Lucha = In the Struggle: A Hispanic Women's Liberation Theology* (Minneapolis: Fortress Press, 1993), 14. She identifies these three groups because they are the most populous of the Spanish-speaking groups in the United States. Mexican Americans or Chicanas include those born in Mexico who live and work in the United States.
8. Ibid., 66–67.
9. Isasi-Díaz, *La Lucha Continues: Mujerista Theology*, 61.
10. Mimi Abramovitz and Tom Hopkins, "Reaganomics and the Welfare State," *The Journal of Sociology and Social Welfare* 10, no. 4 November (1983), 569, http://scholarworks.wmich.edu/cgi/viewcontent.cgi?article=1627&context=jssw.
11. Ada María Isasi-Díaz, *Mujerista Theology: A Theology for the Twenty-First Century* (Maryknoll, NY: Orbis Books, 1996), 128–35.
12. Ibid., 136–37.
13. Isasi-Díaz, *En La Lucha = In the Struggle: A Hispanic Women's Liberation Theology*, 2.
14. Isasi-Díaz, *Mujerista Theology: A Theology for the Twenty-First Century*, 61–2.
15. Isasi-Díaz, *En La Lucha = In the Struggle: A Hispanic Women's Liberation Theology*, 4.
16. Isasi-Díaz, *La Lucha Continues: Mujerista Theology*, 249–50.
17. Isasi-Díaz, *Mujerista Theology: A Theology for the Twenty-First Century*, 89.
18. Isasi-Díaz, *La Lucha Continues: Mujerista Theology*, 116–17.
19. Isasi-Díaz, *En La Lucha = In the Struggle: A Hispanic Women's Liberation Theology*, 35.
20. Ibid., 34–35.
21. Ada María Isasi-Díaz and Yolanda Tarango, *Hispanic Women Prophetic Voice in the Church: Toward a Hispanic Women's Liberation Theology = Mujer Hispana Voz ProfeTica En La Iglesia: Hacia Una Teologia De Liberacion De La Mujer Hispana* (San

Francisco: Harper & Row, 1988), 60–61.

22. Isasi-Díaz, *Mujerista Theology: A Theology for the Twenty-First Century*, 130–31.

23. Ibid., 96.

24. Isasi-Díaz, *La Lucha Continues: Mujerista Theology*, 2.

25. Isasi-Díaz, *En La Lucha = In the Struggle: A Hispanic Women's Liberation Theology*, 45–46.

26. Ibid., 46–47.

27. Ada María Isasi-Díaz, *Women of God, Women of the People* (St. Louis: Chalice Press, 1995), https://users.drew.edu/aisasidi/cd/TOC.html.

28. Ibid.

29. Isasi-Díaz, *En La Lucha = In the Struggle: A Hispanic Women's Liberation Theology*, 149.

30. Ibid., 43.

31. Ibid., 39.

32. Ibid., 40.

10
Disability Vision
The Theology of Nancy Eiesland

A Brief Biography

Nancy Eiesland was born Nancy Lynn Arnold in Cando, North Dakota, with a congenital bone defect.[1] At the age of seven, after she had been fitted with a full-leg brace, her father told her that she would need to get a job that kept her off her feet. "You'll never be a checkout clerk," he told her.[2] As a child she recalls being told by some well-meaning Christians, "You are special in God's eyes, that's why you were given this painful disability" and that God gave her the disability to develop her character. For Eiesland, the thought that God gave her a disability because she was special was illogical. And by the age of six or seven she believed she had enough character to last a lifetime.[3]

Eiesland began undergoing operations to eradicate her birth defect as a toddler even while serving as a poster child for the March of Dimes. However, after her eleventh surgery at the age of thirteen, her doctors stopped telling her that their "cutting" would make her "pain free."[4] Indeed, her disability would prove persistent. Pain would be her constant and lifelong companion. When she was in high school, she became active in the disability rights movement, a worldwide movement to provide basic civil rights for the diversity of people with disabilities. She won a national contest with an essay identifying the inaccessibility of the courthouses in rural North Dakota. She also organized a letter-writing campaign to highlight the issue. Even in her teens, she recognized that while the disability rights movement was necessary, important, and one to which she was committed, it did not address her spiritual and theological questions about her disability.[5] She experienced a disconnect between her faith and the need for civil activism. On the one hand, the disability rights movement afforded her an opportunity to work for social change she had never heard of in her Christian faith. On the other hand, through her Christian faith, she found spiritual fulfillment that she could not find anywhere else.

After enrolling at the University of North Dakota as an undergraduate, she fought for ramps to be installed in the library and parking spots to be designated for the disabled. However, she left the university before she earned her degree after her older sister was killed in an automobile accident.[6] Her sister's unexpected death inspired her family to join an Assemblies of God congregation in Springfield, Missouri. There she enrolled in Central Bible College, trained for and was ordained as an Assemblies of God minister, and graduated class valedictorian in 1986. But she gradually drifted away from the denomination. She went on to Emory University in Atlanta, Georgia, where she earned both her master of divinity in 1991 and PhD in Ethics and Society in 1995.[7] She became an associate professor of Sociology of Religion and Disability Studies at Emory's Candler School of Theology. Eiesland published *The Disabled God: Toward a Liberatory Theology of Disability* in 1994, as well as three other books and numerous articles. She died of genetic lung cancer in 2009.

A Theological Overview

Nancy Eiesland's vision of the reign of God is one in which people with a full range of disabilities are fully liberated from all forms of systemic oppression. In her vision, people with disabilities are no longer marginalized and thought to be helpless. Rather, they are respected and allowed to employ their gifts and skills throughout society and in communities of faith. They are also provided with the resources they need not only to survive but also to thrive and live as independently as possible. In her vision, people with disabilities are not set apart from the wider populations but are intricately woven into it as equals. The justice and equality they seek for themselves is the same equality they want for all of God's people.

The primary purpose of Eiesland's writings about disability is to enable people with disabilities to be integrated fully into the life of the church. To make her case, she argued that people with disabilities of all types form a minority group (both inside and outside of the church) because they are excluded and even persecuted by the majority of people who are (temporarily) able-bodied (see more on this below). There are five common criteria used in sociological studies for determining whether a particular people compose a minority group: they are subordinated by prejudice and pejorative treatment by the majority; they are identifiable by common characteristics; they do not volunteer to be part of the group; they are aware that they are members of that minority group; and they are encouraged to marry within their group by both the majority and other members of their minority.[8]

For much of Christian history, theology has been developed by able-bodied people who considered their physical conditions to be the standard upon which to base and interpret all human experience.[9] The problem with this is that when the unique and varied experiences of people with a range of mental and physical impairments—such as Down syndrome, cerebral palsy, intellectual developmental disorders, autism, paraplegia, complete or partial hearing loss, partial or complete vision loss, muscular dystrophy, and loss of limbs—are ignored, theological traditions and doctrines are incomplete. In addition, when theologies are constructed using particular mental and physical standards, people whose abilities fall outside of those standards are cast as abnormal and unable to represent the image of God. People with disabilities have been excluded not only from theological conversations and traditions but also from full participation and inclusion in the life of many ecclesial bodies, Christian communities, and society-at-large.

In the 1960s persons with disabilities began to demand equal rights through the disability rights movement. The academic field of disability studies officially began in 1982 within the Social Science Association.[10] The founders of disability studies observed that the disabling of persons with physical impairments was a result of society's responses to physical impairments.[11] For example, being in a wheelchair is a disability only if accommodations such as wheelchair ramps and elevators are not readily available. Therefore, disability studies approaches its work with the assumption that disability is a social construct. As a result, full participation and inclusion of people with physical disabilities in all aspects of society can be achieved with proper accommodations.[12] The disability rights movement culminated with the passage of the Americans with Disabilities Act (ADA) in 1990. With the passage of these laws, people with impairments had legal standing to make their cases for full participation and inclusion throughout society.

It was with full participation and inclusion in mind that the new field of disability theology emerged in the latter part of the twentieth century. It was developed by both disabled and non-disabled Christians as they interpreted God, humanity, and the gospel of Jesus Christ in light of historical and contemporary experiences of people with disabilities.[13] Disability theologians have arisen from a diversity of disciplines, including biblical studies, church history, Christian ethics, sociology, and practical theology. While disability theologians such as Nancy Eiesland also contend that disability is a social construct, they have the extra task of making their argument for full participation and inclusion in light of and often in spite of Christian or biblical traditions, interpretations, practices, and beliefs.

Eiesland reminded her readers that while the minority group designated "people with disabilities" has many similarities with other minority groups, it also has a particular uniqueness. "People with disabilities" encompasses those with a wide range of physical, psychological, and intellectual functional impairments, such as deafness, paralysis, dyslexia, multiple sclerosis, and mental retardation. The disabilities can be static or progressive, congenital or acquired. Though each of these disabilities is different, they result in the same type of stigma in the wider society.[14]

The minority group of "people with disabilities" is also unique because unlike other minority groups of people designated by race, gender, ethnicity, or sexual orientation, membership in this group can be achieved by anyone. All currently nondisabled people have a 50 percent chance of becoming permanently or temporarily disabled during their lifetimes.[15] People can become impaired or disabled through illnesses, accidents, or genetic conditions. The probability of becoming disabled increases with age. Racial minorities, the elderly, and people living in poverty or in rural areas have a higher probability of becoming disabled than others. The prevalence of African Americans with disabilities is 16.3 percent compared with 12.8 percent of whites. The severity of impairment is also greater among African Americans than among whites.[16]

Eiesland carefully differentiates between the terms *impairment, disability,* and *handicap.* An impairment is an abnormality or loss of physiological form or function. A disability is the result of an impairment that is evidenced by an inability to perform a physiological function or task that is considered essential and necessary for daily living. A handicap is a social disadvantage or barrier that exists because of impairment or disability. For Eiesland, an impairment does not always result in a disability. A disability does not necessarily have to be a handicap. A disability becomes a handicap when disabled people are not provided with resources, tools, or access needed to function. For example, a person in a wheelchair may be

disabled but becomes handicapped when a building is not accessible because doors are too narrow or it has no wheelchair ramps or elevators.

In *The Disabled God* and her coedited work *Human Disability and the Service of God*, Eiesland highlights the history and importance of the disability rights movement in bringing the issues and concerns of the disabled
into the public square. For much of human history, physical disability was
viewed in many societies as a source of shame. In the United States in the
twentieth century, parents hid their disabled children from public view.
Adults such as President Franklin Delano Roosevelt attempted to conceal
his disability from the American people.[17] It was legislation for veterans
returning from World War I and World War II that reframed disability as
an issue that needed to be addressed through legislation rather than a condition that needed to be hidden and denied. One of the first laws passed
for veterans was the Vocational Rehabilitation Act of 1918, which designated funds for physical therapy and job training programs. Through this
and other legislation, organizations such as Disabled American Veterans
and Paralyzed American Veterans attempted to change perceptions of the
disabled that viewed them as unproductive and pathological. The underlying narrative of this legislation and the narrative of the veterans' associations was that medical science could help "fix" veterans and others
with disabilities. Medical personnel were viewed as the experts and people
with disabilities were the passive recipients of treatments and advice.

The medical model of disability dominated until the disability rights
movement began in the 1960s. A new generation of young people with
disabilities rose up during this period and demanded full social participation. The independent living movement, which began in Berkeley, California, in 1962, was part of this uprising. Ed Roberts, a quadriplegic who
had to have an iron lung to breathe, enrolled as an undergraduate at the
University of California, Berkeley. The headline in the local newspaper
read "Helpless Cripple Attends U.C. Classes."[18] Roberts, along with others
with disabilities, demanded that ramps be installed to make on-campus
housing wheelchair accessible and asked the university to provide them
assistance to complete their degree programs. The efforts of Roberts and
others led to the establishment of the Berkeley Center for Independent Living (Berkeley CIL), an information hub staffed primarily by people with
disabilities. At the Berkeley CIL, people with disabilities received information about housing, education, transportation, and other matters that

enabled them to live more independent lives. By 1996, there were more than three hundred centers for independent living around the country that espoused three core philosophies: the disabled know best the needs of disabled people and how best to meet those needs; the needs of the disabled can be met best through comprehensive programs that provide a variety of services; and disabled people should be integrated as fully as possible into their communities.[19]

The independent living movement was just one of many movements that culminated in 1990 when the Americans with Disabilities Act was signed into law. Modeled after the Civil Rights Act of 1964, the ADA defined the disabled as a group who had been subjected to unequal treatment and had been relegated to a position of powerlessness in society.[20] The ADA prohibits discrimination against and ensures equal opportunities for people with disabilities in employment, state and local government services, public accommodations, commercial facilities, and transportation.[21]

However, even while the battle for basic civil rights was being won in the larger society, some religious groups lobbied for and were granted exclusions from having to accommodate people with disabilities based on the separation of church and state. Many contended that they did not have money to make the accommodations now required by the law. Eiesland linked the desire of some religious communities to seek exclusions from parts of the ADA with their embrace of disabling theology that has roots in the Bible. This disabling theology created at least three theological obstacles for people with disabilities: the conflation of sin and disability, virtuous suffering, and segregationist charity.[22]

Texts such as Paul's "thorn in the flesh" (2 Corinthians 12:7a-10) espouse virtuous suffering in which some physical impairments are viewed as a sign of divine election. Eiesland found the theology of virtuous suffering particularly dangerous because it encourages people with disabilities to yield to social barriers as a sign of devotion to God instead of working to remove them. The theology of virtuous suffering also encourages people to be content with second-class status both inside and outside the church.[23] Eiesland also contends that the church is a leading promoter of charitable practices toward people with disabilities. From the time the church began in the book of Acts, Christian communities have always acknowledged and embraced their godly responsibility for and mission to those who are marginalized and oppressed. People who are physically unable to care for themselves, including some people with disabilities, have been recipients of outreach from the beginning. New Testament passages such as Acts 3:1-3 demonstrates that people with disabilities often begged for money to support themselves financially. People going into the temple to pray and worship were expected to give money to them. In like manner, many churches today have outreach ministries to people with disabilities. However, these same churches do not always actively integrate people with disabilities into all aspects of community life. Eiesland contended that the church had somehow lost sight of its responsibility for the marginalized. When Peter and John healed the disabled man at the Beautiful Gate in Acts 3:1-10, they restored not only his physical health but also his inclusion as a member of the religious community. For Eiesland, political engagement and social inclusion of all of God's people are core tenets of Christianity.[24]

For Eiesland, the church's disabling theology needs to be replaced with a generative and inclusive theology that acknowledges the worth, dignity, and godly embrace of people with disabilities. She had an epiphany that led to her inclusive theology during a Bible study one afternoon in Atlanta at the Shepherd Center, a private, not-for-profit, 152-bed hospital for treatment, research, and rehabilitation of people with spinal cord and brain injuries.[25] At the Shepherd Center she shared her doubts about whether God cared about her. She asked participants how they would know whether God was with them and whether God understood their experiences. A young African American man said, "If God was in a sip-puff maybe he would understand."[26] This image of God was indelibly etched in her memory. Several weeks later she experienced her life-changing insight when reading Luke 24:36-39, in which Jesus encountered the disciples after his resurrection and asked, "Why are you frightened, and why do doubts arise in your hearts? Look at my hands and my feet; see that it is I myself. Touch me and see." Eiesland was struck with the realization that this Jesus was both disabled and divine. The piercings visible in Jesus' hands, feet, and side rendered him severely impaired; yet he was understood to be holy and divine. She believed there were transformative implications for the disabled in the resurrection of a disabled God.

Eiesland believed that a liberatory theology of disability must create new symbols of wholeness and new ways to embody justice. She challenged Christian communities to reconceptualize Jesus Christ in a contextualized Christology based on a disabled God. Through the disabled

God, Christian communities have an opportunity to revise their engagement with people with disabilities:

■ The disabled God eradicates the notion that disability is a consequence of individual sin. The disabled God was persecuted, tortured, and impaired not because of his own sin but because of an unjust system of domination. Therefore, the bodies of people with disabilities participate in the *imago Dei* through their disabilities rather than in spite of them. Thus a new model of wholeness emerges in which disability no longer exists in opposition to divine integrity.

■ The disabled God reconceptualizes bodily perfection as "unself-pitying, painstaking survival."[27] Perfection is therefore no longer a body without blemish. Instead, perfection includes impairments from experiences of injustice and persecution.

■ The disabled God is able to celebrate joy at the same time the disabled God is able to experience pain. The disabled God understands that life is a mixed blessing in which human power has limits.

■ The disabled God does not engage in battles for domination or earthly power. This God engages with people on the margins of society to fight for justice and initiates societal transformation from a nondominant position.

■ The disabled God helps people understand that they are connected to one another through physical impairment and disability rather than in spite of it. Jesus' invitation to friends to touch his wounds after his resurrection offers critique of the social practice of avoiding the physically disabled. Jesus' invitation reminds his friends that they are connected to one another through his physical impairment and the experiences that brought about his physical reality.

■ The disabled God reminds communities of faith that some people have hidden disabilities. The piercing of Jesus' side with a sword likely resulted in internal, hidden damage to Jesus' body. Therefore, Jesus' hidden wounds are symbolic of the hidden disabilities that some people in Christian communities have. Not all disabilities are evident. Some people are suffering in silence, knowing that revealing their disabilities may result is being ostracized by the community of faith.

■ The disabled God understands human interdependence experientially because the disabled God needs care. A God who needs care helps to redefine both human and divine power. Humanity is not powerless and divinity is not all-powerful.

■ The disabled God encourages communities of faith to redefine the term *conversion* to include learning to love our existing bodies, including that which is carnal in them.

■ The disabled God enables the church to rethink the Eucharist. The church needs to physically accommodate people with disabilities so that they can fully participate. Enabling full participation does not mean simply taking the communal elements to people with disabilities wherever they are seated. Rather, it means making space and time for the people with disabilities to participate in all the ways they are willing and able. If people with disabilities want to come forward with personal assistance, wheelchairs, orthotics, leg braces, canes, or scooters, they should be allowed the time and space to do so.

One of the most important aspects of Eiesland's theology of disability is her contention that the disabled God calls on all Christians to recognize and accept the limits of human physical bodies. Jesus' physical body evidenced its limits through impairments acquired by abuse and torture. Eiesland deemed acknowledgment of the physical limits of the human body as *liberatory realism*. Liberatory realism is freedom experienced by accepting the reality that all bodies have limits. It is the truth of being human.

Eiesland highlighted the disconnect between the idealized bodies that are paraded in advertisements and the bodies of real people that fall far short of physical perfection. Attempting to realize the ideal body prevents most people from loving and appreciating their bodies just as they are.[28] When all humans accept the reality that their physical bodies have limits, attention that has been focused on attaining and retaining human perfection can be redirected to issues of justice in order to ensure that all people have access to resources they need to live full lives. Barriers that exclude and humiliate many can be torn down. Hope can be envisioned so that people with bodies outside of the previously accepted norms will realize that their lives are worth living. Those with conventional bodies may be emboldened to embrace their own bodily limitations by acknowledging that even our conventional bodies fail us at times. Those with disabled bodies may be emboldened to affirm their own bodies as good, whole, and beautiful just the way they are.[29]

Eiesland believed that human bodies are not born out of tragedy or sin. Rather, human bodies come from "ordinary women and [are] embodied unexceptionably."[30] In other words, all human bodies are subject to contingency or chance and uncertainty. Therefore, all human bodies come in three forms: temporarily able-bodied, temporarily disabled, or permanently disabled.[31] The term *temporarily able-bodied* acknowledges that even people who live healthy lives without physical or mental impairment (abnormality or loss of physiological form or function) will experience levels of disabilities as they age. With aging comes disintegration of physical and sometimes mental abilities. The term *temporarily disabled* acknowledges that even those who live most of their lives without physical or mental impairment may have a period or periods in their lives in which they are impaired. For example, when people break an arm or leg or suffer a concussion, they become disabled. Once they have healed, they may be able to resume prior levels of physiological or mental function. The *permanently disabled* are those who have permanent abnormalities or loss of physiological or mental function. By highlighting the reality that all people have the potential to be disabled, Eiesland was attempting to enlist all of God's people in her quest.

Implications for Preaching

Nancy Eiesland's work informs, challenges, and critiques all people who claim to be followers of Christ and all institutions and communities who claim to represent Christ in any way. By providing us with a history of the disability rights movement, Eiesland informs us that people with disabilities constitute a minority group that has been ignored, demeaned, ostracized, and marginalized. Before the disability rights movement began, being disabled or having a child or family member who was disabled was viewed as shameful. Parents hid their disabled children from public view. Adults, even the president of the United States, went through great pains to hide physical disabilities from the public. During the disability rights movement, many people with disabilities shed their shame and asserted their personhoods by demanding equal treatment and accommodations to enable them to live fulfilling and productive lives. Eiesland's disappointment was that churches lobbied to be exempt from complying with disability laws rather than seeing the laws as a reminder of their Christian responsibility to treat all people with dignity and respect. Preachers can help educate their congregations and encourage them to welcome people with disabilities into their communities of faith.

Eiesland's overview of the disability rights movement is an informative and necessary element of her work. It is through reference to the movement that she laid the civic foundation for a theological critique of the church and its unexamined treatment of and attitudes toward people with disabilities. While Scripture mandates exclusion, connects disabilities to sin, and espouses virtuous suffering, Eiesland challenged Christians to transcend Scripture and traditional interpretations by embracing a theology from the perspective of a disabled God. Similarly, preachers can revisit texts that include stories of healing while keeping in mind the experiences of marginalization and oppression experienced by those who are not healed as were the people in the biblical texts. (Writings such as Kathy Black's *A Healing Homiletic* can be invaluable resources.[32])

Eiesland's disabled God challenges many long-held beliefs and practices that admittedly need to be confronted and transformed for the good of all of God's people. For example, the disabled God eradicates the belief that disability is a consequence of sin or some moral shortcoming. Jesus was sinless and yet was persecuted, tortured, impaired, and killed. If sin is no longer the reason for disability, Christian communities must redefine wholeness to include disabilities of all sorts. Churches must also rethink their focus on healing. If people are not healed of their impairments, sicknesses, and diseases through prayer, are they bad Christians? Do they lack the faith necessary to receive the healing they seek?

Eiesland's challenge to all people to accept and embrace our bodily limits can be life-transforming. We are constantly bombarded with body images to which many of us aspire. People with disabilities may aspire to be "normal" so they can be accepted rather than pitied or ignored. The temporarily able-bodied may seek to attain the body images they see on television or in magazines—images that have often been photoshopped to perfection. Preachers can help their people understand that while it is important to be cognizant of our bodies as it relates to overall health, it can be detrimental to our physical, emotional, and mental well-being to continually strive to attain some ideal of physical perfection rather than embrace our bodies just the way they are.[33]

Eiesland's challenge to include people with disabilities in our communal rituals, such as the Eucharist and laying on of hands, is another reminder of the ways we have marginalized people who are members or potential members of the body of Christ. Preachers can work with their congregations to welcome people with disabilities to participate in the rituals in the ways they desire.

Eiesland wrote that disability becomes a new model of wholeness when the disabled God becomes the new symbol of the Christian faith. However, she provided no further detail about the tremendous significance of redefining wholeness. In biblical texts such as John 5:6, being made whole means to be healed of disease or infirmity. If one can be whole and be disabled, the standards for wholeness have shifted. What does this new wholeness look like? (Amos Yong's *The Bible, Disability, and the Church: A New Vision of the People of God* could be helpful here.[34])

At the beginning of her work, Eiesland acknowledged the complexity and diversity encompassed by the term *disability*. Disability includes a wide variety of physical, psychological, and intellectual functions such as deafness, paralysis, multiple sclerosis, and mental retardation. While it was necessary and understandable for Eiesland to limit the focus of her work by pursuing issues and concerns related to physical disability, it leaves us with many questions. How should Christian communities effectively and theologically accommodate the needs of all people with all forms of disability? What are some of the cultural differences that exist among various disabled communities? What are some resources to help faith communities successfully navigate some of those differences? Preachers can continue their learning on the subject through interactions and conversations with those with different disabilities and of various races, ethnicities, and cultures. (See John Swinton's *Critical Reflections on Stanley Hauerwas' Theology of Disability*.[35])

As it relates to Eiesland's reference to biblical texts, her work could have benefited from a much deeper study of biblical texts from social, historical, and cultural perspectives. By examining and highlighting the many contexts of the texts and the social and cultural dynamics at work in them, she could have helped her readers understand the role of the holiness codes in Leviticus and why they were important to the community. She could have shared why people with disabilities were such a threat to the daily existence of a nomadic and often-persecuted people. Preachers can use Eiesland's work, and the work of many other inspired biblical scholars such as Jeremy Schipper, Hector Avalos, and Amos Yong, to interpret biblical texts using the lens of disability. Their work and the work of many others can help make an even stronger biblical case for full inclusion of people with disabilities into communities of faith.

One of the most challenging of Eiesland's assertions is that the disabled God is interdependent, that the disabled God needs care and helps redefine power by demonstrating that humans are not powerless and God is not all-powerful. If the disabled God needs care and is not all-powerful, does this God cease to be God? For other marginalized communities, such as African Americans, a core theological tenet is the omnipotence of God. While they may encounter oppression and discrimination at the hands of individuals and social structures, they continue to hope for a new reality based on the belief that God is ultimately in charge and that God is all-powerful. God can change the hearts, minds, and circumstances when God wills. Though many of these communities admit that God does not always intervene in every situation, the belief that God *can* intervene gives them hope. Without hope, life would be difficult to live.

The contention that the resurrected Christ is disabled contradicts Eiesland's own definition of disabled. At the beginning of her work, she differentiated between the terms *impairment* and *disability.* By Eiesland's own definition, Jesus was impaired rather than disabled. He had holes in his hands, feet, and side. However, Jesus suffered no loss of physiological function. In fact, Jesus had powers and abilities after his resurrection that he did not have before his crucifixion. According to John 20:19, Jesus somehow entered a house where the disciples were assembled despite the door being locked. Preachers can remind their people that accuracy and consistency of biblical interpretation is important for every community of faith.

Eiesland encountered the same theological/anthropological quandary that other theologians encounter when they anthropomorphize God: we downsize God to fit into our human conceptions. In John 4:24 we learn that God is Spirit. Yet throughout the Scriptures, in our denominational traditions and in our daily lives, we ascribe human attributes to God in an attempt to better understand the God we serve. Preachers can remind their people that God is Spirit and that God as Spirit is already inclusive.

Questions for Exegesis

1. Are there people in the text who are disabled? If so, how are they treated on a daily basis? Are they marginalized and oppressed? Do they have help to get from place to place?

2. Do disabled people in the text receive healing? If so, is their healing tied to issues of sin or faith?

3. Are there people in the text who are suffering? If so, is their suffering characterized as virtuous or problematic? Is the suffering completely unacknowledged?

4. Do the people in the text experience limitations of their physical bodies? If so, what are the limitations? How do their bodily limitations affect other people in the text?

5. Do the people in the text experience a conversion of some sort? If so, does their conversion impact them spiritually, mentally, or emotionally?

6. Hermeneutical Bridge Question: Are there people in the congregation who are disabled? If so, how are they treated on a daily basis? Do they occupy positions of leadership? Are they allowed to participate fully in worship?

Notes

1. Douglas Martin, "Nancy Eiesland Is Dead at 44; Wrote of a Disabled God," http://www.nytimes.com/2009/03/22/us/22eiesland.html.

2. Ibid.

3. Nancy Eiesland, "Encountering the Disabled God," *British and Foreign Bible Society*, https://www.biblesociety.org.uk/uploads/content/bible_in_transmission/files/2004_spring/BiT_Spring_2004_Eiesland.pdf; Martin, "Nancy Eiesland Is Dead at 44."

4. Nancy Eiesland, "Revealing Pain Undoes a Social Fiction," *Emory Report* 60, no. 28 (2016), http://www.emory.edu/EMORY_REPORT/erarchive/2008/April/April21/FirstPersonNancyEisland.htm.

5. Ibid.

6. Martin, "Nancy Eiesland Is Dead at 44."

7. Ibid.

8. Eiesland, Nancy, *The Disabled God: Toward a Liberatory Theology of Disability* (Nashville: Abingdon Press, 1994), 63. Eiesland references Ellen C. Wertlieb, "Minority Group Status of the Disabled," published in the journal *Human Relations*. https://journals.sagepub.com/doi/10.1177/001872678503801104

9. John Swinton, "Who Is the God We Worship? Theologies of Disability; Challenges and New Possibilities," *International Journal of Practical Theology* 14, no. 2 (2011): 276.

10. Sharon Cuff et al., "The Intersection of Disability Studies and Health Science," *Transformations: The Journal of Inclusive Scholarship and Pedagogy* Volume 25 no. 2 (2016): 37–50.

11. Ibid.

12. Susan Wendell, *The Rejected Body: Feminist Philosophical Reflections on Disability* (New York: Routledge, 1996), 62–64.

13. Swinton, 274.

14. Eiesland, *The Disabled God*, 23–24.

15. Ibid., 110.

16. Ibid., 65.

17. Nancy L. Eiesland and Don E. Saliers, *Human Disability and the Service of God: Reassessing Religious Practice* (Nashville: Abingdon Press, 1998), 202.

18. Ibid., 203–4.

19. "Mission and History," The Center for Independent Living, Inc. (2016), http://www.cilberkeley.org/about-us/mission/.

20. Eiesland and Saliers, 208.

21. "The Americans with Disabilities Act of 1990 and Revised ADA Regulations Implementing Title II and Title III," (2016), http://www.ada.gov/2010_regs.htm.

22. Nancy Eiesland, *The Disabled God: Toward a Liberatory Theology of Disability*, 74.

23. Ibid., 12.

24. "Encountering the Disabled God," *The Other Side*, http://www.dsfnetwork.org/assets/Uploads/DisabilitySunday/21206.Eiesland-Disabled-God.pdf., 12.

25. The Shepherd Center is a private, not-for-profit 152-bed hospital for treatment, research, and rehabilitation of people with spinal-cord and brain injuries in Atlanta, Georgia. More than six thousand people receive outpatient rehabilitation services each year. See http://www.shepherd.org/about/about-shepherd.

26. A sip-puff is a motorized wheelchair for people who do not have control of their hands. It is operated by inhaling or exhaling into a straw.

27. Eiesland, *The Disabled God*, 101.

28. Ibid., 110.

29. Ibid., 95–96.

30. Ibid., 104.

31. Ibid., 110.

32. Kathy Black, *A Healing Homiletic : Preaching and Disability* (Nashville, TN: Abingdon Press, 1996). While making the case that communities of faith need to openly welcome people with disabilities into their midst, she also gives preachers strategies for preaching about faith and disability.

33. In her book *Disability and Christian Theology: Embodied Limits and Constructive Possibilities*, author Deborah Creamer builds on Eiesland's notion of limits to develop a new model of disability theology. For her model, Creamer posits that rather than making some ideal or normal body the standard by which to determine who is disabled or not, we should begin with the notion that all human bodies are limited. We tend to embrace some limits and stigmatize others. She argues that when we deny that limits are normal, we live a lie. We all have limits, our limits increase as we age, and we all have the ultimate limit, which is death. The limits model forces all of us to acknowledge that reality that we prioritize or value some limits over others. Most of all, it challenges what we designate as normal. See Deborah Beth Creamer, *Disability and Christian Theology: Embodied Limits and Constructive Possibilities*, Academy Series (Oxford, New York: Oxford University Press, 2009).

34. Amos Yong, *The Bible, Disability, and the Church: A New Vision of the People of God* (Grand Rapids, MI: W.B. Eerdmans Publishing Company, 2011). Yong challenges pastors and preachers to confront texts in the Bible with people with disabilities in ways that are affirming and liberating.

35. John Swinton, ed., *Critical Reflections on Stanley Hauerwas' Theology of Disability: Disabling Society, Enabling Theology* (Binghamton, NY: Haworth Pastoral Press, 2004). Swinton highlights Hauerwas's personal and academic theological reflections on disability.

11
LGBTIQA / Queer Vision
The Theology of Patrick Cheng

A Brief Biography

Patrick S. Cheng was born in Hong Kong in the late 1960s and moved with his parents to the San Francisco Bay area as a baby.[1] He was baptized and confirmed in the Roman Catholic Church and as a young boy wanted to become a priest. While other children in his neighborhood played cops and robbers, Patrick played Communion using Wonder Bread for wafers and grape juice for wine.[2] He was active in the Boy Scouts, eventually becoming an Eagle Scout. During his time as a scout he learned to tie square knots, overturn a capsized canoe, use an old-fashioned magnetic compass, and perform skits around a campfire. One of the most important virtues he learned during his scouting years was to be trustworthy.[3] As a child, he loved watching the *Wizard of Oz*. His favorite part of the movie, which would become symbolic of many things when he got older, was the part in which the movie switched from black and white into Technicolor.[4]

As Patrick grew older, he realized that he was gay. When he also realized that the Catholic Church he loved so much rejected him because of his sexuality, he was angry and sad. He found it difficult to reconcile theologically being both Christian and gay, and this eventually led to his desire to become a theologian later in his life.[5] Until then, however, he started to slowly drift away from the church.

He attended Yale University, where he came out of the closet. He was elected to Phi Beta Kappa and received a Bachelor of Arts in English language and literature in 1990. He was accepted into Harvard Law School, where he became an executive editor of the *Harvard Law Review*. After graduating in 1993, he served as a law clerk for a judge on the United States Court of Appeals for the Ninth Circuit in Los Angeles. He moved to New York in 1994, where he was an attorney at two different law firms. While he was still in his twenties, he was making a very comfortable salary. However, one day he told his partner (and now husband), Michael, that he did not know what his values were or what he stood for. Though successful in the eyes of the world, he felt spiritually lost.[6]

While still feeling lost, he heard about a church trial in which a bishop of the Episcopal Church was found not guilty of heresy. The priest had been on trial for ordaining an openly gay man. Cheng began researching the Episcopal Church. He liked what he found so much that he started attending The Church of Saint Luke in the Fields, an Episcopal parish in Greenwich Village that welcomed and affirmed people of all racial, sexual, and gender identities. It was there that he fell in love with God all over again. His faith in Christianity was strengthened. It was around this same time that he saw a flier on a street corner advertising a summer intensive course in biblical Hebrew at Union Theological Seminary. He knew nothing about biblical languages and felt compelled to register for the class.[7] The Hebrew class was the start of a long journey in theological education. In 1998 he enrolled in Union Seminary, where he earned a Master of Arts and Master of Philosophy before earning a PhD in systematic theology. His advisor was James Cone.

As the older of two sons in a Chinese immigrant family, Cheng struggled with his choice of vocation even as he pursued advanced degrees in theology. In the eyes of his family, he had already achieved a high level of success as an attorney. He kept working as an attorney full-time even as he worked on his dissertation. On the one hand, he felt filial responsibility to stay with the more lucrative career in law. On the other hand, he felt a call to the church and theological education. Cheng responded to that call and is now an Episcopal priest. From 2010 to 2015, he served on the faculty of the Episcopal Divinity School in Cambridge, Massachusetts. From 2015 to 2019, he served as parish priest at the Church of the Transfiguration, an historic Anglo-Catholic parish in New York City. He currently works for a national agency of the Episcopal Church and is Theologian in Residence at Saint Thomas Church Fifth Avenue in New York City.

A Theological Overview

Patrick Cheng's vision of the reign of God is one in which all people, including those who identify as lesbian, gay, bisexual, transgender, questioning, asexual or intersex and non-binary are treated with equality in the public square. Binary, socially constructed categorizations such as male and female or homosexual and heterosexual would no longer exist. Racial constructs would no longer exist as a means to marginalize some people while privileging others. People would be able move and exist without the need to claim such identities. The human bodies that traditional Christianity and other religions have deemed to be inherently sinful would be seen as good.

Cheng's theology that supports this vision can be classified as queer and rainbow. He uses *queer* as an umbrella term to refer to lesbian, gay, bisexual, transgender, intersex, questioning, and asexual (LGBTIQA) persons who identify with sexualities outside of the sexual or gender norms. The term *queer* can also refer to allies who may not necessarily identify as LGBTIQA but are in solidarity with queer people and work with them to seek a more just world for LGBTIQA people. The term intersex refers to people with the reproductive organs or external sexual characteristics of both males and females.

Cheng's theology is rainbow because it embraces and fully recognizes that many hues of race and ethnicity and many different sexualities and gender identities exist in predominantly straight and cisgender (people whose gender identity matches the sex they were assigned at birth) communities. Rainbow theology draws on the lived experiences of LGBTIQA people of color while reflecting on their positions in the marginalized communities in which they live.

It is with living at intersections in mind that Cheng critiques monochromatic theology, which focuses on a single form of oppression. Monochromatic theology is characterized by the three themes of singularity, staying home, and selecting sides. Some people experience many forms of oppression. However, singularity contends that there is one oppression that is more prevalent than all the others. Staying home contends that people who are oppressed can find a metaphorical home by being in solidarity with others who experience that same singular oppression. As it relates to selecting sides, monochromatic theology understands the world in binary terms such as the oppressor versus the oppressed, or male or female. In this worldview, the job of the oppressed person is to choose sides by selecting liberation over oppression. While selecting liberation over oppression sounds like the best course of action, problems emerge quickly for those who are afflicted with multiple oppressions. Determining which oppression from which they want to be liberated is an untenable choice. Monochromatic theology fails to address the complexities of the experiences of gay people of color.[8]

LGBTIQA people are often treated by the dominant culture and their own marginalized communities as if they should not exist. The advantages of rainbow theology are that it embraces multiplicity versus singularity, middle spaces rather than staying home, and mediation rather than selecting sides.

Cheng differentiates between sexuality and gender identity. Sexuality refers to the emotional and physical attraction people experience toward others, whether it is to those who are of the opposite sex, the same sex, or both sexes. Women who are primarily attracted to other women are known as lesbians. Men who are primarily attracted to other men are known as gay. People attracted to both women and men are known as bisexual. People who are attracted to those of the opposite sex are known as straight or heterosexual. Gender identity refers to the ways in which people identify with respect to gender (traditionally male or female). While many people identify with socially constructed gender identities that coincide with their genitalia, some people do not. People who identify most with a gender that is different from their presenting genitalia are known as transgender even when they do not have medical treatments or surgery to align their bodies with the gender with which they identify most.

In addition to being an umbrella term, *queer* can also refer to a transgressive act. "Queer" has a history of being used to disparage those whom some categorize as strange, odd, or not conforming to societal norms. When LGBTIQA people claim the term "queer," they are transforming the meaning from negative to positive. The new meaning is transgressive and positive. The Oxford English Dictionary defines the LGBTIQA community as a queer nation that is "assertively coed, multi-racial and anti-consumerist." "To queer something" now means to challenge norms and disrupt the status quo.[9] A third meaning of "queer" is grounded in the definition of Paul-Michel Foucault, a French philosopher who viewed sexuality as something to be negotiated and disseminated rather than received as natural fact. Traditional categories of gender and sexuality are social constructions. Foucault highlighted the fact that personal identity was not defined in terms of a person's preference of gender partner until the nineteenth century in Germany. It was then that sexuality became an issue of being rather than doing. Classifications such as this enable some people to exert power over others. Queer theory sees gender as a performative act with socially prescribed and accepted guidelines for gender expression. Those who act outside of the socially accepted guidelines for gender expression are categorized as deviant. The goal of the third meaning of "queer" is to deconstruct or erase categories of gender and sexuality that have traditionally been viewed as fixed by nature or essentialist.

Queer theology has four different sources: Scripture, tradition, reason, and experience. While traditional interpretations of Scripture have been developed to condemn the LGBTIQA people, queer theology reclaims Scripture by developing alternative readings of the Bible. For example, though the story of Sodom and Gomorrah in Genesis 19 has traditionally been interpreted as punishment for same-sex acts, queer interpretations contend that the text is about inhospitality. Hospitality in the ancient world was often a matter of life and death for people who were traveling in harsh desert environments. Queer interpreters point to other texts such as Ezekiel 16:48-49 as evidence that the story of Sodom and Gomorrah was about hospitality rather than sex.

Some queer theologians have argued that LGBTIQA people can be found in relationships throughout the Bible: David and Jonathan; Ruth and Naomi; the Roman centurion; the Ethiopian eunuch; and Mary, Martha, and Lazarus. Queer interpreters of the Bible also incorporate many different hermeneutic approaches, such as feminist, queer, deconstructionist, postcolonial and utopian theories, historical-critical methods, and the social sciences. Church tradition has been decidedly anti-queer. However, over the years some queer scholars have uncovered lost traditions that are inclusive of LGBTIQA people.

The Roman Catholic view that nonprocreative sexual acts are evil and contrary to natural law is largely responsible for excluding LGBTIQ people. Some queer theologians and scholars appeal to scientific evidence to argue that same-sex acts are not unnatural. While queer theologians acknowledge that there are physiological differences and that gender identity and sexuality can be immutable characteristics for some people, they also contend that on some level, gender and sexual identity are also socially constructed. They ask questions such as why a person's genitalia determine the acceptable styles with which one can wear one's hair, the types and colors of clothing one can wear, and the careers one can pursue. Behaviors that are widely accepted by society as being associated with particular biological traits are matters of social convention rather than solely matters of biology.

Queer theologians believe that God acts within the scope of the lives of LGBTIQA people even though many discount the value and worth of LGBTIQA experiences. Queer theologians such as Laurel Dykstra have written about their experiences of God in the in-between spaces of their sexuality and spirituality. Shunning purity codes helps her live a free and joyful existence rather than a life of constraint and socially mandated boundaries. For theologian Justin Tanis, transitioning from female to male was akin to answering a call to ministry. The transition was a deeply spiritual process that allows him to live an authentic life.[10]

In queer theology, the doctrine of revelation can be understood as God's coming out as radical love. By using the term *coming out,* queer theologians liken God's revelation to the self-disclosure that LGBTIQA people do with those with whom they wish to share their sexuality or gender identity. God "comes out" or shares God's self with God's people in order for God's people to know and understand God. God also comes out because God loves God's people and wants them to share in God's eternal life. Patrick Cheng contends that God's coming out is a radical act of love because it dissolves boundaries of all sorts.[11] Boundaries between humanity and God are eliminated because revelation through Scripture demonstrates God's existence within the lives of God's people. In like manner, boundaries between LGBTIQA people and their families and friends can be eliminated when they come out to them. Coming out challenges the notion that some issues of sexuality should remain unspoken or private.

God's revelation or coming out also dissolves boundaries between the powerful and the weak in society by revealing God's solidarity with the marginalized as well as with the powerful. Through Jesus' ministry God revealed God's preferential option for those who are excluded and cast out of various segments of society.

God's coming out can also dissolve boundaries between knowing and unknowing. Knowledge of God can be one of perpetual transformation just like the transgender experience. The transgender experience is not one of definitive knowledge but rather a continual journey fraught with tension and uncertainty. In this sense, God's revelation can be understood as apophatic, or developed with negative statements about the qualities and characteristics of God that God does not possess.

From the days of the early church councils of Nicaea and Constantinople, God's inherent relational nature has been communicated as being composed of one God in three persons: God the begetter, God the Son or the begotten, and God the Holy Spirit or the procession. As such, Cheng contends that God is a community within God's self. As a result, Cheng argues, since God is the manifestation of an internal community, the distinctions between the human self and human others are also disintegrated. Using the Greek term *perichoresis*, which describes the "interpenetration" of the three persons or the Trinity, Cheng makes a connection between the relationships within the Trinity and human relationships. As his point of departure, Cheng contends that the Trinity models passionate friendship. The dominant relationship paradigm into which many of us were socialized posits that there are two types of relationships: sexual and nonsexual. The only acceptable sexual relationships are monogamous ones between two people who were born male and female, accept and assimilate into traditional gender roles prescribed for their gender identities, and are married to one another in civil or religious wedding ceremonies. Sexual relationships based on this paradigm are intended to accommodate reproduction. As a result, relationships that fall outside of this paradigm are deemed unacceptable. Cheng argues that the collapse of distinctions between the self and other, and conceiving of the Trinity as passionate friendship, challenges the divide between sexual and nonsexual relationships. Passionate friendships that are inclusive of same-gender relationships are consistent with the ideals of early Christianity, which were not based on biological families but rather on passionate friendships within the body of Christ.

Cheng also contends that the divine interpenetration of the three persons of the Trinity helps people of color coalesce identities often fragmented by racial or gender oppressions. Often openly gay people of color experience oppression in the community with which they identify racially because of their sexual orientation. Openly gay people of color may experience racial oppression in predominantly white LGBTIQA communities. Openly gay people of color may also experience spiritual oppression in LGBTIQA communities that are suspicious of all people of faith and faith communities in general.

Mind-body dualism has been a dominant paradigm throughout the history of the church. All matters of the flesh, including human bodies and human sexualities, have traditionally been characterized as evil while spiritual things have been characterized as good. Plato is believed to have been the originator of this view. Other early Christian communities such as the

Gnostics and Manicheans also embraced mind-body dualism as doctrine. LGBTIQA people, and women as well, are often believed to be less pure by Christian traditions because of the association of their bodies with sex. However, some Christian theologies have rejected mind-body dualism based on their belief that God created the earth and everything that is in it out of nothing. As a result, everything that God created is good, including human bodies.[12]

Cheng contends that we must understand God as Creator in order to truly understand God. God created the heavens and the earth and everything in them. Since God is inherently relational, as evidenced by the existence of the Trinity, God created humanity as an act of radical love and not because God was lonely. Since God already experienced community in the Trinity, God did not need to create other beings to fill a void or rectify God's solitude. The radical love of God manifests itself in human creative activities in which LGBTIQA engage every day, such as singing, dancing, playing music, acting, playing, writing, or doing theology.

While the doctrine of creation understood as radical love rejects mind-body dualism, it also eliminates the dominant relationship of humanity over the rest of creation. The LGBTIQA experiences of exclusion and oppression heighten the awareness of patterns of domination in their lives and in nature. Violence in society is not inflicted only on humans; it is also inflicted on natural resources and other living things. Therefore, the rainbow covenant that God made with Noah in Genesis 9 can be a symbol for LGBTIQA people of their solidarity with all oppressed people and with all of God's creation.

Having sexualities and gender identities that do not conform to sexual behaviors deemed acceptable in select biblical texts results in LGBTIQA people being deemed sinners. This legalistic approach contends that breaking God's natural law results in punishment. As a result, many LGBTIQA people have been taught all their lives that they will go to hell. Cheng advocates for a new definition of sin: the rejection of God's radical love that is so extreme that it seeks to dissolve the boundaries and divisions that we create for one another. We are sinful, by this new definition, when we reinforce existing divisions as they relate to sexuality, gender identity, and so on.

It is with LGBTIQA people in mind that Cheng argues for the adoption of a Christ-centered model of sin and grace versus a crime-centered model.[13] He contends that the Augustinian view of original sin, in which all of humanity becomes tainted as a result of the sin of disobedience by Adam and Eve, treats sin as a crime against God. Adam and Eve are subsequently expelled from the Garden of Eden and become subject to death. Punishment also included hard labor for Adam and pain in childbirth for Eve. Additionally, the taint of original sin is passed down from generation to generation through sexual intercourse, the goodness of which can be redeemed only through marriage. Infants, for Augustine, are born under the power of the devil because their parents gave in to sexual desire.[14] Sexual organs are evil because lust is more powerful than reason.[15] Augustine's argument is largely responsible for our negative view of bodies and human sexuality. Since sex is acceptable only when used for procreation in the context of marriage, same-sex acts, which are not procreative, are sinful.

Cheng argues that if sin is a crime against God, then grace is acquittal of that crime or a declaration of innocence, and atonement is penal substitution. Grace is a free and unmerited gift from God that frees sinners from the punishment they justly deserve. Grace declares sinners to be righteous before God. Grace also provides an opportunity for sinners to be sanctified or rehabilitated—to turn away from their sinful ways. He highlights the theory of Benedictine monk Anselm of Canterbury when addressing atonement. The penal substitution model of atonement has its impetus in Anselm's theory of satisfaction, in which he argues that Adam and Eve's sin against God was so enormous that only Jesus, who was both human and divine, could satisfy the debt. Anselm's theory was modified by Reformation theologians such as John Calvin to become a theory of penal substitution in which Jesus not only paid the debt humanity should have paid but also bore the punishment humanity should have endured for their sins.

Cheng contends that a fear of collective punishment drives the continued existence of the crime-based model of sin as it relates to LGBTIQA people. Sodom and Gomorrah are destroyed, according to some interpreters, because of the existence of same-sex sexual activity. Some believe that by punishing same-sex activity, the possibility of collective punishment by God will be eliminated. Collective punishment is also a concern in Romans 1 when same-sex behavior is prescribed as punishment by God for idolatry.

Cheng argues for an alternative, Christ-centered model of sin and grace that understands sin as a sign of immaturity rather than a crime. The fall would be viewed as an act by two people in a process of maturation, which is consistent with the Eastern Orthodox reading. According to this reading, Adam and Eve were in the process of growing when the fall occurred—a state that continues with humanity today. The introduction of death into the world is viewed as an end to the ongoing suffering of immature humanity rather than punishment. Adam and Eve are not forsaken by God, nor do they suffer from a lack of grace. Rather, they experienced a "diminution of the effect of grace."[16] The starting point of the Christ-centered model is Christology rather than the doctrine of sin.

The Christ-centered model of grace also conforms to Eastern Orthodox doctrine and takes the form of *theosis*, or deification. In this model humans are seen as "constantly growing in stature towards God in Jesus Christ through the Holy Spirit."[17] Even though we may lose our way sometimes, we always find our way back to God. Cheng cites Psalm 82:6 and 2 Peter 1:4 as evidence of deification. Also, in this view, Jesus Christ is grace itself. He is the greatest unmerited gift given by God.

Atonement for the Christ-centered model is understood as renewal of the cosmos. Since humanity has lost its way, God sent the One in whom all things were created, Jesus Christ, to "gather up all things" and renew all of God's creation. The incarnation was not a plan God put in place in response to the fall. It was part of God's plan from the beginning. Jesus is the grace and the ultimate end to which all of creation is directed.

Using the Christ-centered model of sin and grace as a starting point, Cheng highlights seven models of the Queer Christ, based on reflections of LGBTIQA theologians, that serve as LGBTIQA reflections on sin and grace: the Erotic Christ, the Out Christ, the Liberator Christ, the Transgressive Christ, the Self-Loving Christ, the Interconnected Christ, and the Hybrid Christ. Each model is accompanied by one deadly sin and one amazing grace. Cheng's hope with these models is that they might change the thinking of LGBTIQA Christians in particular and all Christians in general about matters of sin and grace.

Cheng's model of the Erotic Christ reflects Jesus' embodiment of God's deepest desires for humanity. Jesus came to earth to ensure our salvation and not for God's self-gratification. Throughout his ministry Jesus demonstrated his love and desire for the people with whom he came in contact. Jesus was concerned about our needs and desires. The importance of physical touch to his ministry is exemplified when he healed people of sickness and disease through touch and when he washed the disciples' feet. Jesus was also touched by others, such as the woman with the issue of blood and Judas, whose kiss served as a sign of betrayal in the Garden of Gethsemane. Through his love and desire for others and intimate encounters, Jesus embodied African American lesbian feminist writer Audre Lorde's definition of erotic: "a deep relationship with and yearning for another person." In the erotic experience, other people are not used as "objects of satisfaction."[18] Rather, people experience joy in satisfying the desires of others. The erotic can be experienced with friends, lovers, or family members.

The deadly sin or that which opposes the revelation of God experienced in the Erotic Christ is exploitation. Exploitation is the lack of concern for the needs and desires of others, whether those desires are sexual or not. Exploitation denies consent. Consent must be an ethical norm for all LGBTIQA relationships and relationships in general. Exploitation occurs when partners are treated as mere objects of gratification, when people in the LGBTIQA community experience racism, and when LGBTIQA people experience discrimination in the wider society because of their sexuality.

The grace associated with the Erotic Christ is mutuality. Relationships, sexual and nonsexual, should be friendships that embody the values of attentiveness, community building, justice seeking, and generativity. When the grace of mutuality is present in a relationship, each person is concerned about and attends to the well-being of the other.

The Out Christ model understands that God comes out of the closet most fully in Jesus Christ. In the incarnation, ministry, crucifixion, and resurrection of Jesus, God reveals God's nature. God comes out as being in solidarity with the marginalized and the oppressed when he is born in a culture dominated by a foreign power, when he stands up for women and eunuchs, and when he speaks well of Samaritans. God also comes out as a survivor of violent abuse and suffering when Jesus endures the flogging and crucifixion. There are also times in the Bible when Jesus struggles to come out as a divine worker of miracles to those around him (Mark 7:36).

The deadly sin that opposes the Out Christ is the closet. Staying in the closet or refusing to fully reveal oneself to family, friends, coworkers, and loved ones is sin because it prevents people from truly connecting with other people when they cannot share news of intimate relationships. Being in the closet erodes self-esteem and negatively impacts overall well-being because it forces people to keep their lives secret. LGBTIQA people of color have a particularly hard time coming out if they are part of theologically conservative churches. Coming out for people of color may also bring shame upon their family members despite any other life achievements.

The grace associated with the Out Christ is the courage to come out of the closet. Cheng acknowledges that there is not one particular pattern or path for coming out. Some people come out slowly and privately. Others come out quickly and publicly. Whichever approach one chooses to take, coming out is an ongoing, lifelong process. Coming out reflects the nature of God, who is constantly revealing God's self through the Out Christ. Coming out is a gift of God because it encompasses self-love, love for other people, overcoming shame, and overcoming internalized homophobia.

The Liberator Christ model understands Christ as the One who liberates all of those bound by systemic oppressions, including heterosexism and homophobia. Jesus announced at the beginning of his ministry that he had been anointed by God to bring good news to the poor, proclaim release to the captives, and to let the oppressed go free (Luke 4:16-19). Examples of Jesus as the Liberator Christ can be seen in Matthew 25:34-46 when he establishes the mandate to feed the hungry, give drink to the thirsty, clothe the naked, visit the imprisoned, and attend to the sick. Throughout his ministry Jesus challenged the legalism of religious authorities through word and deed.

The Liberator Christ frees humanity from traditional binary thinking as it relates to sexuality and gender identity. Binary thinking is the belief that people must fall into one of two categories. For example, they must either be male or female, heterosexual or homosexual. Cheng believes that in the Liberator Christ traditional gender and sexual binaries are expanded to include bisexual, transgender, and intersex folk.

The Liberator Christ is not found in mistaken notions of liberation such as ex-gay or reparative therapy. Organizations such as Exodus International claim to free LGBTIQA people from their sexualities, gender, and gender identities (the personal sense of one's own gender which may or may not correlate with sex assigned at birth). However, respected psychological and psychiatric professional organizations repudiate those claims. Reparative therapy does not work. The liberation that many LGBTIQA people need is from self-loathing and self-hate that they sometimes learn in church.

The sin associated with the Liberator Christ is apathy. It is a sin to refuse to work to eliminate systemic oppressions that affect LGBTIQA people, including those who are additionally oppressed because of race, class, sex, age, or ability. Cheng reminds people within the LGBTIQA community of the need to be inclusive when fighting for justice. For example, some people question the need for all of the letters in the LGBTIQA acronym that also includes IQQATS—intersex, queer, questioning, allies, and two-spirit people. Apathy often results in the suffering of those who get left behind or are forgotten or intentionally abandoned.

The grace associated with the Liberator Christ is activism. The LGBTIQA rights movement started in the United States with riots at a bar in the Stonewall Inn in Greenwich Village, New York City, on June 27–28, 1968. The customers had grown tired of being routinely harassed by the police because of their sexualities. They fought back that night. Pride parades and marches held in June each year commemorate the Stonewall riots. Many organizations have formed since Stonewall to continue the fight for LGBTIQA rights. Activism is a gift from God that recognizes the interconnectedness within the body of Christ.

The Transgressive Christ model understands that Christ was crucified by the religious and political authorities of his day because he challenged their teaching and behaviors and sometimes undermined their activities. The Pharisees paid strict attention to purity laws. Instead of honoring the laws by avoiding those considered unclean, Jesus interacted with the "unclean" by touching and healing many of them, including the lepers, the disabled, and the demon-possessed. He ate with tax collectors and sinners. He healed on the Sabbath. Jesus refused to conform to conventional behaviors in other aspects of his life. For instance, he was an unmarried rabbi in his early thirties. He rejected his biological family in Mark 3 and was rejected by his hometown in Matthew 13. He told parables about people who were viewed with disdain by the Israelites, such as the Samaritans. The Transgressive Christ is in solidarity with people who decline to conform to the norms of their societies.

The sin associated with the Transgressive Christ is conformity. People who have been marginalized and rejected by society can sometimes mindlessly conform to the ways of the dominant culture. For example, LGBTIQA people of color can disown their own ethnic backgrounds and cultures in an attempt to assimilate into the white dominant

LGBTIQA culture. Conformity can also result in scapegoating. When competing groups in societies become hostile to one another, relief of those hostilities can sometimes be found by blaming problems on a scapegoat—a person, a group of people, or an outsider. After the scapegoat sacrifice has been made, the competing factions can then make peace with one another.

The grace associated with the Transgressive Christ is deviance. Deviance can be defined as transgressing or departing from social, legal, or religious norms. Though deviance can often be met with resistance and hostility and result in crucifixion, it can also include the promise of resurrection when a person seeks to live with integrity—true to their God-given sexual identity and sexuality.

The Self-Loving Christ loved himself enough to maintain that love even in the midst of adversity. Loving God and neighbor is possible only when one loves or has a positive view of the self. Jesus lived in a culture in which honor and shame were key influences. Jesus encountered ridicule and rejection because of his life circumstances, such as being birthed by a mother who was pregnant before marriage, working in the lower-class occupation of carpentry, and being expelled from his hometown. It was self-love that enabled Jesus to resist Satan's temptations in the wilderness. His positive sense of self gave him the inner strength he needed begin his ministry.

It is the same self-love that Jesus exhibited in his day-to-day interactions that enabled him to endure the suffering and persecution of the cross. Even as he was dying, he was able to forgive his persecutors and love them despite their actions. When Jesus healed those who were outcast, "unclean," and sinners, he modeled self-love. They learned from Jesus that breaking through negative social taboos and boundaries is a declaration of love of self.

The sin associated with the Self-Loving Christ is shame. Shame is the feeling that one is not worthy or is somehow defective. Whereas guilt comes from doing something wrong, shame comes from feeling that one *is* something wrong.[19] Cheng contends that the sin of shame is at the root of LGBTIQA suffering in the world. Growing up LGBTIQA in a straight world can be traumatic. Religious teachings purport gender-variant acts to be indicators of a spiritual disorder of some sort. Shame can lead to depression, anxiety, suicide, and addictive behaviors. The sin of shame can be felt even more intensely by people of color who live in a white world. Being LGBTIQA in addition to being a person of color can result in a double sense of shame.

The grace associated with the Self-Loving Christ is pride. Traditionally pride has been understood negatively. According to tradition, the sin of pride caused Adam and Eve to disobey God's direct command not to eat the forbidden fruit. However, for people who are marginalized, the sense of shame is so strong that they lack even enough pride to love themselves. But Jesus did teach that we should love our neighbors *as we love ourselves*.

The Interconnected Christ is the one in whom, according to Colossians 1:16, all things on heaven and earth were made. Therefore all things, including the cosmos, ecosystem, and world religions, are held together in the Interconnected Christ. The Interconnected Christ is very different from the globalized, imperialist, or colonialist Christ who dominates others. Instead, the Interconnected Christ realizes that all people depend on one another for their flourishing. Since the Interconnected Christ holds together the cosmos and everything in it, the Body of Christ can be conceived as including more than just the Christian church, but other religious and spiritual traditions as well.

The sin associated with the Interconnected Christ is isolation or the illusion of self-sufficiency. In this particular view of isolation, people refuse to see how all of creation is connected, how all people of the world breathe the same air, and how all people consume resources from the same planet. Cheng highlights the sin of overconsumption present in the LGBTIQA community. Middle- and upper-class LGBTIQA people, though part of a wider materialistic culture, often have a lifestyle of overspending and overconsumption. There sometimes seems to be a competition among LGBTIQA folk about who can drive the most expensive car, have the best job, or own the biggest house. This lifestyle has a disastrous impact on the entire cosmos.

The grace associated with the Interconnected Christ is interdependence. Through interdependence we recognize that all are part of one cosmic body. According to 1 Corinthians 12:21, no part of the body can say, "I have no need of you." Interdependence encompasses all of humanity regardless of race, gender/gender identity, ethnicity, or any other characteristic used by humanity to separate us or distinguish ourselves from one another. Evidence of interdependence can also be found in interfaith issues and in ecological issues. Interdependence is a central theme for the East

Asian religions and philosophies, such as the oneness found in Hinduism and the interdependence of all things in Buddhism. Through dialogue and interaction among people of different religious traditions, including Judaism and Christianity, the grace of interdependence can be experienced. As it relates to ecological issues, the grace of interdependence can be witnessed in the interaction of various elements of God's creations: humanity, land, plants, animals, water, and air.

The Hybrid Christ occupies a space outside of the traditional binary categories such as divine and human found in the words of Athanasian Creed.[20] Through his hybrid nature, Jesus challenges either/or ways of seeing the world. In his post-resurrection appearances in the Gospels, Jesus occupied yet another hybrid identity as a resurrected person with a human body. He lived between the divine world and the human world. Similarly, racial minorities also challenge either/or ways of seeing the world because though they may inhabit Asian, African, or Latino/Latina bodies, they are no longer purely Asian, African, or Latino/Latina because they live in the United States. Yet they are perceived by some in the dominant culture as foreigners because they are not white. The hybrid nature of their identities is reflected in their double consciousness or awareness of the necessity to live simultaneously in white and non-white worlds.

Bisexuals, those who are attracted to people of various gender identities, challenge the traditional heterosexual/homosexual binaries. Transgendered—those whose gender expression differs from socially constructed norms associated with their genitalia—challenge male/female binaries. Intersex people with the reproductive organs or external sexual characteristics of both males and females challenge the belief that biological sex exists only as a male/female binary.

The sin associated with the Hybrid Christ is singularity. Committing the sin of singularity means simplifying categories such as race, gender, and sexuality into separate or exclusive categories rather than acknowledging the reality that these categories overlap and intersect. Someone's racial identity should not be erased in a predominantly white LGBTIQA community. Someone's LGBTIQ identity should not be erased in predominantly Asian American, African American, Native American, or Latin American communities. The sin of singularity can also be found when sin is understood only from the perspective of the perpetrator but not also for its impact on the victims. Sin sometimes induces suffering that substantively impacts the lives of victims.

The grace associated with the Hybrid Christ is hybridity. Two or more worlds that intersect can be held together. For example, it is vital to the lives of people who exist at the intersections of multiple marginalities that the grace of hybridity be a lived reality. It was by reflecting on the nature of his own hybrid identity as a gay Asian man in his systematic theology class that Cheng realized that neither white queer theologies nor straight Asian American theologies spoke fully to his lived experiences.[21]

Implications for Preaching

Cheng's contention that sexuality and gender are social constructions enables preachers to challenge their congregants' long-held views of what it means to be a man or a woman, gay or straight. Preachers will no doubt find that many of their people have never thought about the rightness or wrongness of their conceptions of gender and sexuality. Preachers may find that if this topic has never been discussed in the congregation, laying some groundwork through their teaching ministries before preaching it from the pulpit may yield more favorable or less antagonistic responses from the congregation.

When challenging views of gender and sexuality, preachers will have an opportunity to remind the congregation of the importance of biblical exegesis. Understanding the situations and circumstances in which the people in the biblical texts lived and the contexts in which the texts were written can help the preacher make the case for congregants to reevaluate their views of gender and sexuality.

To help his readers move from a crime-based model of sin and grace to a Christ-based model, Cheng develops seven models of Christ accompanied by seven deadly sins and seven amazing graces gleaned from the writings of LGBTIQA theologians. These models provide preachers with images of Christ that relate the central figure of their faith to the experiences, plights, and struggles of people who have often been persecuted by adherents of the faith. For example, the Erotic Christ, along with Cheng's critique of mind-body dualism, can help people understand the body as inherently good, and sex, touch, and intimacy as gifts of God. At the same time preachers can warn their congregants not to exploit others in relationships of any kind. All relationships should be based on mutuality or friendship that honors the wishes and desires of all people in all relationships.

Another model of Christ that it is important for preachers to address is the Out Christ. Through Christ, God is continually revealing God's self to humanity. LGBTIQA people should feel supported and loved enough in their communities to come out about their sexualities and gender identities. Some do not come out because of fear of rejection, recrimination, or even threat of physical harm. The shame that some LGBTIQA people experience after being taught that their very existence is sinful does tremendous harm to their self-worth and their self-esteem. No one should be made to feel that their very existence is a crime against God.

Cheng's interpretation of sin as a sign of immaturity is a problematic solution to the crime-based model. He makes his proposal in response to the continued fear of the consequences of Sodom and Gomorrah. However, when making his proposal he does not develop limitations on who qualifies for this new definition by age, mental or emotional development, or experience. He does not suggest that perpetrators must take responsibility for their actions and the consequences thereof. He does not develop parameters that clarify the types of sins that can be attributed to immaturity. As a result, perpetrators of all types of sins are able to sin with impunity while claiming they were not mature enough to know better. Preachers should remind their congregants that all people, except for those with mental or physical developmental issues or of a young physical age, must take responsibility for their actions. Cheng creates more problems than he resolves by suggesting that blaming one's level of maturity for sin is somehow commensurate with the will of God.

Cheng categorizes staying in the closet or refusing to fully reveal one's sexuality as an LGBTQIA person to family, friends, coworkers, and loved ones as sin. He writes that it is sin because it prevents people from truly connecting with other people when they cannot share news of intimate relationships. While it is true that staying in the closet is a roadblock to intimacy, it is also true that many people stay in the closet because coming out can be hazardous to their emotional, mental, physical, and economic well-being. Mothers and fathers can disown their children and/or kick them out of their homes. Coworkers can verbally abuse them. Employers can fire them (though not legally in some states). Families and friends can take on feelings of shame because their loved ones are gay, lesbian, bisexual, or transgender. Rather than categorizing staying in the closet as sin, perhaps Cheng should categorize abusing someone, disowning them, or shaming them as sin. Preachers should let their people know that living by the Golden Rule is not optional. As followers of Christ, we are called to love others the way we love ourselves. Even if and when we disagree with others for any reason, we should treat them with love and respect because that is the way we wish to be treated.

When explaining his model of the Self-Loving Christ, Cheng argues that it was self-love that enabled Jesus to resist Satan's temptations in the wilderness. He believes Jesus' positive sense of self gave him the inner strength he needed begin his ministry. While Jesus undoubtedly had the inner strength he needed, perhaps it is more biblically accurate to believe that being empowered by God gave him the inner strength he needed. With that in mind, as children of God and followers of Christ, we too are empowered by God. Paul wrote in Philippians 4:13 that he could do all things through Christ who gives him strength. We can do all things too— including loving ourselves just as we are.

Questions for Exegesis

1. Does the image of Christ presented in the text reflect the Erotic, Out, Liberator, Transgressive, Self-Loving, Interconnected, or Hybrid Christ? If so, how?

2. Are the sins of exploitation, the closet, apathy, conformity, shame, isolation, or singularity being committed in the text? If so, by whom? What are some of the consequences of the sin?

3. Are the graces of mutuality, coming out, activism, deviance, pride, interdependence, or hybridity manifested in the text? If so, where are they found or experienced? How does this grace impact the lives of the people in the text?

4. Is the radical love of God that tears down existing boundaries evident in the text? If so, how or where does it show up?

5. Are there people in the text who are marginalized or oppressed because of a characteristic or trait that they cannot change? If so, who are they, and why are they being marginalized or oppressed?

6. Hermeneutical Bridge Question: Do we see any of Cheng's seven deadly sins being perpetrated upon or experienced by people in the

LGBTIQA community today? If so, which ones? What should be our response as Christians when we see these sins being perpetrated?

Notes

1. Doris Malkmus, "Rev. Dr. Patrick Cheng," LGBT Religious Archives Network, lgbttran.org.

2. Patrick S. Cheng, *From Sin to Amazing Grace: Discovering the Queer Christ* (New York: Seabury Books, 2012), 16.

3. Patrick S. Cheng, "A Scout Is Trustworthy," The Blog, July 15, 2013, huffingtonpost.com.

4. Patrick S. Cheng, *Rainbow Theology: Bridging Race, Sexuality, and Spirit* (New York: Seabury Books, 2013), Introduction. Kindle edition.

5. Patrick S. Cheng, *From Sin to Amazing Grace: Discovering the Queer Christ*, 16.

6. Ibid., 24.

7. Ibid.

8. Cheng, *Rainbow Theology: Bridging Race, Sexuality, and Spirit*. Kindle edition.

9. Patrick S. Cheng, *Radical Love: An Introduction to Queer Theology* (New York: Seabury Books, 2011), 6.

10. Ibid., 20.

11. Ibid., 45.

12. Ibid., 62–63.

13. Cheng, *From Sin to Amazing Grace: Discovering the Queer Christ*, 48–49.

14. Augustine, *Against Julian*, trans. Matthew Schumacher, *Writings of Saint Augustine*, V 16 (New York,: Fathers of the Church, Inc., 1957), 4.4.34.

15. Ibid., 4.4.35.

16. Cheng, *From Sin to Amazing Grace: Discovering the Queer Christ*, 56.

17. Ibid.

18. Cheng, *Rainbow Theology: Bridging Race, Sexuality, and Spirit*, 70–72.

19. Cheng, *From Sin to Amazing Grace: Discovering the Queer Christ*, 114.

20. The Athanasian Creed is a creed focused on the doctrine of the Trinity and humanity and divinity of Christ. The creed is credited to the fourth-century bishop of Alexandria named Athanasius. See https://www.anglicancommunion.org/media/109017/Athanasian-Creed.pdf.

21. Cheng, *From Sin to Amazing Grace: Discovering the Queer Christ*, 69–149.

12
A Vision of the Reign of God
Perspectives for the Twenty-first Century

Each of the theologians included in this book developed her or his theology in response to their situations and circumstances. They watched and studied closely what was happening in their world and then used their unique theological lenses to develop a vision of the reign of God. John Nelson Darby's vision was motivated by a disdain of scientific approaches for biblical interpretation and rejection of human traditions that sought to replace biblical mandates. Rudolf Bultmann's vision was developed in the wake of World War II while embracing scientific approaches for biblical interpretation. Martin Luther King Jr.'s vision grew out of personal and communal experiences of systemic racism and the civil rights movement. Jürgen Moltmann's view was inspired by his experiences as a prisoner of war in World War II and interactions with disparate theological views from all over the world. The theology of Elisabeth Schüssler Fiorenza grew out of her experiences, the experiences of other women, and sexism in the academy and the Catholic Church. Walter Rauschenbusch's perspective was informed by the lived experiences of poor German immigrants in Hell's Kitchen. The view of James Cone was inspired by personal and communal experiences of systemic racism, the black power movement, the demands of African American students at Philander Smith, and the speeches of Malcolm X. Emilie Townes's vision was inspired by the sexism of black liberation theology, the racism of the feminist movement, and black women's experiences of living at the intersection of gender, race, and class oppression. Ada María Isasi-Díaz's vision was developed in response to the experiences of grassroots Latinas of sexism, racism, and classism in the church and wider society. Nancy Eiesland developed her convictions after experiencing the rejection of disabled people from the life and ministries of churches and after participating in the disability rights movement. Patrick Cheng's vision was informed by his personal experiences and the experiences of LGBTQIA people around the issues of race, gender, and sexual orientation that can lead to discrimination and marginalization inside and outside of the church.

By understanding the vision of each theologian, preachers can broaden their theologies to include people and perspectives they may not have incorporated in the past. For example, many congregations have never thought about how their preaching and teaching, as well as accessibility of their facilities to the disabled, impacts whether people with disabilities feel welcome. Nor have they considered how they relate to people with disabilities. How people relate to LGBTQIA people is shaped by one's theology. Issues of race, gender, and class are matters for theological reflection, as is our vision for the reign of God.

A Holistic Vision of the Reign of God

What follows are just a few of the theological concepts from each theological perspective that can be incorporated into a holistic vision of the reign of God.

Rudolf Bultmann contrasts life in the world with genuine human life or life in the Spirit, which is lived out of what is invisible and nondisposable. Life in the Spirit is made possible through God's grace which we experience as love. Bultmann defines grace as forgiveness of sin and liberation from our pasts which threaten to hold us in bondage. The grace of God allows us to let go of things of the flesh that prevent us from embracing the future that God has in store for us.

Sin for Bultmann is the attitude with which we try to secure our own futures without God. Sin includes being high-handed and rebellious. Sin is grabbing hold of that which we should let go and clinging to that which is in the process of perishing or has already perished. Sin is closing off God's future by refusing to let go of the past. Our sins are forgiven when we open ourselves to grace and renounce all attempts to be acceptable by the standards of the world.

Bultmann concluded that salvation from nihilism can be found in Christianity. In Christianity, humans can experience "radical freedom"—freedom from their own pasts through the grace of God available in the person and work of Jesus Christ. Jesus Christ is the eschatological event by which the old world of believers has come to an end. Once believers accept Christ as their Savior, they are new creatures in Christ Jesus.

As a result of experiencing radical freedom, Christian existence therefore becomes eschatological existence. In this new existence, it is not history and the world that change but rather the newly converted Christian's attitude toward the world.[1] In this new existence, the Christian decides on a new self-understanding for responsible acting. Responsible acting is grounded in Christian love. In this sense, Christian life is one lived from a future where humans find freedom from themselves. This new life of freedom is the result of a conscious decision to accept a new life grounded in the grace of God. For Bultmann, eschatological moments are realized in Christian faith and preaching.[2]

Elisabeth Schüssler Fiorenza calls Jesus' vision of the kingdom of God the *basileia* of God.[3] She prefers to use words such as "domain" or "commonweal" when referring to the Greek *basileia* because those terms underscore how different the Jesus movement was from the Roman Empire in which the movement emerged.[4]

Fiorenza contends that the approach to life and ministry was different for Jesus' renewal movement than for other Jewish renewal movements. People who were part of Jesus' renewal movement did not perceive of God as a divine warrior or king. Rather, they perceived of God as divine Sophia or Wisdom. In the Jewish wisdom tradition, the Sophia goddess language is used to speak about the one God of Israel "whose gracious goodness is divine Sophia."[5] In the Wisdom of Solomon, which is included in the Roman Catholic but not the Protestant canon, Wisdom offers rest, knowledge, salvation, and life for all who accept her. As a result of Jesus' and the movement's very different conception of God, the basileia of God was a radically inclusive reality.

In the basileia of God, all people are welcome, including sinners such as tax collectors and prostitutes. God is on the side of the poor and against all who deny them their basic human rights. Salvation is present in healing moments such as when Jesus cast out demons, healed the sick, and told stories about how the last would be first. In the basileia of God wholeness and holiness are one and the same.

Jesus challenged patriarchal beliefs and structures that oppressed and marginalized women in the domain of God. For example, in Mark 10:2-9, when the Pharisees asked Jesus if it was lawful for a man to divorce his wife, Jesus provided a nuanced response. Jesus asked the Pharisees, "What did Moses command you?" The Pharisees accurately stated that Moses permitted a man to divorce his wife. Jesus then informed them Moses wrote that law because human hearts were hard. He also reminded them that the man was supposed to leave his patriarchal household and join with the woman as one flesh in an equal partnership made possible by the Creator God.

According to James Cone, sin is a way of life in which people cease to be human because of their willingness to participate in the oppression and misery of others. When people live in sin, they live in accordance with their own personal values in pursuit of their personal interests. Cone contends that whiteness is sin that causes whites to believe they are chosen by God to receive special privileges in the world. This sin permeates human beings and renders them incapable of recognizing some structures and conditions as sin.

Cone differs from other theologians who contend that all people are made in the image of God as an unchanging existential reality. While all humans are created in the image of God, he believes that they do not always reflect the image of God in their interactions with others. To be the image of God means being human. Being human means having the freedom to be creative, to treat others humanely, and to oppose acts of inhumanity. Anyone who oppresses others ceases to be human and therefore ceases to be the image of God.[6]

The theological conception of God as Creator has particular significance in black liberation theology. The reality that all humans are created by God means that the purpose and meaning of each human's existence is not found in the oppressors but in God. God is the source of all being. This means that God, not whiteness or how whiteness is perpetuated and embodied in the world, dictates how humans should behave. Humans who claim to follow Christ owe obedience only to God. Black people who are minorities in a world defined by whiteness must resist behavioral dictates that are contrary to the will of God. This is why Cone insists that the term *black revolution* is more apropos than the term *reformation,* which assumes that the system needs only to be cleaned up a bit. The system of whiteness needs to be abolished, not reformed. God as Creator means that the oppressed are free to revolutionize society.[7]

Cone stresses the immanence of God—God's activity in concrete historical situations of human existence. Rather than conceiving of God as a pious feeling in human hearts or believing that God is up in heaven,

Cone contends that God can be found in the world wherever liberation from suffering is occurring.

Using characters from Alice Walker's novel *The Color Purple* and the life of Ida B. Wells-Barnett, Emilie Townes challenges prevailing views of God as exclusive, patriarchal, and wrathful. Instead, she asserts that God is a loving God who celebrates all loving and consensual relationships, including those between people of the same gender. Townes believes that a new heaven and a new earth will not come into being without the exploration and dismantling of evil as cultural production. Stereotypes such as the Mammy were fictionalized depictions of African American women intended to provide cover for white men who raped African American women with impunity. In addition, the commodification of Aunt Jemima on pancake boxes and pancake syrup and in the form of salt and pepper shakers, rag dolls, and cookie jars further ensconced the Mammy image in the psyche of all of those engaging in the public square. Ronald Reagan's use of the Mammy as Welfare Queen demonstrates how damaging stereotypes can be used as pretexts to shape public policy.

Townes argues that human health is a cultural production influenced by many different factors separate and apart from the availability and quality of health care, including poverty, lack of educational opportunities, lack of access to healthy food, and low wages. In a new heaven and new earth, all people will have equal access to comprehensive and affordable health care.

John Nelson Darby believed there are two kinds of love, both of which are divine: downward and upward. Downward love works in human hearts toward other people, while upward love is love toward God and directly affects that state of the human soul.[8] Downward love feels the pain of those who are suffering, just as Christ did. Darby believed that it is not enough for a Christian to love others as they love themselves. They must love in a way that is above all the evil and sin in the world. They must love as Christ loves them.

In addition, Darby did not believe that the impact of faith on the lives of believers was a personal choice. All people who claim to be followers of Jesus Christ are mandated to be obedient to God in every way. The responsibility of Christians in their daily lives is to behave as if they are already Christians rather than as if they are aspiring to be Christians.[9] Therefore, behaving according to one's own will is a sin. Likewise, any human behavior that contradicts the will of God is also sin.

Salvation for Darby is a state of being that occurs when a person becomes conscious of her or his own sin and guilt and through Jesus Christ has past sins erased and assumes a new, righteous condition before God.[10] Being in a new condition means that the believer is now "in Christ" rather than "in the flesh" and lives life anew in obedience to God.

For Martin Luther King Jr., the "image of God" is a biblical phrase that refers to the inherent dignity and innate worth of all humans. Since all humans are created in the image of God, there is "no graded scale of essential worth."[11] No one race has more divine right than any other. The "indelible stamp" of the Creator is etched in the personality of every human.[12]

In addition to treating African Americans like animals, segregation treated them like social lepers—people ostracized or outcast because of physical conditions or characteristics over which they have no control. Being treated as social lepers inflicts immeasurable psychological harm and creates fears, resentments, anxieties, and sensitivities that "make each day of life a turmoil."[13] The ethos of the beloved community further distinguishes itself from secular society for King through its mandate to be guided by love in all things. Since all people are loved by God, they must be respected. It is not a person's intellect, race, or social position that determines human worth. Rather, each person is valued simply because they are valued by God.[14]

King believed that voluntary undeserved suffering is redemptive because it has the potential to educate and transform. He quotes Gandhi when teaching and preaching about suffering: "Things of fundamental importance to people are not secured by reason alone, but have to be purchased with their suffering."[15] For King, suffering is powerful because it has the potential to shame the opponents into a change of heart.[16] When nonviolent adherents refuse to physically attack their oppressors, they expose the barbarity of the oppressor for the world to see.[17] The act of "self-suffering," or suffering as a voluntary act, is the sacrificial offering of a person who sees the misery of people so clearly that she or he is willing to suffer on their behalf to bring an end to it.[18]

Negative peace exists when there is the presence of "stagnant passivity and deadening complacency."[19] When people are too scared or too apathetic to fight for their basic human rights, there exists a negative peace. The beloved community for King is a place of positive peace where the hard-fought battles for justice and equality have been won. It is also a place where people contend in good faith to work with one another to maintain those hard-fought gains.[20] Some of King's harshest words were aimed not only at people who actively try to obstruct the causes of justice but also at those who sit back, watch injustice happen, and say or do nothing while the rights of others are being trampled underfoot.

For King, a nation that was as morally bankrupt as the United States needed to undergo a revolution of values in order to finally become a beloved community. A true revolution of values would cause the United States to shift from a thing-oriented society to a people-oriented society, from a society focused on material prosperity to a nation focused on meeting needs of its people.

According to Jürgen Moltmann, God, the Father of Jesus, cannot be defined in unisexual and patriarchal terms. God is both a motherly father and a fatherly mother of the Son. Therefore, by rejecting the patriarchal doctrine of the Trinity, Christians find the ability to overcome sexist terminology in our language for God. By embracing the Trinity, Christians can fellowship with one another without privilege and subordination. When Christians are in fellowship with their "first-born brother"—Jesus—there is no longer male or female. As Paul contends in Galatians 3:28-29, all are one in Christ and are joint heirs according to the promise.

Moltmann highlights the work of the Holy Spirit in healing when he rejects the notion that health and healing are solely about physical or mental cures or restoration of full physical functioning. The Holy Spirit also heals through restoration of relationships. When Jesus healed people with physical or mental illness, he also restored their relationships with God and with other people. People cannot not fully experience healing and health if their relationships with others are somehow disrupted. Healing happens in restored commitments, reestablished trust, and new sociality.

Rather than approaching nature as something to be dominated or conquered, humanity should see nature as something to be respected. New models of cooperation that seek a partnership with nature should recognize that as a creation of God, nature has rights that need to be respected. When humans finally exist in peace with nature, they will realize liberation. When all people are free and nature is no longer enslaved, the kingdom of God will have arrived.

Moltmann espouses that the theology of the crucified God liberates humanity from idolatry. Humans have the propensity to make idols of ideology and tradition. They worship their own works and bow down to their own gods—such as nationalism, xenophobia, anti-Semitism, racial hatred, class profit, consumption, and anti-social attitudes—thereby becoming neurotic or embroiled in anxiety. These idols produce relative values instead of absolute values. They produce transitory happiness instead of eternal joy. Therefore, when their expectations of joy and happiness do not materialize or are experienced only in the short term, humans resort to ungodly methods to resolve their conflicts. They make their enemies into demons and kill them spiritually. Worship of idols produces a type of slavery that compels humans to act outside of the will of God.

When the church separates itself from politics, it can then coexist easily with any form of social or economic oppression. The freedom that people of God experience in faith can become a substitute for the political freedom they cannot experience in the world. People can be saved spiritually but be in bondage and suffer injustice physically, mentally, and emotionally. For Moltmann, this model does not fully live up to the responsibilities of those who have truly experienced the crucified God.

Walter Rauschenbusch believed that Jesus' most fundamental virtue is love. Love creates fellowship and bonds humans to one another. Love for Jesus is not a fickle emotion. Rather, love for Jesus is "the highest and most steadfast energy of a will bent on creating fellowship."[21] Love creates a sense of worth for those receiving it, pride when those we love advance, pain when they suffer, joy in their happiness and realization of solidarity.[22]

Rauschenbusch defined sin as selfishness. Selfishness has personal, ethical, and social implications that render it very different from the conceptions of sin of the Greek fathers.[23] The Greek fathers viewed sin as sensuousness and materiality. Rauschenbusch believed that clarifying the definition of sin and declaring the doctrine of total depravity unbiblical clears the way for a gospel that better reflects the biblical texts and the life and teachings of Jesus.

Rauschenbusch defines salvation as a change that turns people from self to God and humanity, affirming that "salvation is the voluntary socializing of the soul."[24] Selfish people believe they are the centers of the universe and God and all of humanity are created to serve their pleasures. A person who experiences salvation in the kingdom of God undergoes a reorientation to the common life and good of all humankind. Conversion in the kingdom becomes more than a break with one's own sinful past. Rather, it is also a break with the sinful past of a social group. Regeneration is the creation of new life within us that allows us to see the kingdom of God as it is found in the story of Nicodemus in John 3:1-21. Through regeneration, the light of Christ can shine and create a new religious identity.[25]

One of the most important and needed functions of the social gospel, according to Rauschenbusch, is to reclaim the image of God developed for and by those on the margins or those in solidarity with those on the margins. The image of God needs to be reclaimed because throughout the history of Christianity the images of kings, governors, or others who were the greatest purveyors of earthly powers have been superimposed on God. The image of God has also been tainted by the use of Christianity to colonize world populations. Rauschenbusch cites the proliferation of the myth that Negroes are not descended from Adam but rather from African jungle beasts in order to place Negroes outside of the protection of moral law. Rauschenbusch believes that God has shown God's self to be a barrier breaker.

Ada María Isasi-Díaz believes salvation is a gift of God; it is not earned or won through struggle. Salvation occurs within the realm of human history through God's actions that break into and shape human history, including creation, incarnation, and redemption.[26] For Latinas, experiencing the salvation of God means having a relationship with God that requires them to love their neighbors. These Mujeristas believe that their relationships with God impact every aspect of their lives, and they reject any conception of salvation that does not affect their present and future reality.[27] The state of salvation is contingent not only upon the degree to which people love God but also the degree to which they love their neighbors, which is expressed through solidarity.

The term *kingdom* is packed with gendered language that supports systemic oppression through hierarchical and patriarchal structures. The term also refers to a time and sociopolitical configuration with which few people in the twenty-first century can relate. The metaphor of "kin-dom," however, suggests that the people of God are a family that transcends blood relationships and embraces friendships, love, care, and community. Kin-dom also displaces the primacy of the traditional nuclear family in which the man is the head and chief decision maker for an individualized, inwardly focused, self-contained unit.

Nancy Eiesland believes that human bodies are not born out of tragedy or sin. Rather, human bodies come from "ordinary women" and are "embodied unexceptionably."[28] In other words, all human bodies are subject to contingency and uncertainty and come in three forms: temporarily able-bodied, temporarily disabled, or permanently disabled.[29] "Temporarily able-bodied" acknowledges that even people who live healthy lives without physical or mental impairment (abnormality or loss of physiological form or function) will experience levels of disabilities as they age. With aging comes disintegration of physical and sometimes mental abilities. "Temporarily disabled" acknowledges that even those who live most of their lives without physical or mental impairment may have a period or periods in their lives in which they are impaired. For example, when someone breaks an arm or leg, that person becomes disabled. Once they have healed, they may be able to resume prior levels of physiological or mental function. The "permanently disabled" are those who have permanent abnormalities or loss of physiological or mental function.

Eiesland highlights the disconnect between the idealized bodies that are paraded in advertisements and the bodies of real people that fall far short of physical perfection. Attempting to realize the ideal body prevents most people from loving and appreciating their bodies just as they are.[30] When all humans accept the reality that their physical bodies have limits, attention that is now focused on attaining and retaining human perfection can be redirected to issues of justice to ensure that all people have access to resources they need to live full lives.

The disabled God eradicates the notion that disability is a consequence of individual sin. The disabled God was persecuted, tortured, and impaired not because of God's own sin but because of an unjust system of domination. Therefore, the bodies of people with disabilities participate in the *imago Dei* (image of God) through their disabilities rather than in spite of them. As a result, a new model of wholeness emerges in which disability no longer exists in opposition to divine integrity.

Patrick Cheng contends that the Self-Loving Christ loved himself enough to maintain that love even in the midst of adversity. Loving God and neighbor is possible only when one loves or has a positive view of the self. Jesus lived in a culture in which honor and shame were key influences, and he encountered ridicule and rejection because of his life circumstances, such as being birthed by a mother who was pregnant before marriage, working in the lower-class occupation of carpentry, and being rejected by his hometown. It was self-love that enabled Jesus to resist Satan's temptations in the wilderness. His positive sense of self gave him the inner strength he needed begin his ministry.

The sin associated with the Self-Loving Christ is shame. Shame is the feeling that one is not worthy of unconditional love or somehow defective. Whereas guilt comes from doing something wrong, shame comes from feeling that one's self is somehow wrong.[31] Cheng contends that the sin of shame is at the root of LGBTIQA suffering in the world. Growing up LGBTIQA in a straight world can be traumatic, and religious teachings usually purport gender-variant acts to be indicators of a spiritual disorder of some sort. Shame can lead to depression, anxiety, suicide, and addictive behaviors. The sin of shame can be felt even more intensely by people of color who live in a white world. Being LGBTIQA in addition to being a person of color can result in a double sense of shame.

The grace associated with the Self-Loving Christ is pride. Traditionally pride has been understood negatively. According to tradition, the sin of pride caused Adam and Eve to disobey God's direct command not to eat the forbidden fruit. However, for people who are marginalized, the sense of shame is so strong that they lack even enough pride to love themselves. After all, Jesus did teach that we should love our neighbors as we love ourselves.

Mind-body dualism has been a dominant paradigm throughout the history of the church. All matters of the flesh, including human bodies and human sexualities, have traditionally been characterized as evil, while spiritual things have been characterized as good. Aristotle is believed to have been the originator of this view. Other early Christian communities such as the Gnostics and Manicheans also embraced mind-body dualism as doctrine. LGBTIQA people in general and women in particular are believed to be less pure by Christian traditions because of the association of their bodies with sex. However, some Christian theologies have rejected mind-body dualism based on their position that God created the earth and everything that is in it out of nothing, and that everything that God created is good, including human bodies.[32]

A godly vision of the reign of God will include all of God's people. The visions shared in this text help develop a vision of the reign that honors all of God's people.

Using Visions of the Reign of God for Exegesis

When teaching these diverse visions of the reign of God, I am asked how to use them for preaching. I will briefly outline a process for exegeting a text using Elisabeth Schüssler Fiorenza's perspective as our point of departure. The sermon I developed by using this approach, which I preached in June 2014 while teaching in the ACTS Doctor of Ministry program at the Lutheran School in Chicago, is included in its entirety for reference (see the Afterword). The process of sermon development outlined below has nine steps.

1. Invite the Holy Spirit into the sermon development process.
James Forbes, pastor emeritus of the Riverside Church in New York City, reminds preachers of the importance of the Holy Spirit for preaching. For Forbes, godly preaching is impossible without the Holy Spirit. When empowered by the Spirit of God, all believers become more effective in their ministries.[33] He argues that the presence of the Holy Spirit provides wisdom and knowledge of human situations and circumstances while also providing believers with the power to facilitate abundant life. In addition, those who are confident of the power of the anointing working in their lives will have more confidence that their ministries make a difference in the lives of God's people than those without the anointing.[34]

2. Through the direction of the Holy Spirit, select the text you believe God is calling you to preach.
I chose Mark 1:40-45 after having read it for my personal devotions. I felt that the pastors and preachers who would be attending the worship service would relate well to text. Like all preachers should do, I invited the Holy Spirit into the entire sermon development process.

> A leper came to him begging him, and kneeling he said to him, "If you choose, you can make me clean." Moved with pity, Jesus stretched out his hand and touched him, and said to him, "I do choose. Be made clean!" Immediately the leprosy left him, and he was made clean. After sternly warning him he sent him away at once, ⁵saying to him, "See that you say nothing to anyone; but go, show yourself to the priest, and offer for your cleansing what Moses commanded, as a testimony to them." But he went out and began to proclaim it freely, and to spread the word, so that Jesus could no longer go into a town openly, but stayed out in the country; and people came to him from every quarter. (Mark 1:40-45)

3. Ask questions and research answers to one or more of the questions at the end of the selected chapter to interrogate the text. The Bible, biblical commentaries, Bible dictionaries or encyclopedias, and scholarly books or articles can provide answers to your questions.

I used questions one, three, and five from my chapter about Schüssler Fiorenza to guide my exegesis of the text.

> **Is there evidence of the *basileia* of God in the text (equal opportunities and valuing of all of God's people)? If so, what is it?**
> When Jesus allowed the man with leprosy to approach him, he was defying the conventions of his society that demanded that anyone with leprosy separate himself from others. The man made the request that Jesus heal him, and Jesus honored his request. By treating the man like he treated everyone else, Jesus was giving the marginalized and oppressed man with leprosy the same opportunity he gave everyone else to experience wholeness.

> **Are there any people in the text living under patriarchal domination or oppression? If so, who?**
> The man with leprosy is outcast from his society. According to Leviticus 13:45-46, the leper was considered unclean and must live separate and apart from those who do not have the disease. The leper also had to identify himself as someone who is unclean by crying out "unclean, unclean" when walking among those who were disease-free.

> **Is the salvation of God evident in the text (through healing, wholeness, holiness, etc.)?**
> The salvation of God is evident in the text through Jesus' healing of the man with leprosy restoring him to the wider community. One scholar contends that physical healing is evidence of the reign of God. Disease disrupts the type of existence God has in mind for God's people. By healing people of disease and illness and/or restoring them to their communities, Jesus is anticipating the kingdom that God will establish in full in the future. People who are healed are participants in and forerunners of the new and transformed earthly existence that is to come.[35]

4. Ask and find responses to any other questions that come to mind. Answer fully so they will be helpful in understanding the text.

What was happening in the text before the healing that could help people understand the text better?

Jesus declared, "The time is fulfilled, and the kingdom of God has come near." He told the people to repent and believe in the gospel. Jesus healed a man with an unclean spirit. He also healed Simon's mother who was in bed with a fever.

What conceptions of the kingdom of God can be helpful for understanding this text?

Schüssler Fiorenza writes that the basileia of God is a radically inclusive reality, meaning that all people are welcome, including sinners such as tax collectors and prostitutes. God is on the side of the poor and against all who deny them their basic human rights. Salvation is present in healing moments such as when Jesus cast out demons, healed the sick, and told stories about how the last would be first. In the basileia of God, wholeness and holiness are one and the same.

What are other possible definitions of the basileia of God?

Basileia can mean kingship, dominion, rule, or reign.[36]

5. Review implications for preaching included in the selected chapter for resonance with answers to questions and the leading of the Holy Spirit. Cite the implication(s) that relate to your text.

Using Schüssler Fiorenza's inclusive conception of the basileia of God, preachers can remind their people that the reign of God is both present and yet to come. While many think of the reign or kingdom of God in terms of God's apocalyptic in-breaking into human history, Schüssler Fiorenza focuses our attention on the implication of the basileia for daily living. Therefore, while many eagerly await Christ's Second Coming, we are also reminded that as a redeemed people we have responsibilities for the welfare of God's creation in the here and now.

6. Write a theme in twelve words or less that summarizes what you want people to take away from the sermon.

The succinct theme is used as a guide to keep the sermon focused. Without a succinct theme, it is easy to include thoughts, stories, and illustrations that send the sermon in many different directions.

Theme: God sets the oppressed free in the reign of God.

7. Choose a sermon structure.

I used a version of Paul Scott Wilson's *Four Pages of the Sermon*.[37] In his book, Wilson provides details of a structure that encourages the preacher to identify and develop the trouble or conflict in the Bible while also identifying and developing similar trouble or conflict in our world. By building in the need for the preacher to identify and develop grace in both the text and our world, preachers are reminded of the importance of grace in the lives of the people of God. My structure took the following form:

> Introduction
> Trouble in the text
> Grace in the text
> Trouble in the world
> Grace in the world
> Conclusion

8. Write the sermon.

I write out a full manuscript for every sermon I preach. I require my students to do the same. By writing out a manuscript, I have to think through every move of the sermon. I have to think through my transitions from one part of the sermon to the next. Writing out the sermon forces me to think through my wording and phrasing so that it will be well-received by the intended congregation.

Another advantage of a manuscript is that it can be posted on websites and blogs after it is preached. Some people like to read sermons. Though I write a complete manuscript, I don't preach from it. I convert the manuscript into an outline. An outline frees me from being tied to the text so I can better interact with the congregation during the sermon. An outline also provides enough of a guide to help me stay on point. I tell my students that though they too are required to write out a manuscript, they don't have to preach from it. They can convert their sermons to an outline, format the manuscript into bullet points, or condense the manuscript to main points that can be written on small sticky notes. They can also preach without any notes. But writing out a manuscript starts the internalization process that continues in the rehearsal.

9. Rehearse the sermon.

In order to deliver a sermon with confidence, I have to rehearse it out loud many times. Two things happen when I rehearse the sermon: I hear flaws in the general flow of the sermon, and I change language that worked well in the written manuscript to language more suitable for oral communication. It is also in this phase of the sermon development process that I finalize the introduction and conclusion by making sure they work well together. It is after I have established the rhythm of the sermon that I am able to develop an appropriate introduction and conclusion.

After inviting the Holy Spirit into the sermon development process, selecting and exegeting the biblical text, developing a theme, choosing a sermon structure, and writing and rehearsing the sermon, the preacher is ready to deliver it. Though it may be tempting to continue tweaking the sermon up until the time of delivery, the preacher must decide consciously when to let go of the sermon and invite the Holy Spirit to have its way with it.

Notes

1. Rudolf Bultmann, *History and Eschatology: The Presence of Eternity* (New York: Harper Torchbooks, 1957), 153.

2. Ibid., 154.

3. Elisabeth Schussler Fiorenza, *In Memory of Her: A Feminist Theological Reconstruction of Christian Origins*, 10th anniversary ed. (New York: Crossroad, 1994), 120.

4. Elisabeth Schussler Fiorenza, "To Follow the Vision: The Jesus Movement as Basilea Movement," in *Liberating Eschatology: Essays in Honor of Letty M. Russell*, Margaret A. Farley and Serene Jones, eds. (Louisville: Westminster John Knox Press, 1999), 134–35.

5. Ibid., 135.

6. James H. Cone, *A Black Theology of Liberation*, 20th anniversary ed. (Maryknoll, NY: Orbis Books, 1990). 90–94.

7. Ibid., 74–76.

8. John Nelson Darby, "1 Corinthians 13," *Stem Publishing*. http://stempublishing.com/authors/darby/EXPOSIT/26020-6E.html#a13.

9. John Nelson Darby, "What Is the Responsibility of the Saints?," *Stem Publishing*, http://stempublishing.com/authors/darby/PRACTICE/17012E.html.

10. John Nelson Darby, "Salvation and Separation," *Stem Publishing*, http://stempublishing.com/authors/darby/NOTESJOT/40010E.html.

11. Martin Luther King Jr., "The Ethical Demands for Integration," *A Testament of Hope: The Essential Writings and Speeches*, ed. James M. Washington (New York: HarperCollins, 1986), 119.

12. Ibid.

13. Ibid., 121.

14. Ibid.

15. Martin Luther King Jr., "An Experiment in Love," *A Testament of Hope: The Essential Writings and Speeches*, ed. James H. Washington (New York: HarperCollins, 1986), 18.

16. Martin Luther King Jr., "My Trip to the Land of Gandhi," *A Testament of Hope: The Essential Writings and Speeches*, ed. James M. Washington (New York: Harper-Collins, 1986), 26.

17. Martin Luther King Jr., "Stride toward Freedom," *A Testament of Hope: The Essential Writings and Speeches*, ed. James M. Washington (New York: HarperCollins, 1986), 485.

18. Martin Luther King Jr., "Nonviolence: The Only Road to Freedom," *A Testament of Hope: The Essential Writings and Speeches*, ed. James H. Washington (New York: HarperCollins, 1986), 57.

19. Martin Luther King Jr., "Love, Law, and Civil Disobedience," *A Testament of Hope: The Essential Writings and Speeches*, ed. James M. Washington (New York: Harper-Collins, 1986).

20. Ibid.

21. Walter Rauschenbusch, *Christianity and the Social Crisis in the 21st Century: The Classic That Woke Up the Church*, Paul B. Raushenbush, ed. (New York: HarperOne, 2007), 55–57.

22. Walter Rauschenbusch, *Dare We Be Christians?* (Cleveland: Pilgrim Press, 1993).

23. Walter Rauschenbusch, *A Theology for the Social Gospel* (New York: The Macmillan Company, 1917).

24. Ibid., 99.

25. Ibid., 100.

26. Ada Maria Isasi-Diaz, *En La Lucha = In the Struggle: A Hispanic Women's Liberation Theology* (Minneapolis: Fortress Press, 1993), 35.

27. Ibid. 34–35.

28. Nancy Eiesland, *The Disabled God: Toward a Liberatory Theology of Disability* (Nashville: Abingdon Press, 1994), 104.

29. Ibid., 110.

30. Ibid.

31. Patrick S. Cheng, *From Sin to Amazing Grace: Discovering the Queer Christ* (New York: Seabury Books, 2012), 114.

32. Patrick S. Cheng, *Radical Love: An Introduction to Queer Theology* (New York: Seabury Books, 2011), 62–63.

33. James Forbes, *The Holy Spirit and Preaching* (Nashville: Abingdon Press, 1989), 50.

34. Ibid.

35. Warren Carter, "Jesus' Healing Stories: Imperial Critique and Eschatological Anticipations in Matthew's Gospel," *Currents in Theology and Mission 37*, no. 6 (December 2010): 496.

36. Walter Bauer, *A Greek-English Lexicon of the New Testament and Other Early Christian Literature*, ed. Frederick W. Danker, 3rd ed. (Chicago: University of Chicago Press, 2000).

37. Paul Scott Wilson, *The Four Pages of the Sermon: A Guide to Biblical Preaching* (Nashville: Abingdon Press, 1999).

Afterword
A Chance of Reign
Mark 1:40-45

A leper came to him begging him, and kneeling he said to him, "If you choose, you can make me clean." Moved with pity, Jesus stretched out his hand and touched him, and said to him, "I do choose. Be made clean!" Immediately the leprosy left him, and he was made clean. After sternly warning him he sent him away at once, saying to him, "See that you say nothing to anyone; but go, show yourself to the priest, and offer for your cleansing what Moses commanded, as a testimony to them." But he went out and began to proclaim it freely, and to spread the word, so that Jesus could no longer go into a town openly, but stayed out in the country; and people came to him from every quarter.

I have a Weather Channel app on my phone. I look at it several times a day especially during the spring and summer to check on the chance of rain. I plan my activities at home around it. When I don't have to be at the seminary and when I don't have a pile of papers to grade or an article to write, I look at my phone to decide whether it is a good day to be outside. I check to see if it is a good day to go for a walk, weed the garden, or mow the lawn. When the chance of precipitation is 30 or 40 percent, I know it may rain lightly or for a short while. When the chance is more than 70 or 80 percent, I know it is not just likely to rain a little. It will probably rain hard. That means it's a nice day to stay inside and read some eschatology.

In the title of my message today, I am not talking about that kind of rain. I'm talking about the kind of reign that Jesus declared at the beginning of his ministry. In this first chapter of the Gospel of Mark, after a season of preparation, Jesus declared that the *basileia* of God had come near. After calling his disciples, he healed the man with an unclean spirit.

Then he healed Simon's mother-in-law who had been in bed with a fever. Then he healed the man with leprosy. He made one declaration of the *basileia* and followed it up with three acts of healing—all in a relatively short period of time.

What was this *basileia* of God and what did it have to do with healing? The Greek word *basileia* can be translated as kingship, dominion, rule, or reign. Therefore, the *basileia* of God is the place where the power of God reigns over all of creation. It is not just hope for good things in the distant eschatological future, but it is a place pregnant with eschatological possibilities in the present. You may say, "That sounds good, preacher, but what did this have to do with healing?"

For biblical scholar and feminist theologian Elisabeth Schüssler Fiorenza, the *basileia* of God is about wholeness. In the *basileia* of God people are whole, healthy, and strong. In the *basileia* of God, debilitating, dehumanizing, oppressive systems and structures are overthrown. In the *basileia* of God, affirming relationships that were once severed are completely restored.

In Mark 1, we don't know the precise nature of the man's leprosy, but since he was living outside the community, we can assume it was somewhat severe. He was forced by the Mosaic law to live outside his community because of the condition of his skin. While he was living the solitary existence of an outsider, he could not share in the day-to-day, ordinary life events of his faith community. He could not celebrate the joys of the community, such as the birth of a new baby or the yield of an abundant harvest. Nor could he share in the sorrows of his community such as mourning the death of loved ones. When he needed advice about what to do in his own life, he could not just go show up at someone's house and ask for help. He had been kicked to the curb, ostracized, marginalized, treated as one who had no intrinsic worth—all because of the condition of his skin.

In addition to living a life of marginalization, he lived a life of humiliation. Whenever this man went out in public, he was supposed to cry out in a loud voice "unclean, unclean," a warning for other adherents of Mosaic law to move out of the way, so they would not become unclean themselves. How humiliating.

Humans are relational creatures. We thrive most when we are part of a community that loves us dearly and challenges us regularly to be the people God is calling us to be. To be kicked out of the community was dehumanizing. To be left out of the community's most sacred moments was oppressive. To be abandoned and shunned by family and friends was debilitating and alienating. To have to declare constantly to others that he was unclean was humiliating. I would imagine there were days when this man did not want to get out of bed. I would imagine there were days when he questioned his own existence. I would imagine there were many times when he did not want to live—not for one more moment.

But I also like to imagine that what happened next in this text happened just in the nick of time. Just as he was about give up hope completely, just when he was about to throw in the towel, just when he was about to make peace with his own mortality, along came Jesus. Jesus, about whom John had prophesied. Jesus, who had been declared "well pleasing" by God. Jesus, who had been traveling throughout Galilee preaching and teaching. Jesus, about whose healing power this man had undoubtedly heard.

When this man with leprosy saw Jesus, he didn't just see a prophet; he saw a chance of reign. He saw an opportunity for wholeness. He saw a chance for restoration. He saw a chance of being welcomed back into his community. And having seen his chance of reign, he seized it. He went up to Jesus and stated plainly, "If you choose to, if you want to, if it is your will, you can make me clean."

This was a definitive statement. There was not a hint of doubt in this statement. He did not waver. He did not hesitate. He truly believed in his heart that Jesus could make him clean. He had faith that Jesus could make a difference in his life. Jesus heard this man's plea and instantly declared, "I do choose. Be made clean."

Immediately (in good Markan fashion), the reign fell. Immediately, it fell hard. The reign fell so hard, the man was immediately made whole. The reign fell so hard it swept away Jesus' admonition not to tell anybody. The reign fell so hard the man was carried away in its flood. He told everybody who would listen what Jesus had done for him.

The world in which we live today is sorely in need of people of faith like the man cleansed of leprosy. The world needs people who believe that through the person and work of Jesus Christ, their lives in particular, and the world in general, can be different.

The world needs people like Ida B. Wells-Barnett, who believed that God could do all things. She believed lynching was wrong. She stood on her faith and started an anti-lynching campaign. Thanks to her faith and work, and the faith and work of many others in her day, the world became a safer place.

The world in which we live needs people like Nelson Mandela, who believed that apartheid was against the will of God. Mandela was willing to put his life on the line to attain freedom for all. Thanks to his faith and work, and the faith and work of people all over the world, apartheid was dismantled.

Do you believe that through God all things are possible? Do you believe God can heal the physical body? Do you believe God can heal broken relationships? Do you believe God can heal broken communities? Do you believe God can heal our broken world?

If you believe in the power of God to do all things, let it reign. Let the power of God reign in your home. Let the power of God reign in your churches. Let the power of God reign in your communities. Let the power of God reign throughout the world. Let it reign.

Wherever there are people of faith, people who believe in God's ability to do all things, there is a chance for the reign of God to manifest itself in the world. Let it reign!

Bibliography

"About Dr. King." The King Center (2014). http://www.thekingcenter.org/about-dr-king.

Abramovitz, Mimi and Tom Hopkins. "Reaganomics and the Welfare State." *The Journal of Sociology and Social Welfare* 10, no. 4 November (1983). http://scholar works.wmich.edu/cgi/viewcontent.cgi?article=1627&context=jssw.

Achtemeier, Paul J., and Eldon Jay Epp, ed. *1 Peter: A Commentary on First Peter*. Hermeneia—A Critical and Historical Commentary on the Bible. Minneapolis: Fortress Press, 1996.

The Acts of Paul and Thecla. Translated by Jeremiah Jones. New York: The St. Pachomius Orthodox Library, Forham University, 1995. https://legacy.fordham.edu/ halsall/basis/thecla.asp.

"The Americans with Disabilities Act of 1990 and Revised ADA Regulations Implementing Title II and Title III." (2016). http://www.ada.gov/2010_regs.htm.

Aristotle. *Politics*. Medford, MA: Perseus Digital Library Project, 1987. http://www.perseus.tufts.edu/hopper/text?doc=Perseus%3Atext%3A199.01.0058%3Abook%3D1%3Asection%3D1254b.

Augustine. *Against Julian*. Translated by Matthew Schumacher. *Writings of Saint Augustine, V 16*. New York: Fathers of the Church, Inc., 1957.

Baker-Fletcher, Karen. "Anna Julia Cooper and Sojourner Truth: Two Nineteenth-Century Black Feminist Interpreters of Scripture." *Searching the Scriptures*, vol. 1. New York: Crossroad Publishing Company, 1993.

Bard, Mitchell G. "World War II: Denazification." *Jewish Visual Library* (2008). http://germanculture.com.ua/germany-history/the-nureberg-trials/.

Bauer, Walter. *A Greek-English Lexicon of the New Testament and Other Early Christian Literature*, ed. Frederick W. Danker, 3rd ed. Chicago: University of Chicago Press, 2000.

Betz, Hans Dieter. *Galatians: A Commentary on Paul's Letter to the Churches in Galatia*. Hermeneia—A Critical and Historical Commentary on the Bible. Philadelphia: Fortress Press, 1979.

Black, Kathy. *A Healing Homiletic: Preaching and Disability*. Nashville: Abingdon Press, 1996.

The Black Panther Party. "What We Want, What We Believe." *The Digital Public Library of America* (1966). https://dp.la/primary-source-sets/sources/388.

Browning, W. R. F., ed. "Pastoral Epistles." *A Dictionary of the Bible*. http://www.oxfordbiblicalstudies.com/opr/t94/e1424.

———. "Paul's Letter to the Colossians." *A Dictionary of the Bible*. http://www.oxfordbiblicalstudies.com/article/opr/t94/e2117.

Brueggemann, Walter. *The Prophetic Imagination*, second ed. Philadelphia: Fortress Press, 2001.

Buckland, Patrick. "The Act of Union, 1800." *The Warrington Project* (1998).http://www.iisresource.org/Documents/0A5_02_Act_Of_Union.pdf.

Bultmann, Rudolf. *History and Eschatology: The Presence of Eternity*. New York: Harper Torchbooks, 1957.

———. "Is Exegesis without Presuppositions Possible? (1957)" *New Testament and Mythology and Other Basic Writings*, edited by Schubert M. Ogden. Philadelphia: Fortress Press, 1984.

———. "New Testament and Mythology (1941)." *New Testament and Mythology and Other Basic Writings*, edited by Schubert M. Ogden. Philadelphia: Fortress Press, 1984.

———. "On the Problem of Demythologizing (1952)." *New Testament and Mythology and Other Basic Writings*, edited by Schubert M. Ogden. Philadelphia: Fortress Press, 1984.

———. "On the Problem of Demythologizing (1961)." *New Testament and Mythology and Other Basic Writings*, edited by Schubert M. Ogden. Philadelphia: Fortress Press, 1984.

Carter, Warren. "Jesus' Healing Stories: Imperial Critique and Eschatological Anticipations in Matthew's Gospel." *Currents in Theology and Mission* 37, no. 6 (December 2010): 488–96.

Centers for Disease Control and Prevention. Opiod Overdose: Understanding the Epidemic. Atlanta: U.S. Department of Health and Human Services, 2018.

Cheng, Patrick S. *From Sin to Amazing Grace: Discovering the Queer Christ*. New York: Seabury Books, 2012.

———. *Radical Love: An Introduction to Queer Theology*. New York: Seabury Books, 2011.

———. *Rainbow Theology: Bridging Race, Sexuality, and Spirit*. New York: Seabury Books, 2013.

———. "A Scout Is Trustworthy." The Blog, July 15, 2013. huffingtonpost.com.

Collins, Adela Yarbro, and Harold W. Attridge. *Mark: A Commentary*. Hermeneia A Critical and Historical Commentary on the Bible. Minneapolis: Fortress Press, 2007.

Collins, Sara R., Munira Z. Gunja, Michelle M. Doty, and Herman K. Bhupal. "First Look at Health Insurance Coverage in 2018 Finds ACA Gains Beginning to Reverse." *To the Point: Quick Takes on Health Care Policy and Practice*. 2018. https://www.commonwealthfund.org/blog/2018/first-look-health-insurancecoverage-2018-finds-aca-gains-beginning-reverse?redirect_source=/publications/blog/2018/apr/ health-coverage-erosion.

Cone, James H. *Black Theology and Black Power*. Maryknoll, NY: Orbis Books, 1997.

———. *A Black Theology of Liberation*. 20th anniversary ed. Maryknoll, NY: Orbis Books, 1990.

———. *The Cross and the Lynching Tree*. Maryknoll, NY: Orbis Books, 2011.

———. *For My People: Black Theology and the Black Church*. Maryknoll, NY: Orbis Books, 1984.

———. *God of the Oppressed*. Rev. ed. Maryknoll, NY: Orbis Books, 1997.

———. *My Soul Looks Back*. Nashville: Abingdon Press, 1982.

Coote, Robert B., and Mary P. Coote. *Power, Politics, and the Making of the Bible: An Introduction*. Minneapolis: Fortress Press, 1990.

da Costa, Pedro Nicolaci. "The Richest US Families Own a Startling Proportion of America's Wealth." Business Insider (2017). https://www.businessinsider.com/richest-us-families-own-a-startling-proportion-of-americas-wealth-2017-6.

Creamer, Deborah Beth. *Disability and Christian Theology: Embodied Limits and Constructive Possibilities.* Academy Series. New York: Oxford University Press, 2009.

Cuff, Sharon, Kathleen McGoldrick, Stephanie Patterson, and Elizabeth Peterson. "The Intersection of Disability Studies and Health Science." *Transformations: The Journal of Inclusive Scholarship and Pedagogy* Volume 25 no. 2 (2016): 37–50.

Darby, John Nelson. "The Apostasy of Successive Dispensations." *Biblecentre.org.* http://biblecentre.org/content.php?mode=7&item=613.

———. "Christ in Heaven, and the Holy Spirit Sent Down." *Stem Publishing.* http://stempublishing.com/authors/darby/DOCTRINE/31018E.html.

———. "The Christian's Life in Christ: Colossians 1," *Stem Publishing.* http://stempublishing.com/authors/darby/DOCTRINE/31015E.html.

———. "The Closing Days of Christendom." *Sound Teaching on Electronic Media.* http://www.stempublishing.com/authors/darby/New7_96/Closing_Days.html.

———. "The Dispensation of the Kingdom of Heaven." *Stem Publishing.* http://stempublishing.com/authors/darby/PROPHET/02004E.html.

———. "Evidence from Scripture of the Passing Away of the Present Dispensation." *Stem Publishing.* http://www.stempublishing.com/authors/darby/PROPHET/02007E.html.

———. "Not of the World." *Sound Teaching on Electronic Media.* http://stempublishing.com/authors/darby/EXPOSIT/27008E.html.

———. "Obedience." *Stem Publishing.* http://stempublishing.com/authors/darby/ PRACTICE/16001E.html.

———. "1 Corinthians 13." *Stem Publishing.* http://stempublishing.com/authors/ darby/EXPOSIT/26020-6E.html#a13.

———. "The Public Ruin of the Church." *Stem Publishing.* http://www.stempublishing.com/authors/darby/MISCELLA/32026E.html.

———. "The Rapture of the Saints and the Character of the Jewish Remnant." *Stem Publishing.*http://www.stempublishing.com/authors/darby/PROPHET/11007E.html.

———. "Salvation and Separation." *Stem Publishing.* http://stempublishing.com/authors/darby/NOTESJOT/40010E.html.

———. "Scripture: The Place It Has in This Day." *Stem Publishing.* http://www.stempublishing.com/authors/darby/DOCTRINE/23005E.html.

———. "Signs of Antichrist." *Stem Publishing*. http://www.stempub lishing.com/authors/darby/PROPHET/05038E.html.

———. "What Is the Responsibility of the Saints?" *Stem Publishing*. http://stempublishing.com/authors/darby/PRACTICE/17012E.html.

———. "What Saints Will Be in the Tribulation?" *Stem Publishing* .http://stempublishing.com/authors/darby/PROPHET/11006E.html.

Demby, Gene. "The Truth Behind the Lies of the Original 'Welfare Queen.'" *All Things Considered* (2013). https://www.npr.org/sections/codeswitch/2013/12/20/255819681/the-truth-behind-the-lies-of-the-original-welfare-queen.

Dennison, William D. *The Young Bultmann: Context for His Understanding of God, 1884–1925*. American University Studies VII, Theology and Religion. New York: P. Lang, 2008.

DuBois, W. E. B. *The Souls of Black Folk*. Greenwich, CT: Fawcett Books, 1961.

Ehrman, Bart D. *Lost Christianities: The Battle for Scripture and the Faiths We Never Knew*. New York: Oxford University Press, 2003.

Eiesland, Nancy. *The Disabled God: Toward a Liberatory Theology of Disability*. Nashville: Abingdon Press, 1994.

———. "Encountering the Disabled God." British and Foreign Bible Society, https://www.biblesociety.org.uk/uploads/content/bible_in_transmission/files/2004_spring/BiT_Spring_2004_Eiesland.pdf.

———. "Encountering the Disabled God." *The Other Side*, http://www.dsf network.org/assets/Uploads/DisabilitySunday/21206.Eies land-Disabled-God.pdf.

———. "Revealing Pain Undoes a Social Fiction." *Emory Report* 60, no. 28 (2016). Published electronically April 21, 2008. http://www.emory.edu/EMORY_REPORT/erarchive/2008/April/April21/FirstPerson NancyEisland.htm.

Eiesland, Nancy L., and Don E. Saliers. *Human Disability and the Service of God: Reassessing Religious Practice*. Nashville: Abingdon Press, 1998.

Enander, Glen. *Elisabeth Schussler Fiorenza (Spiritual Leaders and Thinkers)*. Philadelphia: Chelsea House, 2005.

Evans, Christopher Hodge. *The Kingdom Is Always but Coming: A Life of Walter Rauschenbusch*. Library of Religious Biography. Grand Rapids: William B. Eerdmans Pub., 2004.

"Fast Fact: Child Protection and Development." UNICEF USA (2018). https:// www.unicefusa.org/mission/protect.

Field, Marion. *John Nelson Darby: Prophetic Pioneer*. Surrey: Highland Books, 2008.

Fontenot, Kayla, Jessica Semega, and Melissa Kollar. "Income and Poverty in the United States: 2017 Current Population Reports, United States Department of Commerce." Washington, DC: U.S. Census Bureau, 2018.

Forbes, James. *The Holy Spirit and Preaching*. Nashville: Abingdon Press, 1989.

Foster, Paul. "Is Q a 'Jewish Christian' Document?" *Biblica* 94, no. 3 (2013): 368–94.

Gill, N. S. "Six Vestal Virgins: Obligations and Rewards of the Thirty Year Commitment the Vestal Virgins Made." *About Education* (2016). http://ancienthistory.about .com/cs/rome/a/aa1114001.htm.

Glanton, Dahleen. "The Myth of the 'Welfare Queen' Endures, and Children Pay the Price." Chicago Tribune (2018). http://www.chicagotribune.com/news/columnists/glanton/ct-met-dahleen-glanton-welfare-queen-20180516-story.html.

"Gospel of John." *A Dictionary of the Bible* (2009). http://www.oxfordbiblical studies.com/article/opr/t94/e1018.

Hammann, Konrad, and Philip E. Devenish. *Rudolf Bultmann: A Biography*. First English edition. ed. Salem, OR: Polebridge Press, 2013.

Hockenos, Matthew D. "The Church Struggle and the Confessing Church: An Introduction to Bonhoeffer's Context." *Journal of the Council of Centers on Jewish-Christian Relations* 2, no. 1 (2007).

Hughes, Philip Edgcumbe. *Creative Minds in Contemporary Theology: A Guidebook to the Principal Teachings of Karl Barth, G. C. Berkouwer, Emil Brunner, Rudolf Bultmann, Oscar Cullmann, James Denney, C. H. Dodd, Herman Dooyeweerd, P. T. Forsyth, Charles Gore, Reinhold Niebuhr, Pierre Teilhard De Chardin, and Paul Tillich*. Grand Rapids: Eerdmans, 1966.

Isasi-Díaz, Ada María. "Biographical Information," Drew University Theological School Graduate Division of Religion. Last modified 2009. https://users.drew.edu /aisasidi/bioInfo.htm.

———. *En La Lucha = In the Struggle: A Hispanic Women's Liberation Theology*. Minneapolis: Fortress Press, 1993.

———. *La Lucha Continues: Mujerista Theology.* Maryknoll, NY: Orbis Books, 2004.

———. *Mujerista Theology: A Theology for the Twenty-First Century.* Maryknoll, NY: Orbis Books, 1996.

———. *Women of God, Women of the People.* St. Louis: Chalice Press, 1995. https://users.drew.edu/aisasidi/cd/TOC.html.

Isasi-Díaz, Ada María and Yolanda Tarango. *Hispanic Women Prophetic Voice in the Church: Toward a Hispanic Women's Liberation Theology = Mujer Hispana Voz ProfeTica En La Iglesia: Hacia Una Teologia De Liberacion De La Mujer Hispana.* San Francisco: Harper & Row, 1988.

"James H. Cone." (2017). https://utsnyc.edu/faculty/james-h-cone/.

Jukes, Andrew. "The Way Which Some Call Heresy or Reason for Separation from the Established Church." *Brethren Archive* (1844), http://brethren archive.org/media/357772/the_way_which_some_call_heresy_or_reason.pdf.

King Jr., Martin Luther. Selections from *A Testament of Hope: The Essential Writings and Speeches*, edited by James M. Washington. New York: HarperCollins Publishers, 1986.

———. *Where Do We Go from Here: Chaos or Community?* Boston,: Beacon Press, 2010.

King Jr., Martin Luther, Clayborne Carson, Peter Holloran, Ralph Luker, and Penny A. Russell. "The Papers of Martin Luther King, Jr." Berkeley, CA: University of California Press, 1992. https://king institute.stanford.edu/sites/mlk/files/publications/vol1intro.pdf.

"The King Philosophy." The King Center (2014). http://www.theking-center.org/king-philosophy#sub4.

King Sr., Martin Luther, and Clayton Riley. *Daddy King: An Autobiography.* Boston: Beacon Press, 2016.

Kreis, Steven. "A Note on Protestant Dissent and the Dissenters." *The History Guide* (2004). http://www.historyguide.org/intellect/dissenter.html.

LaRosa, Patricia E. "Finding Aid for Emilie M. Townes Papers, 1971–2005," New York: Union Theological Seminary, 2006. https://library.columbia.edu/content/dam/libraryweb/locations/burke/fa/awts/ldpd_59072 00.pdf.

Lefkowitz, Mary R., and Maureen B. Fant. *Women's Life in Greece and Rome*. Baltimore: Johns Hopkins University Press, 1992. http://www.stoa.org/diotima/anthology /wlgr/wlgr-romanlegal120.shtml.

Lorde, Audre. *Sister Outsider: Essays and Speeches*. The Crossing Press Feminist Series. Trumansburg, NY: Crossing Press, 1984.

Lou, Michelle and Christina Walker. "There Have Been 22 School Shootings in the US So Far This Year." CNN (2019). https://www.cnn.com/2019/05/08/us/school-shootings-us-2019-trnd/index.html.

Malkmus, Doris. "Rev. Dr. Patrick Cheng." LGBT Religious Archives Network. lgbttran.org.

Martin, Douglas. "Nancy Eiesland Is Dead at 44; Wrote of a Disabled God." http://www.nytimes.com/2009/03/22/us/22eiesland.html.

Mather, Ruth. "The Impact of the Napoleonic Wars in Britain." *Discovering Literature: Romantics and Victorians*, May 15, 2014, https://www.bl.uk/romantics-and-victorians/articles/the-impact-of-the-napoleonic-wars-in-britain.

McClintock, Louisa. "Facing the Awful Truth: Germany Confronts the Past, Again." *Problems of Post Communism* 52, no. 6 (2005).

Minus, Paul M. *Walter Rauschenbusch, American Reformer*. New York: Macmillan, 1988.

"Mission and History." The Center for Independent Living, Inc. (2016). http://www.cilberkeley.org/about-us/mission/.

Moltmann, Jürgen. *A Broad Place: An Autobiography*. 1st Fortress Press Edition. Minneapolis: Fortress Press, 2008.

———. *The Crucified God: The Cross of Christ as the Foundation and Criticism of Christian Theology*. 1st Fortress Press Edition. Minneapolis: Fortress Press, 1993.

———. *The Spirit of Life: A Universal Affirmation*. 1st Fortress Press Edition. Minneapolis: Fortress Press, 1992.

———. *Sun of Righteousness, Arise! God's Future for Humanity and the Earth*. Fortress Press Edition. Minneapolis: Fortress Press, 2010.

———. *Theology of Hope: On the Ground and the Implications of a Christian Eschatology*. San Francisco: HarperSanFrancisco, 1991.

———. *The Trinity and the Kingdom: The Doctrine of God*. 1st Fortress Press Edition. Minneapolis: Fortress Press, 1993.

Montagna, Joseph A. "The Industrial Revolution." (1981), http://teachersinstitute.yale. edu/curriculum/units/1981/2/81.02.06.x.html.

Muddiman, John. *A Commentary on the Epistle to the Ephesians*. New York: Continuum, 2001.

National Council of Negro Churchmen. "'Black Power': Statement by the National Committee of Negro Churchmen." *The New York Times*, Sunday, July 31 (1966). https://www.episcopalarchives.org/Afro-Anglican_history/exhibit/pdf/blackpowerstatement.pdf.

Nix, Elizabeth. "Tuskegee Experiment: The Infamous Syphilis Study." *History* (2017). https://www.history.com/news/the-infamous-40-year-tuskegee-study.

Patzia, Arthur G. *The Making of the New Testament: Origin, Collection, Text & Canon*. 2nd Edition. Downers Grove, IL: IVP Academic, 2011.

Ramsey, Paul. *Christian Ethics and the Sit-In*. New York: Association Press, 1961.

Rauschenbusch, Walter. *Christianity and the Social Crisis in the 21st Century: The Classic That Woke Up the Church*. Edited by Paul B. Raushenbush. New York: HarperOne, 2007.

———. *Dare We Be Christians?* The William Bradford Collection from the Pilgrim Press. Cleveland: Pilgrim Press, 1993.

———. *The Righteousness of the Kingdom*. Nashville: Abingdon Press, 1968.

———. *A Theology for the Social Gospel*. New York: The Macmillan Company, 1917.

Ricœur, Paul. "Freud and Philosophy: An Essay on Interpretation." The Terry Lectures. New Haven, CT: Yale University Press, 1970.

Russell, Letty M. *Household of Freedom: Authority in Feminist Theology*. 1st ed. The 1986 Annie Kinkead Warfield Lectures. Philadelphia: Westminster Press, 1987.

Schüssler Fiorenza, Elisabeth. "Feminist Theology as a Critical Theology of Liberation." *Theological Studies* 36, no. 44 (1975).

———. *In Memory of Her: A Feminist Theological Reconstruction of Christian Origins*. 10th Anniversary Edition. New York: Crossroad, 1994.

———, ed. *Searching the Scriptures: A Feminist Introduction*. Volume 1. New York: Crossroad, 1993.

———. "To Follow the Vision: The Jesus Movement as Basilea Movement." *Liberating Eschatology: Essays in Honor of Letty M. Russell*, edited by Margaret A. Farley and Serene Jones. Louisville: Westminster John Knox Press, 1999.

————. *Transforming Vision: Explorations in Feminist The*logy.* Minneapolis: Fortress Press, 2011.

Sharpe, Dores Robinson. *Walter Rauschenbusch.* New York: The Macmillan Company, 1942.

Söelle, Dorothee. *Suffering.* Philadelphia: Fortress Press, 1975.

Stanton, Elizabeth Cady, Carrie Chapman Catt, and National American Woman Suffrage Association Collection (Library of Congress). *The Woman's Bible.* 2 Volumes. New York: European Publishing, 1895.

Swinton, John, ed. *Critical Reflections on Stanley Hauerwas' Theology of Disability: Disabling Society, Enabling Theology.* Binghamton, NY: Haworth Pastoral Press, 2004.

Swinton, John. "Who Is the God We Worship? Theologies of Disability; Challenges and New Possibilities." *International Journal of Practical Theology* 14, no. 2 (2011): 273–307.

Townes, Emilie M. "A Conversation with AAR President Emilie Townes." *Religious Studies News,* March 2008.

————. *In a Blaze of Glory: Womanist Spirituality as Social Witness.* Nashville: Abingdon Press, 1995.

————. *Womanist Ethics and the Cultural Production of Evil.* New York: Palgrave Macmillan, 2006.

————. *Womanist Justice, Womanist Hope.* American Academy of Religion Academy Series. Atlanta: Scholars Press, 1993.

Townes, Emilie Maureen. *Breaking the Fine Rain of Death: African American Health Issues and a Womanist Ethic of Care.* New York: Continuum, 1998.

Trible, Phyllis. "The Creation of the Feminist Theology." *The New York Times.* May 1, 1983. http://www.nytimes.com/1983/05/01/books/the-creation-of-a-feminist-theology .html?pagewanted=all.

Turner, Melissa. "James Hal Cone." *Blackpast.* http://www.blackpast .org/contact.

"U.S. Defense Spending Compared to Other Countries." Peter G. Peterson Foundation (2016). http://www.pgpf.org/Chart-Archive/0053_defense-comparison.

Vitello, Paul. "Ada María Isasi-Díaz, Dissident Catholic Theologian, Dies at 69." *The New York Times* (2012). https://www.nytimes.com /2012/06/06/nyregion/ada-maria-isasi-diaz-dissident-catholic-theologian -dies-at-69.html.

Waggoner, Ben. "Aristotle (384–322 B.C.E.)." (1996). http://www. ucmp.berkeley.edu/ history/aristotle.html.

Wagner, Peter and Wendy Sawyer. "Mass Incarceration: The Whole Pie 2018." Prison Policy Initiative (2018). https://www.prisonpolicy.org/re ports/pie2018.html.

Walker, Alice. *The Color Purple.* New York: Harcourt Brace Jo-vanovich, 1970.

Washington, Joseph R. *Black Religion: The Negro and Christianity in the United States.* Boston: Beacon Press, 1964.

Wendell, Susan. *The Rejected Body: Feminist Philosophical Reflections on Disability.* New York: Routledge, 1996.

Weremchuk, Max S. *John Nelson Darby.* Neptune, NJ: Loizeaux Brothers, 1992.

Wertlieb, Ellen C. "Minority Group Status of the Disabled." *The Disabled.* https://journals.sagepub.com/doi/10.1177/001872678503801104.

Wilson, Paul Scott. *The Four Pages of the Sermon: A Guide to Biblical Preaching.* Nashville: Abingdon Press, 1999.

X, Malcolm. *The Autobiography of Malcolm X: As Told to Alex Haley.* 1st Ballantine Books hardcover ed. New York: Ballantine Books, 1992.

Yong, Amos. *The Bible, Disability, and the Church: A New Vision of the People of God.* Grand Rapids: W.B. Eerdmans Publishing Company, 2011.

Index

A

A Chance of Reign (sermon), 213–216

A Theology for the Social Gospel (Rauschenbusch), 90

Aaron, 8

Abernathy, Ralph, 36

Abihu, 8

Abraham, 8

Abrahamic promise, 55–56

activism, 188

The Acts of Paul and Thecla (Jones), 77

Adam, 184, 190

Africa, immigration in, vii

African Americans

    agape love of, 39–40, 48, 49

    Aunt Jemima and, 134–135

    black religion and, 109

    challenges of, 44

    The Color Purple and, 133–134

    conditions of, 118

    disabled, 164

    feminist theology and, 69

    health and, 136–138

    heaven viewpoint of, 118–119

    legal progress of, 108

    liberation and, 114–115

    lynching and, 128, 215–216

    oppression of, 105

    poverty of, 108

    racism and, 37–38

    rape of, 128

    segregation and, 38–39

    social ills of, 135–136

    as social lepers, 38–39, 48

    syphilis and, 137

    violence against, 118

    Welfare Queen and, 135–136

    womanist, 126–127

agape love, 39–40, 48, 49

Aid to Families with Dependent Children (AFDC), 147

alcohol, 94

Americans with Disabilities Act (ADA), 163, 166

Anglican Church, 4

Anslem of Canterbury, 96, 100, 184

anthropological poverty, 155–156

Antichrist, 12

Aquinas, Thomas, 112

Aristotle, 59, 80–81, 206

Arnold, Nancy Lynn. *See* Eiesland, Nancy

Athanasian Creed, 191

atonement, 100, 101, 184, 185

Augustine, 112, 184
Augustus, 78
authority, 129–130
Avalos, Hector, 172

B
baptism, 23, 26, 98
basileia, iv, vi, 73–74, 83–84,
198, 214
beloved community, 37, 38, 39,
41, 43, 47, 201, 202
Berkeley Center for Independent
Living, 165–166
binary thinking, 187
black liberation theology, 107,
108, 111, 113–114, 115, 119–
120, 121
Black Matriarch, 135
black power, 109–111
black religion, 109
Black Religion (Washington),
109, 110
black revolution, 117, 199
*Black Theology and Black
Power* (Cone), 107
Bonaparte, Napoleon, 3
Book of Common Prayer, 4
Brooks, Gennifer, viii
Brotherhood of the Kingdom,
90
Buddhism, 191
Bultmann, Arthur Kennedy, 17–
18
Bultmann, Rudolf
biography of, 17–19
concerns of, 30–31
demythologizing and, 20–21

History and Eschatology,
25, 30
honors given to, 19
influence of, 118
lectures of, 25–26
*New Testament and
Mythology,* 30
preaching and, 20
theological terms of, 21–22
vision of, 196, 197–198
works of, 25

C
Cannon, Katie, 145
Carmichael, Stokely, 109
Catholicism, 2, 4, 180
charity, 149, 156
Cheng, Patrick S.
atonement viewpoint of, 185
biography of, 176–177
grace viewpoint of, 184,
185, 206
oppression viewpoint of,
178–179
preaching implications of,
192–194
sin viewpoint of, 183–184,
185, 206
solidarity viewpoint of, 178
vision of, 196–197, 205–206
children, crises of, vii
Christ. *See* Jesus
Christian Ethics and the Sit-In
(Ramsey), 113
Christian missionary movement, 75, 83

Christianity and the Social Crisis (Rauschenbusch), 90
Christians/Christianity
  black power and, 109–111
  colonization and, 97–98
  criticism of, 43
  cross and, 56, 57–58
  Day of Judgment and, 26
  discipleship of equals model of, 81
  Enlightenment and, 17
  Hispanics and, 152–153
  hope of, 7
  ideological thinking within, 112
  injustice and, 37
  John Nelson Darby's viewpoint of, 5–6
  radical freedom of, 19–20, 27, 28–29, 197–198
  Renaissance and, 17
  role of, 29, 30, 200
  social order and, 103
  society and, 90
  white theology within, 112
Christ-Sophia, 75–76
Chrysostom, John, 72
Church of England, 4
churches
  black liberation theology and, 119–120
  communal rituals within, 171–172
  disabled people within, 162–163
  division within, 106, 109
  Enlightenment and, 4

failures of, 95
healing and, 171
house, 76
as "in ruin," 7, 13
people with disabilities and, 166–167
politics and, 62–63, 203
role of, vi–vii
sacramentalism in, 27
start of, 76
unity within, 59
worship within, 79
Civil Rights Act, 36, 108, 166
Civil Service Reconstruction Law, 54
collective punishment, 184–185
The Color Purple (Walker), 133–134, 200
The Coming of God: Christian Eschatology (Moltmann), 54
coming out, 181, 193–194
communities of faith, 154–155
compassion, 45
Cone, Charlie, 105
Cone, James
  biography of, 105–108
  black liberation theology and, 107, 108, 111, 115
  Black Theology and Black Power, 107
  freedom viewpoint of, 115
  God of the Oppressed, 131
  ideology viewpoint of, 111–112
  influence of, 130–131, 132
  liberation viewpoint of, 113–114, 115

preaching implications of, 120–123

quote of, iv

reformation viewpoint of, 117

sin viewpoint of, 116

vision of, 196, 199–200

Confessing Church, 18–19, 54

conformity, 189

conscience, 153–154, 158

conscientization, 151

consent, 186

conversion, 169, 204

Cooper, Anna Julia, 69–70

creation, 80–81, 183

Creator, God as, 117, 183, 199

crises, vii

cross/crucifixion, 23, 56, 57–59, 65, 67

cultural production, 136–137, 139, 140, 200

D

Daly, Mary, 70

Daniel, book of, iv

Darby, John, 1

Darby, John Nelson

  biography of, 1–3

  Christian viewpoint of, 5–6

  church viewpoint of, 7

  dispensations viewpoint of, 7–10

  Great Commission viewpoint of, 9

  Great Tribulation viewpoint of, 11–12

  kingdom of God viewpoint of, 6–7

  love viewpoint of, 6, 12

  objections of, 4–5

  preaching implications of, 12–14

  premillennial dispensationalism and, 3

  Rapture viewpoint of, 10–11

  salvation viewpoint of, 5, 201

  sin viewpoint of, 201

  vision of, 196, 200–201

David, 8

Davis, George Washington, 36

Day of Judgment, 26

death, 121

deification, 185

demythologizing, 20–21, 23–25, 29

denazification process, 19

depravity, 101

deviance, 189

disabilities

  defined, 164–165, 172

  image of God and, 205

  obstacles for, 166–167

  preaching implications for, 172

  of veterans, 165

  vision, 162–170

disability rights movement, 161, 163

disabled

  God, 168–169, 171, 172, 173, 205

  integration of, 162–163

  as minority, 164

preaching implications for,
170–173
Disabled American Veterans,
165
The Disabled God (Eiesland),
165
dispensations, 7–9, 10, 13
Dissenters, 4, 5
downward love, 6, 200
drugs, vii
Dykstra, Laurel, 181

E
economics, 27, 63, 91, 147
Eiesland, Nancy
    biography of, 161–162
    The Disabled God, 165
    disabled God viewpoint of,
        168–169
    *Human Disability and the
    Service of God,* 165
    liberatory realism viewpoint
        of, 169
    preaching implications of,
        170–173
    vision of, 196, 205
Eleazar, 8
emancipation, 109
end times, iv
England, 4
Enlightenment, 4, 17
equality, 74, 77–79
Erotic Christ, 186
eschatology
    Biblical views of, 26
    defined, iv–v
    realized, 19–20

role of, vi
social orientation of, 99–100
terms of, iv
waiting for, 26–27
womanist, 126–138
Eucharist, 23, 98, 169
Europe, immigration in, vii
Eve, 184, 190
existential interpretation, 23–25
Exodus International, 187–189
exploitation, 186
Ezekiel, book of, iv

F
The Fall, 93, 184, 190
familia, 149, 157
feminism, 148
feminist movement, 64
feminist theology, 69
Festchrift, 19
fiestas, 150
flesh, 21–22
Forbes, James, 207
forgiveness, 13, 49
Foucault, Paul-Michel, 179–180
Four Pages of the Sermon (Wilson), 210
Frank, Leonhard, 18
freedom, 115, 132
freedom of faith, 62–63
Freud, Sigmund, 62
fruits of the Spirit, 22

G
Gandhi, Mahatma, 40, 41
gender equality, 66, 72
gender identity, 179–180

Gentiles, 9, 77–78
Germany, 19, 20
Gladden, Washington, 89
God
  as barrier-breaker, 98
  basileia of, iv, vi, 73–74,
    83–84, 198, 214
  characteristics of, 202
  Christians and, 6
  as Creator, 117, 183, 199
  as disabled, 168–169, 171,
    172, 173, 205
  empowerment by, 194
  faithfulness of, 55–56, 62
  forgiveness and, 13
  grace of, 22
  humanity of, 58–59
  image of (*See* image of God)
  immanence of, 117, 121,
    122–123, 198–200
  Jewish people and, 11
  justice of, 37
  kingdom of, iv, 6–7, 10, 92,
    148–149, 204
  liberating acts by, 112
  love of, 59, 130
  mythology and, 21
  the oppressed and, 113–114
  poverty and, 113–114
  power of, 216
  queer theology and, 181–182
  relational nature of, 182
  throne of, 11
  transcendence of, 117–118,
    121
  Trinity and, 56–58
  understanding of, 139

God of the Oppressed (Cone),
131
  Good Samaritan, story of, 39–
40, 45
  Gospels, reign of God in, v
  grace, 22, 184, 185–194, 197,
206
  Graham, Billy, 116
  The Grandparents Who Care
Support Network, 138
  Great Britain, 3
  Great Commission, 9
  Great Tribulation, 11–12

H
handicap, 164–165
healing, 60, 66, 171, 202
health, 136–138, 140, 200
health care, 137
heaven, 118–119
Hezekiah, 9
Hinduism, 191
Hispanics, 146–155, 158
historical project, 151–152
History and Eschatology
(Bultmann), 25, 30
  Hitler, Adolf, 18
  Hitler Youth, 53
  Holy Spirit
    dispensation of, 9
    healing and, 60, 202
    importance of, 83
    preaching and, 207–208
    preaching implications for, 66
    role of, 6
    sanctification through, 63
    Shekinah-like nature of, 60

Trinity and, 56–58, 59–60
hope, viii, 12, 55
hopelessness, 25–26
Horden, William, 106
house churches, 76
household codes, 79–81, 83
*Human Disability and the
Service of God* (Eiesland), 165
humanity
bodies of, 139–170, 205
characteristics of, 214–215
connections within, 60–61
disabled within, 164
dispensations of, 7–9
free will of, 123
of God, 58–59
health and, 136–138
idolatry and, 61–62, 203
image of God and, 37, 48
nihilism and, 25–26
redemption of, 13
suffering of, 130–132
Trinity and, 182
Hybrid Christ, 191–192
hybridity, 192

I

ideology, 111–112
idolatry, 8–9, 61–62, 203
image of God
disabilities and, 205
humans as, 37, 48
James Cone's viewpoint
of, 199
Martin Luther King, Jr.'s
viewpoint of, 201
meaning of, 37, 47–48

preaching implications for,
102–103
reclaiming of, 96–97
reflection of, 116–117
Walter Rauschenbusch's
viewpoint of, 96–97, 204
immanence of God, 117, 121,
122–123, 198–200
immigration, vii, 91
impairments, 163, 164–165
In Memory of Her (Schüssler
Fiorenza), 71, 72
"in ruin," church as, 7, 13
Industrial Revolution, 3–4,
90–91
injustice, 37, 48
Interconnected Christ, 190–191
interdependence, 190–191
Ireland, 4
Isasi-Battle, Domingo G., 144
Isasi-Díaz, Ada María
Bible teaching of, 153
biography of, 144–146
kin-dom of God viewpoint
of, 146, 148–149
liberation viewpoint of, 149
preaching implications of,
155–159
salvation viewpoint of, 150,
204
sin viewpoint of, 155
solidarity viewpoint of, 149
suffering viewpoint of,
150–151
vision of, 196, 204
isolation, 190

Israelites, 6, 8–9, 55
Ithamar, 8

J
jails, crises of, vii
Jemima, Aunt, 134–135, 200
Jericho Road, 45
Jeroboam, 8–9
Jerome, 73
Jerusalem Countdown
(movie), iv
Jesus
    basileia of God and, 74
    black liberation theology and,
        113–114
    challenges given by, 198–199
    compassion of, 13, 114
    crucifixion of, 58–59
    demythologizing of, 23
    as disabled, 173
    as eschatological event,
        27–28
    Eucharist and, 98
    example of, 13, 30
    forgiveness and, 13
    God and, 102
    hope of, viii
    influence of, 84
    kingdom of God teaching
        by, iv
    leper story and, 213–215
    love of, 59, 92, 130
    mythology and, 21
    as Out Christ, 186–187
    prayer teaching by, v
    as Queer Christ, 185–192
    renewal movement of, 198

resurrection of, 117–118, 122
revolutionary nature of,
    91–92
sacrifice of, 100
Second Coming of, 7, 10–11
as Self-Loving Christ,
    189–190, 205–206
Sermon on the Mount by, v
sin and, 100–101
solidarity of, 100–101
Sophia and, 75
suffering of, 114, 131, 152
as Transgressive Christ,
    188–189
Trinity and, 56–58
white man's, 111
works of, 213–214
wounds of, 168
Jesus movement, 75–76, 81
Jewish movement, 83
Jewish people, 4, 10, 11,
77–78, 114
Judaism, 74–75
Judith, story of, 74–75
Jülicher, Adolf, 18
justice, 37, 122

K
Kant, Emmanuel, 27
kin-dom of God, 146, 148–149,
157, 204
King, Alberta Christine
Williams, 34
King Jr., Martin Luther
    assassination of, 107
    beloved community view
        point of, 37, 38, 39, 41,

43, 47, 201, 202
biography of, 34–37
criticism from, 43
image of God viewpoint
  of, 201
love viewpoint of, 39
preaching implications
  from, 46–49
racism and, 38
salvation viewpoint of, 42–43
speech of, 36, 46
suffering and, 41
Vietnam War and, 43–45
vision of, 196, 201–202
voluntary suffering and, 201
King, Sr., Michael, 34, 42
kingdom of God, iv, 6–7, 10,
92, 148–149, 204
kingdom of heaven, 7
Kingly, dispensation of, 8–9

L
last days, iv
Latin America, 146–155
Latinas, 152–153, 154–155,
204. *See also* Hispanics
the Law, dispensation of, 8
leadership, 132
Left Behind (movie), iv
leper(s), 38–39, 48, 213–215
LGBTIQA, 178, 182, 187–188,
192–194, 206
liberalism, 17
liberating gospel, 119
liberation, 113–114, 115, 132,
149, 157, 197

Liberator Christ, 187–189
liberatory realism, 169
life in the Spirit, 22, 197
Lorde, Audre, 131, 186
Lord's Supper, 23, 98, 169
love
  agape, 39–40, 48, 49
  characteristics of, 92
  of God, 59, 92, 130
  guidance of, 39–40
  John Nelson Darby's view
    point of, 6, 12
  Martin Luther King Jr.'s
    viewpoint of, 39
  suffering and, 130
  types of, 6, 200
  Walter Rauschenbusch's
    viewpoint of, 203
Luther, Martin, 34, 112
Lydia, 76
lynching, 128, 215–216

M
Malcolm X, 109, 111
Mammy, story of, 134–135
Manasseh, 9
Mandela, Nelson, 216
Martha, 82
Marx, Karl, 27
Mary Magdalene, 82
Matthew, Gospel of, v
Mays, Benjamin, 35
The Memphis Free Speech
(newspaper), 128
mind-body dualism, 183, 206
minorities, 166. *See also*
specific groups

Moltmann, Elisabeth, 54
Moltmann, Jürgen
  biography of, 52–54
  The Coming of God:
    Christian Eschatology, 54
  feminist movement viewpoint
    of, 64
  freedom of faith viewpoint
    of, 62–63
  implications for preaching,
    65–67
  oppression viewpoint of, 63
  quote of, vii–viii
  salvation viewpoint of, 64
  sanctification viewpoint of,
    63
  Theology of Hope, 54
  viewpoint of, iv–v
  vision of, 196, 202–203
monochromatic theology, 178
Montgomery bus boycott, 36
Moses, 8
Moss, Thomas, 128
Mujerista theology, 146–155,
157, 158
myth, 21

N
Nadab, 8
National Committee of Black
Churchmen (NCBC), 110
  natural knowledge, 58
  Nazi Party, 18–19
  negative peace, 201–202
  Nelson, Lord Horatio, 1
  New Testament and Mythology
    (Bultmann), 30

New York Times (newspaper),
110
Niebuhr, Reinhold, 108, 112–
113
nihilism, 25–26, 29
Noah, 8
nonviolent resistance, 40–41
North America, immigration in, vii

O
obedience, 26, 129–130
objective realm of reconciliation, 132
opioids, crises of, vii
oppressions
  challenges of, 48–49
  consequences of, 136–137
  God and, 113–114
  Jürgen Moltmann's
    viewpoint of, 63
  of Latinas, 154–155
  of LGBTIQA communities,
    182
  Patrick S. Cheng's viewpoint
    of, 178–179
  preaching implications
    of, 122
Origen, 72
Out Christ, 186–187

P
pain, 131–133
paradisiacal state, 7
Paralyzed American Veterans,
165
  pastoral voice of leadership, 132
  Paul, 76–79, 98, 166, 194

peace, 41–42, 201–202
perfection, 168
perichoresis, 56
permanently disabled, 170, 205
perspective, 25
Peter, 9
Philemon, 77
Plato, 183
Plymouth Brethren, 3
politics, 62–63, 203
Politics (Aristotle), 80–81
Poor People's Campaign, 36–37
pope, veneration of, 2
poverty
  of African Americans, 108
  anthropological, 155–156
  crises of, vii
  God and, 113–114
  of Hispanics, 150
  during the Industrial Revolu
    tion, 91
  preaching implications for,
    155–156
  race and, 122
  in the United States, 48
prayer, v
preaching
  challenges of, 20
  exegesis for, 207–211
  role of, 24–25, 28, 47–48
prejudice, 25
premillennial dispensationalism,
  3, 11, 12–14
pride, 190, 206
priesthood, 8
Prisca, 76
prisons, crises of, vii

promises, 55–56
prophetic voice of leadership,
132
Protestantism, 2

Q

queer, 178, 179
Queer Christ, 185–192
queer theology, 180–181

R

racial ideology, 120–121
racism, 37–38, 116
radical freedom, 19–20, 27,
28–29, 197–198
rainbow, 183
rainbow theology, 178, 179
Ramsey, Paul, 113
Rapture, 10–11
Rauschenbusch, August, 88
Rauschenbusch, Caroline, 88
Rauschenbusch, Walter
  alcohol viewpoint of, 94
  biography of, 88–90
  *Christianity and the Social
    Crisis,* 90
  Eucharist viewpoint of, 98–99
  The Fall viewpoint of, 93
  image of God viewpoint of,
    96–97, 204
  love viewpoint of, 203
  preaching implications of,
    101–103
  salvation viewpoint of,
    94–95, 203–204
  sin viewpoint of, 92–95, 203
  suffering viewpoint of, 97

*A Theology for the Social
Gospel*, 90
vision of, 196, 203–204
war viewpoint of, 94
Reagan, Ronald, 135–136,
147, 200
Reaganomics, 147
realized eschatology, 19–20
reconciliation, 132
Reconstruction Law, 19
reformation, 117, 199
regeneration, 95, 204
Rehoboam, 8–9
relationships, v, 60, 202
Renaissance, 17
reparative therapy, 187–188
resurrection, 23, 40, 117–119,
122
Revelation, book of, iv
revolution, 45, 48
revolutionary, 91
Revolutionary War, 3
righteous social order, 92
Roberts, Ed, 165
Roman Empire, 78
Roosevelt, Franklin Delano,
165
Ruether, Rosemary Radford, 70
Rumors of Wars (movie), iv

S
sacramentalism, 27
saints, 10–11
salvation
Ada María Isasi-Díaz's
viewpoint of, 150, 204

Elisabeth Schüssler Fiorenza's
viewpoint of, 74
John Nelson Darby's view
point of, 5, 201
Jürgen Moltmann's
viewpoint of, 64
Martin Luther King Jr.'s
viewpoint of, 42–43
preaching implications for,
102, 157
role of, 29
Rudolf Bultmann's
viewpoint of, 197
Walter Rauschenbusch's
viewpoint of, 94–95,
203–204
Samaritan, story of, 39–40, 45
sanctification, 63
satyagraha, 40
scapegoating, 189
Schipper, Jeremy, 172
Schnackenburg, Rudolf, 71
Schreiner, Josef, 71
Schüssler Fiorenza, Elisabeth
basileia viewpoint of, 73–74
biography of, 70–71
as feminist theologian, 70
influence of, ix, 73
In Memory of Her, 71, 72
preaching implications of,
82–84, 207–211
salvation viewpoint of, 74
vision of, 196, 198–199
Scott, Coretta, 36
Second Coming, 7, 10–11
segregation, 38–39
selfishness, 93, 203

Self-Loving Christ, 189–190, 205–206
self-suffering, 41
Sermon on the Mount, v
sexual orientation, 177–178, 192–194
sexuality, 178–180, 191, 192–194
shame, 189–190, 206
Shepherd Center, 167
sin
  Ada María Isasi-Díaz's viewpoint of, 155
  black liberation theology and, 121
  consequences of, 116
  James Cone's viewpoint of, 116, 199
  Jesus and, 100–101
  John Nelson Darby's viewpoint of, 201
  Mujerista theology and, 155
  original, 184
  Patrick S. Cheng's viewpoint of, 183–184, 185, 206
  preaching implications for, 121, 156, 192–194
  Queer Christ and, 185–192
  Rudolf Bultmann's viewpoint of, 22, 197
  Walter Rauschenbusch's viewpoint of, 92–95, 203
white people and, 116
singularity, 178, 191–192
slavery, 77, 80
social change, 41
social gospel, 97, 100, 204

social lepers, 38–39, 48
social order, 103
Social Science Association, 163
Society of United Irishmen, 4
Sodom and Gomorrah, 180, 184–185
solidarity, 64, 100–101, 149, 156, 178, 204
Sölle, Dorothee, 130–131, 140
Solomon, 8
Sophia (wisdom), 73–74, 198
Southern Christian Leadership Conference (SCLC), 36, 42
Stanton, Elizabeth Cady, 69
Stephen, death of, 9
Stern, Helene, 17
Strong, Josiah, 89
subjective realm of reconciliation, 132
suffering
  Ada María Isasi-Díaz's viewpoint of, 150–151
  Hispanics and, 150–151
  humanity and, 130–132
  as part of nonviolent resistance, 41
  preaching implications for, 102, 139, 140, 156–157
  role of, 49
  virtuous, 166
  Walter Rauschenbusch's viewpoint of, 97
syphilis, 137

T

Tanis, Justin, 181
Tarango, Yolanda, 145
temporarily able-bodied, 170, 205
temporarily disabled, 170, 205
Tertullian, 73
Thecla, 77
Theology of Hope (Moltmann), 54
    throne of God, 11
    Tillich, Paul, 108
    total depravity, 93
    Townes, Emilie
        authority viewpoint of, 129
        biography of, 125–126
        obedience viewpoint of, 129
        preaching implications for, 138–140
        vision of, 196, 200
        Womanist Justice, Womanist Hope, 127
    Townes, Mary McLean, 125
    Townes, Ross E., 125
    Transgressive Christ, 188–189
    Trinity, 56–58, 59, 65–67, 182
    Truth, Sojourner, 69
    Tuskegee Institute, 137
    Tuskegee syphilis study, 137

U

United States
    as beloved community, 45, 202
    civil rights issues within, 42
    defense spending of, 48
    disability in, 165
        Hispanics and, 147
        political climate of, 108
        poverty in, 48
        Public Health Service, 137
        racial ideology of, 120
        revolution of, 202
        riots in, 108–109
        Vietnam War and, 43–45
        Vocational Rehabilitation Act of 1918, 165
        white theology within, 114–115
upward love, 6, 200

V

values, revolution of, 45
Vaughan, Anne, 1
Vestal Virgins, 78
veterans, 165
Vietnam War, 43–45, 108
virtuous suffering, 166
vision, 47, 157
Vocational Rehabilitation Act of 1918, 165
voluntary suffering, 49, 140, 201
    Voting Rights Act, 36, 108

W

Walden, Mary, 145
Walker, Alice, 133–134, 200
war, 41, 44, 45, 94
Washington, Joseph, 109
Weiss, Johannes, 18
Welfare Queen, 135–136, 200
Wells-Barnett, Ida B., 127–132, 138–129, 200, 215–216

West African slave trade, 3
Wilhelm, Dawn Ottoni, viii
Williams, A. D., 34, 42
Williams, Delores, 133
Wilson, Paul Scott, 210
wisdom (Sophia), 73–74, 198
Wiseman, Karyn, viii–ix
womanist eschatology, 126–138
Womanist Justice, Womanist Hope (Townes), 127
The Woman's Bible (Stanton), 69
women
    church father writings about, 72–73, 82
    church roles of, 72, 76, 81
    dedication to service by, 81–82
    Hispanic, 147–148
    image of, 75
    poverty of, 150
    role of in Judaism, 74–75
    Roman laws for, 78
Women's Ordination Conference (WOC), 145
Working Girl Luncheon, 138
World War II, 19
worship, 79

Y
Yong, Amos, 172